Paradoxy of Modernism

Paradoxy *of* Modernism

ROBERT SCHOLES

Yale University Press   New Haven and London

Set in Minion type by Integrated Publishing Solutions.
Printed in the United States of America.

Library of Congress Cataloging-in-Publication Data
Scholes, Robert E.
    Paradoxy of modernism / Robert Scholes.
        p.   cm.
    Includes bibliographical references (p.   ) and index
    ISBN-13: 978-0-300-10820-0 (cloth : alk. paper)
    ISBN-10: 0-300-10820-6 (cloth : alk. paper)
    1. Modernism (Art)   2. Modernism (Literature)   3. Arts,
Modern—20th century.   4. Criticism—History—20th century.
I. Title.
NX456.5.M64S36   2006
700′.4112—dc22

A catalogue record for this book is available from
the British Library.

The paper in this book meets the guidelines for permanence
and durability of the Committee on Production Guidelines
for Book Longevity of the Council on Library Resources.

10 9 8 7 6 5 4 3 2 1

This book is dedicated to the first friend
I made in graduate school at Cornell,
Carl H. Klaus, my colleague and collaborator
at the University of Iowa, a gifted writer
and a steadfast friend.
And to the memory of Kate Franks Klaus,
who proved definitively, against much evidence
to the contrary, that it can be a very good idea
to marry a poet. I can see her smiling,
getting ready to respond to that,
with a wisecrack of her own.
To Carl and Kate, then,
with love

Contents

Preface   ix

PART I Paradoxies

ONE   High and Low in Modernist Criticism   3

TWO   Old and New in Modernist Art   33

THREE   Poetry and Rhetoric in the Modernist Montage   95

FOUR   Hard and Soft: Joyce and Others   120

PART II Paradoxes

FIVE   Durable Fluff: The Importance of
Not Being Earnest   143

SIX   Iridescent Mediocrity: Dornford Yates and Others   162

SEVEN Formulaic Creativity:
Simenon's Maigret Novels   195

PART III **Doxies**
EIGHT Model Artists in Paris:
Hastings, Hamnett, and Kiki   221

NINE The Aesthete in the Brothel: Proust and Others   257

Works Cited   281
Index   285

Preface

I have a personal stake in this book, which I want to mention here, partly because I think you have a right to know about it and partly as a way of explaining why I have written the book and what kind of result I am hoping to achieve with it. I have loved stories for as long as I can remember, and loved them rather indiscriminately—high and low, serious and funny, long and short—so long as they did what stories can do: hold my interest and provide the pleasures that we all derive from emotional investment in artificial beings. Moving from those (relatively) innocent pleasures through various academic modes of studying literature and art, I have regularly run into ways of dividing the texts I enjoyed into those that I should indeed enjoy and those that I shouldn't be enjoying at all. Offended at this regular correction of my taste, I have naturally sought to justify my choices, and, over the years, have written about science fiction, about crime stories, and about other kinds of texts that I like. Part of my motivation in writing this book, then, is just a continuation of that project, but there is a second part as well.

Born in 1929, I grew up with Modernism as a part of my heritage, and, attending Yale just before the midcentury, I was more or less indoctrinated into the New Critical account of aesthetic value, which I see now as a distinctly Modernist account. At Yale, too, I encountered a great teacher of art history, George Kubler, who directed me to the Museum of Modern Art in New York, which, as it happens, was also born in 1929. Visiting MoMA in the late 1940s, I absorbed semiconsciously the museum's doctrine that "modernism is the art that is essentially abstract" (now made explicit on MoMA's Web site). I shall return to both of these views (that of the New Critics and that of MoMA) later in this work, which may be seen as a continuation of my long attempt to extricate myself from these views while continuing to learn about Modernism.

On the literary side, my further academic studies, partly by design and partly by accident, led me deeper into Modernism as a field of scholarship, with special emphasis on writers like James Joyce, whose papers I catalogued at Cornell University, and William Faulkner, who was at the University of Virginia when I first taught there (when I taught *Absalom, Absalom!* in an undergraduate honors seminar, he sat in on the class). My pedigree in Anglo-American literary Modernism was strong enough, then, but my contact with these major writers, whose work I admired, never prevented me from continuing to be interested in their less exalted contemporaries— as they were, of course, themselves. There is no real equivalent for visual abstraction in the literary arts, though a number of attempts have been made to provide literary studies with a notion of Modernism as clear and powerful as MoMA's "art that is essentially abstract." Even so, critics and scholars kept attempting to define literary Modernism in terms of verbal experimentation or some form of departure from grammar, representation, or narrative structure.

Thinking about all this, studying the verbal and visual texts from the modern period, and discussing them with stu-

dents, colleagues, and friends, I sensed that my own understanding of Modernism, and the understanding of it by other
people as well, was far from accurate, and, even more important, far from useful in sorting out our own situation and
understanding the art and culture of our own time. So I began
to reconsider Modernism, casting a wider net for useful texts—
and to recognize that this was not my time but a very different
time, when other views and values prevailed, which could be
understood only by an immersion in the texts of that time, accompanied by a critical acceptance of my own position as a
foreigner, an alien in that territory, who needed to make a serious effort to understand the ways and values of the original
inhabitants. As I did this, over a period of many years, I began
to be more and more aware of a problem which has shaped
this book as a whole and every chapter within it—the problem
I have named in my title.

   We have been familiar with the notion of paradox as a literary value ever since the New Critics popularized it a half-
century or more ago. But paradoxy? What is that? I am using
the word to indicate a kind of confusion generated by a terminology that seems to make clear distinctions where clear distinctions cannot—and should not—be made. In particular, I
shall be examining the terminology that has been deployed in
definitions and discussions of Modernism in literature and the
other arts—a terminology generated at the time when what
we know as Modernism was establishing its place in the culture of the English-speaking world, and sustained by the critics and scholars who sought to interpret Modernism and teach
others about it. This terminology was based on apparently
clear and simple binary oppositions—high/low, for instance,
or old/new—which turn out, upon examination, to be far
from simple and anything but clear. Taken together, these oppositions often function to suppress or exclude a middle term,

forcing many admirable works into the lower half of an invidious distinction. The four chapters constituting Part I of this
book are devoted to explorations of four major paradoxies
that have shaped Modernist critical discourse.

These paradoxies share a tendency to reject or suppress
any middle term that might mediate between their extremes.
My project, then, has been to look into this critical terminology
and explore the confusions and contradictions lurking there,
hoping, among other things, to recover the middle that they exclude. In doing this I regularly capitalize the first letter of key
terms as a way of calling attention to their status as objects of
investigation rather than solid critical assumptions on which to
build—capitalization being less intrusive than such alternatives as scare quotes or italics. I shall begin with a chapter on the
distinction between High and Low, which has been the founding binary opposition for all Modernist critical terminology.

In the second chapter, I propose an examination of the
paradoxy of Old and New in the visual arts, not from MoMA's
perspective but from that of a weekly magazine appearing in
the crucial years from 1910 to 1914. In these excerpts from *The
New Age*, we will hear the voices of artists and critics as those
voices argued about what should be the proper art for modern
culture—and we will look at images of the works they were discussing. The critical vocabulary of Modernism began with the
visual arts, and was to some extent—and not always happily—
adopted by literary artists and critics. Writers like Joseph Conrad and Ford Madox Ford, for example, borrowed the term Impressionism to describe their own literary work, and Virginia
Woolf was discussing Cézanne with her sister and Roger Fry
even as she began her own career as a novelist.

After the investigation of Old and New in art, we shall
conclude Part I with two more considerations of the workings

of paradoxy in the definition of Modernism in literature: the distinction between Poetry and Rhetoric in Chapter 3, and that between Hardness and Softness or sentimentalism in Chapter 4. In Part II the focus will shift to discussions of works of modern literature that are excluded or marginalized by Modernist paradoxy. Part of what we miss when we regard Modernism through the lenses provided by its polemicists and writers of manifestos is the importance of traditional values in establishing the durability of works of literature and visual art. And by traditional values I mean things like empathy with characters and concern for their fates in fiction, the pleasures of recognition and seeing freshly in visual art, and the defamiliarizing effects of poetic language. I also mean wit and grace, whether verbal or visual. The one thing that distinguishes the arts from other kinds of texts is that their aim is pleasure. They can please by representing pain and ugliness, but please they must—or they are not art but something else. We do not take pleasure seriously enough, I believe, and Modernism, with its emphasis on the connection between greatness and difficulty, is to some extent responsible for this. Therefore I shall have something to say in the following pages about the importance of being earnest about pleasure, assuming the risk of paradoxical discourse myself.

The emphasis in Part II, then, will be on pleasurable writers and texts, best described by paradoxical categories—with paradox itself functioning here as a kind of antidote to paradoxy: Oscar Wilde and "Durable Fluff" in Chapter 5, Dornford Yates and "Iridescent Mediocrity" in Chapter 6, and Georges Simenon and "Formulaic Creativity" in Chapter 7. Then, finally, in Part III, we will consider what I call "Doxies": lives and texts concerned with prostitution or the bohemia that exists on the border of the brothel, where artists and models exchange places and aesthetes get down and dirty. Some of these texts are journalistic or cast in the form of casual memoirs. Such texts are the doxies of Modernism, represented in Chapter 8 by letters and memoirs from women who modeled for Modernist painters. Others reveal High Modernist authors descending to low places, as with Proust and Joyce in the world of prostitutes and brothels in Chapter 9.

This whole book, then, will constitute a sort of *descensus ad avernum*. (Did I mention that Virgil came to my class when I taught the *Aeneid*? Actually, he didn't, but the ghost of Miss Jennings, my high school Latin teacher, was there, I assure you.) Anyway, the descent is easy, the poet said, and I hope you will find it so. Parts of Chapters 1, 4, and 6 appeared in an essay published in *Narrative* (vol. 11, no. 3 [October 2003]). I am grateful to the editor, James Phelan, for very helpful advice at that time and also for permission to use those materials in this book, where they appear in extensively revised and expanded versions. Part of Chapter 8 appeared in the *Hemingway Review* (September 22, 1999), and I thank Susan Beegel for permission to use it here. All materials drawn from *The New Age* have been taken from the digital edition of that journal available at <www.modjourn.brown.edu>, where they may be accessed and used freely by anyone, and I strongly recommend that site to all those who share my interest in modernity and Modernism. The manuscript of this book was read by John Kulka, of Yale University Press, by Carl Klaus, James Phelan, and an anonymous reader for the Press. They saved me from many follies, and I am grateful to them all. The faults that remain are, I am afraid, necessary aspects of whatever virtues this book may claim.

Paradoxy of Modernism

Part I
Paradoxies

In this part we shall explore the major oppositions that have structured discussions of Modernism in literature and the arts: High and Low, Old and New, Poetry and Rhetoric, Hard and Soft. In Modernist critical discourse, each of these sets of terms has operated to exclude a middle ground or to obscure complications and combinations of the basic oppositional terms. My main goal in these chapters will be to recover what has been excluded or to restore complications that have been lost. These discussions are meant, among other things, to set the stage for later chapters that focus primarily on artists and texts that have been marginalized if not excluded by the manifestos and critical dogmas of Modernism, though we shall return to High texts in Low places in the final chapter.

1

High and Low
in Modernist Criticism

I want to insist on the existence of badness in poetry and so
to establish an antithetic point of reference for the discussion
of goodness. . . . The purpose of my essay is . . . to show
the relationship between examples acknowledged
to lie in the realms of the good and the bad.
—*W. K. Wimsatt*

My objectives in this chapter are to look into the way the terms High and Low were deployed in the critical discourse around Modernism, and how they slide easily into absolute notions of Good and Bad. I shall also try to situate that discourse in relation to some earlier versions of the High/Low distinction, and

to use the results of that investigation to argue that the paradoxy we find when we look into these matters should lead us
to rethink the Modernist canon and curriculum, opening up
both of these to accommodate texts formerly excluded, and
should make us more alert to the way that texts we think of as
belonging to one or the other of these categories often have
crucial elements that our critical discourse associates with its
opposite.

In a recent article Andreas Huyssen finds it necessary to
clarify the interpretation of the "Great Divide" between High
and Low Modernism that he advanced to such great effect in
his book, *After the Great Divide:*

> Much valuable recent work on the editing, marketing,
> and dissemination of Modernism has misconstrued my
> earlier definition of the Great Divide as a static binary
> of high Modernism vs. the market. My argument was
> rather that there had been, since the mid-nineteenth cen-
> tury in Europe, a powerful imaginary insisting on the di-
> vide while time and again violating that categorical sepa-
> ration in practice. After all, the insight that all cultural
> products are subject to the market was already advanced
> by Theodor Adorno, key theorist of the divide, in the late
> 1930s. (366–67)

Huyssen goes on to say that he was mainly interested in how
the divide played out in the context of Post-Modernist attempts to break down the wall between High and Low, and that
he now wishes to reconfigure or reconsider the divide in terms
of a global approach to comparative literary studies. This is all
well and good, but it seems to me that certain aspects of the divide have never been properly understood, and that in order to
understand them we need to reexamine some of the internal

contradictions and other problems that I am calling paradoxy in the work of those who theorized the divide during the Modernist period—not just Adorno but others, ranging from Georg Lukács and Clement Greenberg to the literary New Critics. It will also help, after this, to consider briefly some previous formulations of the High/Low opposition, from which the Modernist version evolved.

We can start with Lukács, who was insisting on the distinction as early as 1914–15, when he wrote *Theory of the Novel*. In the preface he wrote for the 1963 edition of this book, Lukács points out that he had composed the work during World War I, in a mood of profound depression as he contemplated the future of Europe. First published in a journal, it appeared as a book in 1920. In this work, Lukács wished to make an argument for the novel as a major form of literary art—a motivation that he shared with such illustrious predecessors as Gustave Flaubert and Henry James, though his reasoning was very different from theirs. For Lukács the novel succeeded the epic as the proper narrative mode for an age after the death of God, a narrative grounded in what he called a "transcendental homelessness" (61). Lukács felt that the dignity of the novel was threatened by the presence of a number of similar but trivial narrative modes, the most prominent among them being "mere entertainment literature" (71). The novel, he asserted, unlike other literary genres, was cursed by having an evil twin: "a caricatural twin almost indistinguishable from itself in all inessential formal characteristics: the entertainment novel, which has all the outward features of the novel but which, in essence, is bound to nothing and based on nothing, i.e. is entirely meaningless" (73).

Lukács wanted the novel to do serious cultural work, which meant, for him, a Hegelian project, in which characters would embody the workings of a progressive historical dialectic. This led him, as similar concerns led Erich Auerbach, to privilege novels that offered a coherent and historicized narrative position (omniscience) and dealt with social and economic forces from a progressive perspective, exposing the evils of capitalistic society in the manner of Balzac or pointing the way toward a better social system. The pessimistic naturalism of Zola he did not approve, and, indeed, Lukács linked naturalism to aestheticism as excessively concerned with sensual details. Granting these concerns their seriousness, his attack on "the entertainment novel" is still shocking in its vehemence: "the entertainment novel . . . is bound to *nothing* and based on *nothing*, i.e. is *entirely* meaningless" (emphasis added). The double nothings, and the unnecessary adverb intensifying the already absolute "meaningless" to a presumably lower level of inanity, reveal a serious problem here.

This man was protesting too much. Which suggests that he was fond of the guilty pleasure found in these works and was trying to exorcize the demon from his consciousness. But my serious point here is that multiplying the zeroes and intensifying the meaninglessness simply will not work. Literary texts cannot be classified so rigidly. The divide that Lukács was trying so strenuously to create never existed and could not exist, because narratives are essentially entertaining, whether epics or novels, and because a narrative cannot be entirely meaningless or based on nothing. In asserting that novels are "essentially entertaining," I mean to insist that narrative structures are linked to a distinctly human psychology of pleasure at a very fundamental level of existence. Lukács was too thoughtful a critic to ignore this, and in his later work he modified his extreme position. But the question of the purity or rigidity of the divide is the most important issue we shall face. If we were to follow Lukács, we might define the opposition in terms of entertainment versus representation (allowing the word "representation" to stand for the complex issues Lukács addressed using terms like "realism" and "narration"), but before accepting any single view, we must look more deeply into the ways in which various critics have defined the divide. We can begin with the powerful formulation articulated by the American art critic Clement Greenberg in the 1930s.

In his 1939 essay "Avant-Garde and Kitsch," Greenberg made a frankly class-based assessment of the High/Low divide. Great art—high culture—depends, he argued, on a class with leisure and education: "No culture can develop without a social basis, without a source of stable income. And in the case of the avant-garde, this was provided by an elite among the ruling class of that society from which it assumed itself to be cut off, but to which it has always remained attached by an umbilical cord of gold" (8). But these proper patrons of the highest art, "the rich and the cultivated," were being wooed away from supporting the avant-garde artists who kept the flame of culture alive—wooed away by a spurious commercial or academic substitute: "that thing to which the Germans gave the wonderful name of *Kitsch:* popular, commercial art and literature with their chromeotypes, magazine covers, illustrations, ads, slick and pulp fictions, comics, Tin Pan Alley music, tap dancing, Hollywood movies, etc., etc." (9). In a brief historical excursus, Greenberg blamed the birth of kitsch on "peasants who settled in cities as proletariat and petty bourgeois." These wretches "learned to read and write for the sake of efficiency, but they did not win the leisure and comfort necessary for the enjoyment of the city's traditional culture" (10). Thus they demanded—and got—something less elevated than the art that the rich and cultivated had supported:

> To fill the demand of the new market, a new commodity was devised: ersatz culture, kitsch, destined for those who,

insensible to the values of genuine culture, are hungry nevertheless for the diversion that only culture of some sort can provide.

Kitsch, using for raw material the debased and academicized simulacra of genuine culture, welcomes and cultivates this insensibility. It is the source of its profits. Kitsch is mechanical and operates by formulas. Kitsch is vicarious experience and faked sensations. Kitsch changes according to style, but remains always the same. Kitsch is the epitome of all that is spurious in the life of our times. Kitsch pretends to demand nothing of its customers except their money—not even their time. (10)

Just how this cheap stuff manufactured to please half-educated peasants succeeded in luring the rich and cultivated away from their support of high art is left a bit unclear by Greenberg, but we can tease out his reasoning if we look closely enough at what he is saying. We can note, as in Lukács, the vehemence of the denunciation of what is being designated as Low in this formulation and the insistence that the distinction be absolute, despite some awkward cases that seem to claim a middle ground. This is apparent, for example, in Greenberg's description of *The New Yorker* as "fundamentally high-class kitsch for the luxury trade" (11). Genuine art, for Greenberg, is "necessarily difficult" and requires work from the cultivated consumer (15), while kitsch offers the pleasures of art without the work. High equals difficult; Low equals easy. High art offers pain, which the cultivated can transmute, with effort, into pleasure; Low art offers its pleasures directly. Greenberg compares T. S. Eliot to Edgar Guest (whom he patronizingly calls "Eddie"), Braque to a *Saturday Evening Post* cover (read Norman Rockwell), and Michelangelo to Maxfield Parrish. We, the cultivated ones, know better, yet we will put the lower pictures on our walls and read the lower books as well. Why should this be the case? Greenberg's answer to that question seems to be this:

- Avant-garde art is necessarily critical of late capitalism ("capitalism in decline").
- The cultivated ruling class does not want to hear this message.
- Therefore this class turns away to cheap and easy satisfactions.

Greenberg's assumed connection between avant-gardism in art and a socialist or anticapitalist avant-gardism in politics is no longer a viable assumption—if it ever was one. That is, we can no longer easily assume that violating aesthetic conventions contributes to the alteration of social structures. That is one reason why Greenberg's distinction is not useful for us, though the more nuanced version of this position developed by Adorno and Horkheimer must be considered. Another reason lies in Greenberg's insistence that kitsch is "mechanical and operates by formulas." We can clarify this problem by rethinking Walter Benjamin's distinction between works of mechanical reproduction and works that retain the aura of the oral storyteller. The actual oral storyteller, whether epic or more humble, worked with formulas at every level of production from verbal to structural and thus was formulaic without being mechanical.

Formulas belong to crafts; mechanical reproduction belongs to industry. They are very different things, and the tendency of Modernist critics to equate them is a major aspect of Modernist paradoxy. What it comes down to, perhaps, is a distinction between works that are virtually identical—truly mechanical—and works that are individualized productions of a formulaic craft. It seems to me that the novels of Jane Austen are formulaic in plotting and even to some extent in characterization (all those villains whose names begin with W, for example), but are nonetheless clearly the products of a crafty individual rather than a factory. Perhaps Clement Greenberg considered Jane Austen's novels "high class kitsch"—I do not know. But my point is that formulas have a place in almost all art, and sometimes an important place, as E. H. Gombrich demonstrated so powerfully in *Art and Illusion*. Much of the pleasure we derive from works of art has to do with our recognition of formulaic patterns—and this includes music, visual art, and verbal art. This is an important and complex matter that deserves a chapter of its own, which it shall receive, but I must make two observations about it at this point.

1. There is undoubtedly a sliding scale between the highly formulaic (call it mechanical) and the highly original in aesthetic texts, but the absolute ends of the scale are impossible to occupy, since they would yield no new text at one end and an unintelligible text at the other.

2. Modernist discourse often insists that aesthetic value is distributed perfectly along this scale, with the best work at the original end and the worst at the formulaic end. This discursive position has played a major role in creating and sustaining the Great Divide and the paradoxy of Modernism. A lifetime of reading, looking at images, and listening to music on both sides of the divide has convinced me that interesting work (and uninteresting work) may be found all along this scale. I shall argue, then, that we have something to gain by at-

tending to the works of the modern period without accepting the presuppositions of many Modernist critics.

A second problem in Greenberg's formulation is in that snappy put-down at the end of the passage I quoted above: "Kitsch pretends to demand nothing of its customers except their money—not even their time." Now if kitsch is in fact a remedy for boredom, time is precisely what it demands—or, rather, what it fills. It is, to some extent, there to fill empty time with pleasure. Matei Calinescu shows a keen awareness of this in his own discussion of kitsch in *Five Faces of Modernity:*

> To understand the nature of kitsch we should, then, analyze the particular hedonism characteristic of middle-class mentality. Its primary feature is perhaps that it is a middle-of-the-road hedonism, perfectly illustrated by the "principle of mediocrity" that always obtains in kitsch (this all-pervading mediocrity is easier to notice in the more elaborate and exaggeratedly complicated forms of kitsch). (244)

> Kitsch is the direct artistic result of an important ethical mutation for which the peculiar time awareness of the middle classes has been responsible. By and large, kitsch may be viewed as a reaction against the "terror" of change and the meaninglessness of chronological time flowing from an unreal past into an equally unreal future. . . . The fun of kitsch is just the other side of terrible and incomprehensible boredom. (248)

"Fun," of course, is a word that trivializes the pleasure to be obtained by works labeled kitsch, but the notion of a kind of existential boredom, a fear of the meaninglessness of a life without hope for human progress or a heavenly reward, is far from trivial. Calinescu, I believe, may exempt himself too easily from "middle-class mentality" and disparage too readily the need of modern human beings for pleasure. (I am rejecting the notion that there is a real distinction between "fun" and "pleasure." I see Calinescu's "fun" as a term meant to trivialize rather than describe.) But by pointing toward a "terrible and incomprehensible boredom" as an aspect of the modern situation, he offers us a major clue to the function and power of works composed by modern writers who accept "mediocrity" (a word I hope to redeem) as their portion and the pleasure of audiences as their goal. I would thus distinguish between works that attempt to pass themselves off as high art by aping the superficial signs of superior achievement—true kitsch, if you will— and works that decline the masterpiece gambit and aim at a lower but genuine level of artistic production—the level of craft, as opposed to art, perhaps, or the level of entertainment, as opposed to what I called "representation" in discussing Lukács above.

Lukács returns to this question himself in the essay "Narrate or Describe," included in the American collection of his essays, *Writer and Critic:*

There has probably never been a time like the present when so much empty literature of pure adventure has flourished alongside the official, serious literature. Nor can there be any illusion that this literature is read simply by the "uneducated" while the "elite" stick to the significant artistic literature. Rather the opposite is the case. Modern classics are read partly out of a sense of duty and partly out of an interest in the content—to the extent that they deal with the problems of the time even hesitantly and with distortion. For recreation and pleasure, however, the public turns to detective stories.

While working on *Madame Bovary*, Flaubert complained that his novel failed to provide entertainment. We encounter similar complaints from many outstanding modern writers; they note that the great writers of the past combined the representation of significant human beings with entertainment and suspense, for which modern art has substituted monotony and tedium. (124–25)

Unlike Greenberg, Lukács sees the rise of entertainment as a result of the nature of Modernist fiction itself, which repudiated entertainment and suspense at the cost of introducing monotony and boredom. (Some of this difference results from the different objects the critics are considering—mainly visual art for Greenberg and verbal for Lukács—but the problem cuts across all the media.) The problem posed by Lukács is the real problem of the High/Low divide—how the contemporary writer can recover or find an equivalent for that combination of significance and entertainment so abundantly present in the works of the great nineteenth-century novelists. In the visual arts, as we shall see in the next chapter, the problem takes the form of how artists should proceed after Impressionism, which had offered a combination of significance and entertainment that still works powerfully in museums and auction houses alike. That is why the question of "Post-Impressionism" looms so large in debates on the visual arts in the period during which Modernism was taking shape.

It seems to me that Lukács, more than any other critic, put the problem in a form that is still useful to us, by asking how entertainment and suspense could be combined in fiction with the serious representation of modern life. In later chapters, I shall look into some attempts to achieve this, on both sides of the High/Low divide as we have been seeing it, but first we must continue to stare into the abyss itself. Theodor Adorno and Max Horkheimer will help us. Their essay, "The Culture Industry: Enlightenment as Mass Deception," was written in America during World War II and first appeared in print in 1947. In recent years it has been essential reading in cultural studies programs, but I am not sure that it is really being "read." Rather, we all too often emerge from reading or studying the essay with a simple moral about the evils of the culture industry that ignores the Adornian complexities of the text. We cannot remedy this situation here and now, but we can look a bit more closely at some of those complexities, as in the following passage:

> "Light" art as such, distraction, is not a decadent form. Anyone who complains that it is a betrayal of the ideal of pure expression is under an illusion about society. The purity of bourgeois art, which hypostasized itself as a world of freedom in contrast to what was happening in the material world, was from the beginning bought with the exclusion of the lower classes—with whose cause, the real universality, art keeps faith precisely by its freedom from the ends of the false universality. Serious art has been withheld from those for whom the hardship and oppression of life make a mockery of seriousness, and who must be glad if they can use time not spent at the production line just to keep going. Light art has been the shadow of autonomous art. It is the social bad conscience of serious art. The truth which the latter necessarily lacked because of its social premises gives the other the semblance

of legitimacy. The division itself is the truth; it does at least express the negativity of the culture which the different spheres constitute. Least of all can the antithesis be reconciled by absorbing light into serious or vice versa. But that is what the culture industry attempts. (135)

The first and the penultimate sentences of this passage are perhaps the most important. Adorno and Horkheimer argue that light art is not a betrayal of serious art but a social necessity for those who have been left out of serious art, despite its claims to universality. The artistic Great Divide, in this view, expresses an important truth about a great social division between the exploiters, whose leisure is based on the exploitation of others, and the exploited, whose lives are not expressed in serious art and who are incapable of attending to that art because of the pressures of mere existence. Seen from this angle, the divide is not the problem; the culture industry's attempts to disguise it are the problem. For Adorno and Horkheimer, art has always been a commodity since its invention as an autonomous sphere of activity patronized by Renaissance bankers, but it preserves its critical autonomy even while being patronized: "What is new is not that it is a commodity, but that today it deliberately admits that it is one; that art renounces its own autonomy and proudly takes its place among consumption goods" (157).

There is a problem hidden in the Adorno/Horkheimer formulation—a problem of paradoxy that we need to notice at this point—and that is the unjustified assumption that all light art is produced by the "culture industry," and that it is produced for the masses who are too tired from exploitation to enjoy the serious art that is consumed by the leisured members of society, whose leisure is based on the exploitation of those working masses. Actually, there is—and has been in ancient, medieval, and modern times—light art produced by very skilled literary artists for the more favored classes of society. Part of the problem in the Adorno/Horkheimer formulation, and in other variations of that view, is in the serious/light opposition itself. The opposite of "light" in our language is "heavy," and the opposite of "serious" is "comic"—as in the traditional distinction in Mozart's time between *opera seria* and *opera buffa*—which Mozart himself did so much to undo. And we shall see these matters more clearly if we remain aware of those distinctions. The word "light" can be used to trivialize the comic as the word "fun" is used to trivialize pleasure. Both the comic and the serious are interpretive gestures toward a world that is neither comic nor serious, a world that is neutral, indifferent. Like pain and pleasure—which are responses to the world by the beings who inhabit it—the comic and the serious are human interpretations of the world, ways of humanizing that world which help us to deal with it. And that is why we call the studies that deal with these modes of interpretation "the humanities."

The most basic problem in the Adorno/Horkheimer formulation, then, is the use of serious and light as a binary opposition. But even if we were accept that formulation, there would remain another problem in the mapping of the terms of this opposition onto such class distinctions as upper and lower, or elite and mass, or bourgeoisie and proletariat—or any other set of social signifiers. This problem is that the privileged group in every one of these formulations has always enjoyed light literature. That much is obvious. What is perhaps less obvious is that the unprivileged group has also always enjoyed serious literature. But here is where the false opposition between light and serious really inhibits our vision. We can take a cue here from Matthew Arnold, who frequently referred to "high seriousness" in literature, implying, perhaps unwittingly, that there might be a low seriousness as well. And so there is, if we only look for it. There is a serious quality found in folk tales, in melodrama, in crime fiction, in a lot of soap opera, and in many other genres, which we may call "low seriousness" if we choose. But if we respond to this notion by saying, "Oh, but those are not really serious," the game is up. We need, instead of making that thoughtless response, to think harder about what High and Low seriousness might actually mean, as we may have already thought about the difference between High and Low comedy.

I would go further in this matter, and I shall do so later, but now I want to make just one more observation before returning to the main topic of this chapter: If we can distinguish between High and Low comedy, as we might, for example, between Oscar Wilde's *The Importance of Being Earnest* and *Pop Goes the Easel* by the Three Stooges, we have not necessarily made a distinction between good and bad. Chaplin's *Modern Times* probably belongs in the low-comedy category, but we might wish to argue that it is better than the work of the Three Stooges. And what about *Fawlty Towers?* Low, surely, but good or bad? My point is that categorical terms ought to be descriptive and apply to whole groups of works, whereas evaluation should always be a unique judgment of a particular work by a particular person. We run into difficulties when we apply evaluative terminology to entire categories, whether these be literary, artistic, social, or racial. And we run into enormous difficulties when we try to map one category onto another, as in any mapping of Low or light literature onto the masses and High or serious literature onto the privileged. But let us return to the attempts of Modernist critics to do just that.

All of the critiques of the situation of art and literature that we have so far considered have been drawn from critics on the political left, as the critics themselves would certainly have acknowledged. And they all have certain features in common, but the differences among them are at least as important as the similarities. Let us see (at the cost of further oversimplification) whether we can sort these out:

- For Lukács, serious literature moved away from narrative pleasure, thus opening the divide.
- For Greenberg, the cultivated class got lazy and abandoned high art for kitsch.
- For Adorno and Horkheimer, art for the cultivated was always a lie, but its existence, along with that of entertainment, indicated the truth of the social divide. The culture industry's easy bridges over the divide are a worse lie, because they conceal the invidious class structure itself.
- For Calinescu, kitsch is a peculiarly modern form of entertainment, generated by the existential terrors of Modernity, which justify, to some extent, the work of the culture industry.

If we can accept these rather brutal summaries as at least sketching the range of views of the Great Divide from the left side, they may serve for benchmarks as we turn to see how things look from the vantage point of the right.

Actually, things don't look very different—to the point of causing us to wonder about the usefulness of right and left as ways of thinking about these matters. We shall find paradoxy there, too, if we look, but that investigation must be put off while we focus on other matters. The right is seldom as bla-

tant, however, about the connection of High culture with elevated social and financial position as is Clement Greenberg.
But let us look at some examples. I take Allen Tate's essay
"Tension in Poetry" as a quintessential instance of the view of
the divide from the right. In this essay, which, as I have argued
elsewhere (*The Crafty Reader*, chapter 1), was seminal for the
New Criticism, Tate argues for a sharp distinction between
good poetry, marked by the quality he called "tension," and
bad poetry, which comes in a number of debased forms:

> political poetry for the sake of the cause; picturesque po-
> etry for the sake of the home town; didactic poetry for
> the sake of the parish; even a generalized personal poetry
> for the sake of the reassurance and safety of numbers. This
> last I suppose is the most common variety, the anony-
> mous lyricism in which the common personality exhibits
> its commonness, its obscure and standard eccentricity, in
> a language that seems always to be deteriorating; so that
> today many poets are driven to inventing private lan-
> guages, or very narrow ones, because public speech has
> become heavily tainted with mass feeling.
>   Mass language is the medium of "communication," and
> its users are less interested in bringing to formal order
> what is today called the "affective state" than in arousing
> that state. (55)

The word "common" beats like a drum in this passage and
leads to the notion of mass communication in the last sentence. Our language has been debased by the mass media, and
this debasement has driven the modern poet to new heights of
obscurity in order to avoid the common. Tate locates the roots
of this process of debasement in 1798 (the year of the first edi-

tion of *Lyrical Ballads,* among other things) and labels it "the fallacy of communication in poetry" (56). From the perspective of the right, the Great Divide seems to have been caused by what José Ortega y Gasset called "the revolt of the masses," with the ensuing corruption of the common tongue by the mass media, which drove serious poets into private languages at worst or, at best, into the difficulties and obscurities Tate praises as poetic "tension." As W. K. Wimsatt put it, "Every real poem is a complex poem" (81). In this scenario mass-mediated kitsch *caused* the avant-garde to appear and thus created the Great Divide. Most of those who looked into the Great Divide from the right saw the High as a necessary refuge from the Low, though they attributed the low to different causes.

The New Humanists, for example, led by T. S. Eliot's teachers Irving Babbitt and Paul Elmer Moore, blamed the deterioration of culture on Rousseau, Baudelaire, and other advocates of self-expression. These critics condemned self-expression under the general label of Romanticism, to which they opposed a Classicism of restraint—a restraint that expressed itself through objective correlatives for subjective emotions, thus bringing order, in Tate's terms, to the "affective state," controlling emotion rather than arousing it. But the divide, expressed frequently in terms derived from Tate's influential essay, continued to manifest itself in the critical prose of Eliot himself and all the New Critics. The problem behind all these formulations, of course, is the preference of many readers for "bad" poetry. Wimsatt addressed this issue in his essay "The Concrete Universal," in which he mentioned (like Greenberg) the name of Edgar Guest as the author of "newspaper poems" that lack "artistic unity." To this comment he appended a footnote to the effect that a reader he esteemed had complained that Guest's name should not even be uttered in a

serious discussion of poetry, that "such a name appears in a serious discussion of poetics anomalously and in bad taste" (81).
(One is tempted to see Allen Tate behind the mask of this esteemed reader.) But Wimsatt defended himself by saying that
he kept the name because he wanted to insist on the existence
of "badness" in poetry as a point of reference for talking about
"goodness," and he explicitly rejected such euphemisms as
"mediocrity."

The critics of the right certainly helped to create and sustain the Great Divide, and they did it in the name of poetry. The
problem they faced, of course, was that far too many readers
were unable or unwilling to follow the poets of tension across
the divide to the heights of "good" poetry. There was a solution, however. It came to be called "The New Criticism," and it
taught the art of reading the works of poets driven to obscurity by the depredations of the mass media and the vulgariza-
tion of the common tongue. The difficulties of the poetry of
"tension" required and sustained the efforts of critics and teachers who could lead less gifted people across the divide to the
heights of critical appreciation. In the marketplace of ideas, the
Great Divide could be used to generate cultural and economic
capital for the literary critic, whose role Wimsatt defined as
that of "a teacher or explicator of meanings" (34). In a revealing moment he mentioned an anecdote recounted by Thomas
Mann: "Mann and a friend came out of a movie weeping co-
piously—but Mann narrates the incident in support of his
view that movies are not Art. 'Art is a *cold* sphere'" (31).

Not all of the New Critics were so visibly on the political
right as Allen Tate, whose Tory disdain of the common man
and (especially) woman was all too obvious, but the New Critics, like their New Humanist predecessors, preferred the "cold"
or restrained in art and literature, which they defined as Good.

The New Humanists, based primarily at Harvard, and the New Critics, based primarily at Yale, shared a sense of their special educational mission: the training of a social elite in the virtues proper to a ruling class. These virtues were dominated by Classical restraint for the New Humanists and by a judicious appreciation of irony and paradox for the New Critics, but the general outlook was similar. The Great Divide in literature would be used to maintain a social divide. Teachers of literature would work to ensure the perpetuation of a class of cultured leaders for the uncultured mass of common people. Or, in a more democratic formulation, such teachers would work to elevate as many of the uncultured mass as could be saved from their enslavement to the media and the Bad literature of which they were too fond. Thus elevated, they might join the ruling class, though there was some question about whether women *could* be so elevated.

The Great Divide as seen from the right does not look so very different from the Great Divide as seen from the left. Adorno was as ready to reject any aesthetic bridging of the gap as was Wimsatt or Tate. In this, perhaps, they were all very much products of their time, which was the time of Modernism itself, and, in particular, the moment of Modernist reflection, which came after the great achievements of Modernist art and literature. The Great Divide, it is now apparent, was a basic element of Modernist critical theory and Modernist pedagogy. For the most part, critics from both the left and the right attributed the divide to a prior social or economic divide, though they differed about the possibility—or even the desirability—of diminishing the socioeconomic gap. But we can learn something from the different ways in which the abstract notions of high and low were filled by more concrete descriptive terms. Consider, for example, the following table:

high	low
good	bad (Wimsatt)
avant-garde	kitsch (Greenberg)
tension (private)	communication (mass) (Tate)
classic	romantic (Babbitt, Hulme)
serious	light (Adorno/Horkheimer)
representation	entertainment (Lukács)

I have arranged the table not from left to right, but from the most abstract and extreme to the most nuanced and complex, which as it happens goes from America to Europe as well. Only the latter two formulations allow any virtue at all to the term on the right, and only the last (Lukács) saw the union of the two sides as both possible and desirable. But even Lukács gave priority to the term on the left, seeing entertainment and suspense as something that representation once possessed but had lost. For Adorno and Horkheimer, mixing the two modes is all too possible and the result was deplorable. For most of the others, a mixture was neither possible nor desirable. But the question had been in the air since at least 1914. An illuminating exchange of views on this very matter may be found in the correspondence of Max Beerbohm and Virginia Woolf.

When Woolf's famous polemic on behalf of Modernist writing, "Mr. Bennett and Mrs. Brown," was published as a pamphlet in 1924, Beerbohm responded with what a perceptive critic has called "preemptive senescence" (Danson, 22): "In your novels you are so hard on us common readers. You seem to forget us and to think only of your theme and your method. Your novels beat me—black and blue. I retire howling, aching, sore; full, moreover, of an acute sense of disgrace. I return later, I re-submit myself to the discipline. No use: I am carried out half-dead" (165). "You certainly are very like your father," he says, turning himself into a contemporary of Leslie Stephen—and lending Woolf a kind of Victorian severity as well. In fairness to her, of course, we should note that in "Mr. Bennett and Mrs. Brown" Woolf herself had emphasized the need for the reader and the writer to share certain values, both social and aesthetic. In that essay she took James Joyce and T. S. Eliot to task, respectively, for indecency and obscurity. We may find her wrong on both counts, if we choose, but we should also find food for thought in the way she posed the problem of Joyce and Eliot. She saw it as a function of an unfortunate social gap between the Modernist or "Georgian" writer and the readers she addressed directly in this essay and in her own fiction: "It is this division between reader and writer, this humility on your part, these professional airs and graces on ours, that corrupt and emasculate the books which should be the healthy offspring of a close and equal alliance between us" (118).

What Woolf meant by "professional airs and graces" may be glossed by her earlier comment on the experience of reading T. S. Eliot's poetry:

> I think that Mr. Eliot has written some of the loveliest single lines in modern poetry. But how intolerant he is for the old usages and politenesses of society—respect for the weak, consideration for the dull. As I sun myself upon the intense and ravishing beauty of one of his lines, and reflect that I must make a dizzy and dangerous leap to the next, and so on from line to line, like an acrobat flying precariously from bar to bar, I cry out, I confess, for the old decorums, and envy the indolence of my ancestors who, instead of spinning madly through mid-air, dreamt quietly in the shade with a book. (116)

Woolf was clearly seeking in this essay—as she sought in writing her own fiction—for a compromise between the avant-gardist ambitions of Modernism and the traditional pleasures that earlier literature had offered its readers. It is both ironic and amusing, then, for Beerbohm to appear in the guise of one of those ancestors, putting her in the place where she had put Eliot—as one who is hard on "common readers"—just two years after the appearance of her collection of reviews and essays called *The Common Reader* (which Beerbohm admired), in which she observed in her concluding essay that "Mr. Beerbohm, in his way, is perfect, but it is not a big way" (240). Woolf, in her persona as a common reader, kept hoping for what she called, in the closing phrase of her book, "the masterpiece to come" (246)—and it is clear that, for her, the masterpiece, when it came, would be "big."

Acutely aware of the Great Divide, Woolf seemed to be trying to position herself on both sides of it—as an uncommon writer for common readers—while Beerbohm was saying, in effect, "No, Virginia, you are entirely uncommon as a writer of fiction." For the purposes of our present inquiry, however, what may be most important is the way Woolf shared the feeling of Lukács that modern writing need not and should not abandon the pleasures provided by the great Victorian novelists. For Lukács, of course, Woolf represented that inward turn to subjectivity he called "description" as opposed to "narration," and of which he disapproved. But Woolf tried repeatedly to cross the divide from the modern or uncommon side and reach those common readers, succeeding often enough to lead a committed Modernist critic like Hugh Kenner to deny Woolf's writing a spot in the Modernist canon. If Woolf is not a Modernist we are indeed in the land of paradoxy. And Woolf, to be sure, made her own attack on the middle in some intemperate musings on the "Middlebrow," to which we shall return more than once in the course of this book. An attempt to exclude the middle can be seen as the engine driving Modernist paradoxy itself, so that my hope is to recover the middle without destroying that engine, without which there would be no Modernism at all. That such a hope may itself be paradoxical (or oxymoronic) should go without saying. Before moving on to other aspects of Modernist paradoxy, however, it will be useful to look back a bit farther into the history of the High/Low distinction, which has existed in some form or other since Aristotle.

Aristotle thought about these matters in ways that are still instructive for us, or can be, if we pay attention to him. We have, fortunately, lost his treatise on comedy, or people like me might find nothing new to say about it, but what he says about tragedy in the *Poetics* can be useful to us here. He found the stuff of tragedy in Homer, though not the dramatic form which he believed to be the best medium for tragic subject matter and found perfected in Aeschylos and Sophocles. And tragic subject matter required characters and situations he referred to as *spoudaios*. Here we can use some help from recent scholarship on Aristotle. Paul Cantor tells us,

> The Greek word *spoudaios* is normally translated as *good* or *serious*. However one chooses to understand the term, the essential point is that Aristotle understands *spoudaios* in contrast to *phaulos,* and that together the two terms reflect the hierarchy of aristocratic society in ancient Greece. *Spoudaios* characterizes the way of life of the Greek hero or warrior or noble; *phaulos* the way of life of the ordinary man, the slave, or the commoner. (Cantor in Perkins, 65)

In other words, the literary terminology that European culture derived from Aristotle linked social position with literary value.

Critical terms like noble and base, High and Low, good and bad have ever since mixed social and aesthetic qualities, sometimes concealing the one behind the other.

In eighteenth-century Britain the High/Low distinction became a function of a new discourse on Taste, in which the aesthetic and the social are wonderfully mixed. We can find an exemplary instance of this in a passage in Lord Kames's *Elements of Criticism*. Taste entered English discourse as a serious critical term in David Hume's essay of 1757, "On the Standard of Taste," and was transmitted to the schools by Lord Kames's adaptation of Hume's views in 1762. Kames took up the question of taste in the introduction to his three-volume textbook and returned to it in his final lecture. In the introduction he argued that "the God of nature" has constructed the world so that humans may pass from "corporeal pleasures to the more refined pleasures of sense; and not less so, from these to the exalted pleasures of morality and religion" (1: 5–6). He continued in this vein:

> We stand therefore engaged in honour, as well as interest, to second the purposes of nature, by cultivating the pleasures of the eye and ear, those especially that require extraordinary culture, such as are inspired by poetry, painting, sculpture, music, gardening, and architecture. *This chiefly is the duty of the opulent, who have leisure to improve their minds and their feelings.* . . . A taste in the fine arts goes hand in hand with the moral sense, to which indeed it is nearly allied. Both of them discover what is right and wrong. . . . They are rooted in human nature.
> (1: 6–7, emphasis added)

It is painfully clear how powerfully the social and economic are commingled with the aesthetic and moral in this formulation. Human nature reaches its peak among the opulent, who have the leisure to cultivate their taste. And good taste is closely connected to good behavior, making the rich not just richer but ethically better than their inferiors in opulence. The function of *The Elements of Criticism* as a textbook, however, suggests that this process might be reversible. Cultural capital, demonstrated by means of a cultivated taste, could lead in the direction of opulence and hence to virtue. Thus Kames concluded his third volume with a lecture on "The Standard of Taste," in which he indicated that the major purpose of his book was "to lay a foundation for this valuable branch of knowledge" (3: 374). To learn what Kames called "the elements of criticism" was to acquire "a standard of taste."

Some of Kames's views on taste were still alive and well, as we have seen, in the writing of Clement Greenberg two centuries later, and, mixed with something else, in the theories of Horkheimer and Adorno. This "something else" was added to the discourse of High and Low in the Romantic period. We can find a powerful instance of it, for example, in Wordsworth's preface to the second edition of *Lyrical Ballads* in 1800. In this passage Wordsworth brings the High/Low distinction together with the Old/New distinction in a way that we must recognize as modern. For English and American readers, here is where Modernist critical discourse begins.

> A multitude of causes, unknown to former times, are now acting with a combined force to blunt the discriminating powers of the mind, and, unfitting it for all voluntary exertion, to reduce it to a state of almost savage torpor. The most effective of these causes are the great national events which are daily taking place, and the increasing accumulation of men in cities, where the uniformity of their oc-

cupations produces a craving for extraordinary incident, which the rapid communication of intelligence hourly gratifies. To this tendency of life and manners the literature and theatrical exhibitions of the country have conformed themselves. The invaluable works of our elder writers, I had almost said the works of Shakespeare and Milton, are driven into neglect by frantic novels, sickly and stupid German Tragedies, and deluges of idle and extravagant stories in verse.—When I think upon this degrading thirst after outrageous stimulation, I am almost ashamed to have spoken of the feeble endeavour made in these volumes to counteract it; and, reflecting upon the magnitude of the general evil, I should be oppressed with no dishonourable melancholy, had I not a deep impression of certain inherent and indestructible qualities of the human mind, and likewise of certain powers in the great and permanent objects that act upon it, which are equally inherent and indestructible; and were there not added to this impression a belief, that the time is approaching when the evil will be systematically opposed, by men of greater powers, and with far more distinguished success. (935–36)

There is very little in the positions of Greenberg, Adorno, and the others that was not here, already, in Wordsworth's reflections of 1800. Modernity itself had arrived and become visible. For Wordsworth it was embodied in "great national events," like the French Revolution, and in great social changes brought about by urbanization ("the increasing accumulation of men in cities, where the uniformity of their occupations produces a craving for extraordinary incident") and by "the rapid communication of intelligence" (through the nascent mass media). These historical events and social changes, according to Wordsworth, had led to a "degrading thirst after outrageous stimulation"—a thirst that was satisfied by a new popular culture that found expression in "frantic novels, sickly and stupid German Tragedies, and deluges of idle and extravagant stories in verse." This Low popular culture of stimulation, in turn, threatened to drive into neglect the Old cultural monuments provided by Shakespeare and Milton.

We should note, of course, that Wordsworth conveniently forgot that Shakespeare had once been regarded as satisfying a thirst for outrageous stimulation, and we should be aware that Wordsworth's preface is essentially an advertisement for the curative powers of his own work against this new cultural plague. What Wordsworth's world lacked, of course, were the media of mass communications as we now know them. But his critical discourse was already aware of "the rapid communication of intelligence," and his vocabulary was readily adapted to suit later developments. What critic of contemporary television does not inveigh against the "degrading thirst after outrageous stimulation" in language that lacks only Wordsworth's elegant syntax? Even so, there is an important difference between the menace Wordsworth saw and the kind of critical discourse generated by Greenberg and the other apologists for High Modernism. Wordsworth thought he could achieve what he was attempting without resorting to situational or linguistic extremes:

> The principal object, then, proposed in these Poems was to choose incidents and situations from common life, and to relate or describe them, throughout, as far as was possible in a selection of language really used by men, and, at the same time, to throw over them a certain colouring of

imagination, whereby ordinary things should be presented to the mind in an unusual aspect; and, further, and
above all, to make these incidents and situations interesting by tracing in them, truly though not ostentatiously,
the primary laws of our nature: chiefly, as far as regards
the manner in which we associate ideas in a state of
excitement. (935)

Here Wordsworth seeks his own solution to the paradoxy of
Modernism by taking the common and the ordinary (Low)
in language and life, and linking them to "imagination" and
"the primary laws of our nature" (High). Coleridge, of course,
came along a bit later and pointed out that Wordsworth's language wasn't all that common, but we know what Wordsworth
meant. He was not a poet of tension, which is why the New
Critics, for the most part, did not like him, though they could,
and occasionally did, show that when his work was good, it
was riddled with paradox and ambiguity. You will remember
that Allen Tate dated the decline of literary standards precisely
to 1798, the date of the first edition of *Lyrical Ballads*, effec-
tively putting Wordsworth himself into the Low category.

For me—and I have stood inside the ruins of Tintern
Abbey and read Wordsworth's lines on that place, trying to
control my own emotions—Wordsworth's greatest poems are
driven by that Low emotion, sentimentality, though these feelings are controlled by great syntactic and semantic powers.
And so are many of the monuments of Modernism, if we can
only get through the paradox of Modernist critical discourse
and see them for what they are. That point is part of the large
case I am trying to make in this book. And that point has a
corollary as well, which is that we need the full range of Modernist literature and art in order to understand Modernism—

and we need Modernism to understand modernity and hence to see ourselves from the other side. Many of the lighter and less extreme forms of Modernism have their own master-pieces, masterpieces of mediocrity, perhaps, and I hope to make the case for taking a serious interest in them before I am done with this project. I shall also argue that we need to know texts that are not masterpieces—things like jokes, cartoons, and parodies—in order to grasp that fascinating lost world of Modernism that we cannot enter but only gaze at from the other side of the truly great divide between the past and the present.

2

Old and New in Modernist Art

*Mr. Thomas T. Baxter presents what appears to be a figure
of Christ teaching a dickey-bird to chew worms. This work
is labelled "St. Francis" (D'Asise). I cannot concede his
background but the face is remarkable; it is painted with
very great skill, and* the frenetic modernist who rushes by
the picture merely because of the demoded subject-matter
will miss one of the best pieces of detail in the exhibition.
—Ezra Pound, *in* The New Age, *1918 (emphasis added)*

*Among the many kinds of artists, it may be that there are some
who are hybrid. Some, that is to say, bore deeper and deeper
into the stuff of their own art; others are always making
raids into the lands of others. Sickert, it may be, is among
the hybrids, the raiders. . . . But . . . he is probably
the best painter now living in England.*
—Virginia Woolf, *1933 (emphasis added)*

In 1918 we find Ezra Pound worrying about "the frenetic modernist" who will miss something of great beauty because its subject matter, which Pound himself has mocked, is "demoded." And as late as 1933 we find Virginia Woolf, reporting on a conversation in "Bloomsbury" about Walter Sickert, in which a consensus is reached that this derivative painter, whose work is often naturalistic in its content, and might well have been associated by Woolf with the despised Edwardians, is the best that England has to offer. I begin with these texts as a way of pointing to a certain complexity or paradoxy in the way that professed Modernists viewed Modernism in the visual arts, involving the notions of Old and New, in relation to Realism and Abstraction in painting, drawing, and sculpture.

In pursuit of this paradoxy, I intend to travel back in time and eavesdrop on a conversation about Old and New that took place in the pages of *The New Age,* a weekly magazine devoted to politics, literature, and the arts, edited by A. R. Orage in London from 1907 to 1922. As the title of this journal proclaimed, it aspired to be the proper voice for a new age, helping that age to find its way, and, among other things, directing artists, writers, and their audiences toward an adequate response to the conditions of modernity and the events of the time, a time that saw a transition from the last vestiges of the Victorian world—preserved for a decade in Edwardian Britain—to something new, signified by the accession of George V after the death of Edward VII in 1910, and by the horrendous war that broke out in 1914, leaving a different world behind when it ended in 1918. This was the period, then, in which writers and artists were trying to define a Modernist aesthetic practice that would be an adequate response to the new conditions of life, the conditions of modernity. These con-

ditions included increasing industrialization and urbanization, the growing power of materialistic capitalism which generated labor unrest, the rise of new media of communications,
and the struggle of women for equality and independence.

Should the conditions of modernity be accepted or resisted? And how should this changed world be represented in literature and art? Should the past be utterly rejected? Or should
it be mined, selectively, for inspiration? Was the New to be a
continuation of the Old—and, if so, which parts of the Old
could serve as points of departure? Or should the New be based
on a rejection of the Old—and, if so, which parts should be
singled out as most offensive? In the five years before the out-
break of war in 1914, the visual arts played a central role in discussions of Modernism, leading the way, to some extent, for the
other arts. Writers were already borrowing terms like Impressionism from the visual arts to describe their work. The debates
over Old and New in visual art that took place during this crucial period set the tone and established many of the terms that
have been used since that time in discussions of Modernism.
For these reasons I propose to look into the debates about visual art as they played out in the crucial pages of *The New Age*
in the first years of Georgian England, paying particular attention to the paradoxy surrounding the terms Old and New,
along with such variations as Modern and Contemporary, and
such descriptive terms as Realistic and Abstract. (The images
from the magazine included here are drastically reduced from
their original folio size, and are offered for reference rather
than study. I urge all concerned to examine the originals in the
digital edition of *The New Age*, available on line from the Modernist Journals Project at <www.modjourn.brown.edu>.)

Some months before the famous "Manet and the Post-
Impressionists" show organized by Roger Fry at the end of the

year 1910, the debate over a proper visual art for the modern
world began in the pages of *The New Age*. It was started by
Huntley Carter, who was doing both art and drama criticism for
the magazine at that time. Carter organized an art supplement
for the issue of April 7, 1910, in which artists and critics joined
to discuss "all that concerns the welfare and prospects of art."
Among the artists who contributed to this supplement were
Walter Sickert, who continued to write about art for the magazine for many years, William Shackleton, a symbolist painter,
and Cecil French, an associate of Shackleton—but the most
interesting contribution came from a critic and historian of art
then living in Paris: Victor Reynolds. Reynolds argued that

> people still continue to talk of neo-impressionism and of
> newer movements in impressionism, quite regardless of
> the fact that the fundamental principle of impressionism
> (at the best of times never one of very vital aesthetic im-
> port) has already been exemplified and developed to its
> extreme limits, and that as a force or a starting point for
> anything new it is as dead as the Pharaohs. Deader, in-
> deed. Nothing is more hopeless than a moribund tradi-
> tion, while on the other hand the oldest, most primitive
> sources, such as Egyptian art itself (partly because they
> survive only in a condition so fragmentary as to preclude
> any possibility of direct imitation), have ever been the
> seeding ground and the hope of future progress. (*NA*
> 6.23supp:7)

This is the note of radical Modernism, sounded half a year
before "Manet and the Post-Impressionists" opened. And
Reynolds went on to observe that critics had sneered at Pablo
Picasso's work in a recent salon, comparing it to Aztec art. His

defense of Picasso is the first full appreciation of this artist
to appear in English:

In him one sees an almost isolated instance of the power
to react against the current tradition, and one of the very
few men in modern France whose work can in any real
sense be called progressive. I believe that at a very early
age he was producing work in the manner of the Spanish
classics like Velasquez and Goya. After he came to Paris,
however (he is a native of Barcelona), his work took a
wholly different aspect. In the collection of Mr. Leo Stein
there are several exquisite studies of heads painted in a
bluish monochrome on millboard, strange and delicate
as Lionardo, and with something of that master's use of
line. These are, however, still the work of a transition
stage. Such also is the painting of a girl in a blue dress,
with its curious ritualistic or religious air, which seems
to suggest a profound influence of Piero della Francesca,
or possibly Puvis de Chavannes. There is a nobility about
this painting which he hardly seems to have recaptured in
any later effort. To these succeed a number of the strangest
decorations, in which all element of representation is
thrown overboard, and an attempt made to express emotion of form by the use of an extremely large and simple
curve. I believe that these were actually produced under a
combined influence of Ingres and of negro carving; they
are, in fact, like "Aztec decorations" or the statues from
Easter Island. (6.23supp:8)

Reynolds went on to discuss Henri Matisse, whom he thought
less interesting, as being too close to Paul Gauguin, and, finally,
the sculptures of Aristide Maillol,

whose exquisite little bronze, "Coureur Cycliste," was perhaps the dominant feature of an exhibition of singular interest from a sculptural point of view. The power to react immediately against the force of such a personality as that of Auguste Rodin alone argues an extraordinary vitality of talent. The work of this latest of French masters shows the influence of Egyptian or very early Greek work. Austere, unimpassioned, exquisitely simple, it is as far removed in feeling from that of Rodin as is the latter in his turn from the bronze or marble twaddle which chokes his masterpieces in the Gallery of the Luxembourg. (6.23supp:8)

For Reynolds, Impressionism is the Old, that which must be rejected by a clean break, and the New is to be achieved by a linkage with an earlier Old: Egyptian, very early Greek, or Primitive. Already, in April 1910, the definitions of Old and New are complicated, and these complications would deepen over the next few years. But Reynolds had, as it were, set certain oppositions in stone, and these would recur in various ways in the years to come. For Roger Fry and his Bloomsbury friends, we should note, Impressionism was very much alive and could be continued, as it was in the Post-Impressionist works of Fry himself, Duncan Grant, and Vanessa Bell. Thus we have two modes of the New, one breaking with Impressionism in a radical way, and another attempting to extend it.

Moreover, in addition to these two modes of the New, we have two attitudes toward the Old and the New embodied in the writing of two critics, Huntly Carter, who initiated the discussion to which Reynolds contributed so tellingly, and Anthony Ludovici, who replaced Carter in 1912 as the major art critic of *The New Age* and reversed the evaluative polarity of Old and New. After April 1910 Carter continued to review exhibitions at home and abroad, constantly searching for works that would express the New Spirit of Modernity, producing several books on theater with the words "New Spirit" in their titles, and ultimately editing an anthology of essays on spiritualism itself, which, upon investigation, turns out to be a recurring element of Modernism, from the Symbolists to Gauguin and Wassily Kandinsky. Carter was sympathetic to the work of the Rhythmistes, who gathered around the short-lived little magazine *Rhythm*, edited by John Middleton Murry, with the Fauvist painter John Duncan Fergusson handling the art. The Rhythmistes included a number of artists who later joined the Vorticists. This magazine, which operated from 1911 to 1913, printed art by Picasso and Henri Gaudier-Brzeska, among others. Carter was quick to note the power of the designs being made for the stage in Europe, especially the work of Bakst for the Russian Ballet.

Ludovici, Carter's replacement at *The New Age*, brought to the debate over Old and New a certain conservative strain of Modernist critical discourse. The son and grandson of painters named Albert Ludovici, Anthony Ludovici was born in England in 1882 and studied abroad, where he discovered the works of Nietzsche. For a time he acted as a private secretary to Rodin, after which he returned to England. His name first appeared in the pages of *The New Age* in advertisements for lectures on Nietzsche, whom he translated into English and discussed in a book which was favorably reviewed in the pages of the magazine. His first editorial contribution to the magazine was a review of a translation of a biography of Nietzsche in 1911, and he wrote his first column as an art critic for *The New Age* in July 1912. He used the occasion to make an invidious distinction between the Old and the New in favor of the Old, and he maintained that position rigorously for several years, until he had a head-on collision with T. E. Hulme in the pages of the magazine. Ludovici's Old was virtually feudal, and he looked in art for representations of Greatness, often muttering about portraits of people who were not worthy of being painted. He was the sort of conservative who took race and class seriously, mixing Nietzschean notions with a more traditional Royalism that we may find also in T. S. Eliot.

Ludovici's debut as an art critic for *The New Age* was a review of a show in Cologne, Germany. He began by making a historical claim of a large order, to the effect that a unified Catholic European sensibility had been broken by the Reformation, leaving European culture prey to various sorts of later fragmentation. In Ludovici's hands, this distinction was used as a weapon against most of the varieties of Modernism in the arts. We can pick up his argument as he shifts from religion to art in the Cologne review:

> So it was with art. Once it had been divorced from the traditional law that it was the voice of a certain kind of life expressing its view of all life, there was no end to the chaos and the muddle that resulted. There may not have been five hundred sects, as in Protestantism; but there were certainly a hundred. For who doubts that the Impressionists, the Neo-Impressionists, the Post-Impressionists, the Futurists, the Cubists, the Synthesists, the Pointillistes, and their ancestors the Transcriptists, Naturalists, Pre-Raphaelites, etc., are anything else than the Puritanical Baptists, Anabaptists, Methodists, Wesleyan Methodists, Plymouth Brethren, Quakers, Unitarians, Presbyterians, and Congregationalists of a Grand Rebellion in art? He who doubts this wants guidance. He who denies it wants enlightenment. (*NA* 11.13:307)

For a time, as he continued to review exhibitions of new artworks, Ludovici abandoned the restrictive Cavalier/Roundhead distinction and settled into a Nietzschean vocabulary which was more flexible and useful for him: here the key binary opposition was Sick/Healthy. The culture was sick, he was certain, which made it virtually impossible for art to be healthy. Knowing this, he promised to be gentle with the younger generation of artists, but he continued to hope for an artistic superman to arrive and offer leadership to lesser beings. And he also indicated that he would deal with the really sick, such as the Futurists, as a surgeon deals with cancer or a gardener with blight. With the Rhythmistes and other younger artists, however, he would be kinder, blaming their failings on the Mediocrity of Modernity itself. And he sent up a cry for a strong leader: "Oh, why is there not someone strong enough, trust-inspiring enough, to be able to say to them all, with some hope of being listened to: 'Put down your palettes and follow me!'" (11.25:596).

Ludovici was critical of art that he called "mere transcription" and impatient with Mediocrity. He was looking for a master painter who would produce masterpieces and help to cure the sickness of the age. But as he observed when reviewing the second Post-Impressionist show in November 1912, "This is the heyday of the mediocre person. Let him profit while he may from the confusion and doubt that prevail about him. But do not let him try to convince us that his work is anything more than the pot-boiler paramount" (12.3:67). Ludovici was fond of the High/Low distinction, but he did not align High with New—quite the contrary. He was a Modernist who despised modernity, which for him took the form of "Capitalist Industrialism," as he called it in a piece on the white slave traffic, which was the subject of a bill then under discussion in

Parliament. Appearing in the same issue of *The New Age* as
Ludovici's review of the Post-Impressionists was a short piece
by Muriel Wells in which she imagined a Futurist superman as
a kind of robotic Frankenstein's monster, devouring the Futurist leader Marinetti and waiting to greet the rest of the Futurists, hungrily. Ludovici no doubt approved, though he thought
the Futurists were far from being supermen. He was certain,
however, that artists had not resisted modernity sufficiently. As
he put it, "Artists have been on the side of modernity for over
a century; one or two exceptions apart, they have even believed
that modernity was right. How could they help but suffer in
the end for this treacherous alliance with the enemy of taste?"
(12.4:89).

The precise nature of Ludovici's conservatism emerges
clearly in a review he wrote in August 1913:

At the Doré Gallery there is an interesting show the proper
title of which is the "Post-Impressionist Poster Exhibition." It is interesting and sad at the same time, because it
shows how utterly the last possible opponent of this age
and all its vulgarity has become enslaved to the very
power which it ought to have done its utmost to under-
mine and to overthrow. The despotism of the last hundred and fifty years, if such there has been, has consisted
of the uncontested supremacy of uncontrolled industry
and commerce. This despotism has been one of vulgarity,
the unscrupulous spurning of all that constituted flourishing and desirable life, the deliberate flouting of all that
made for desirable humanity, the tasteless abuse of power
in bad taste. The last really vigorous attempt to arrest the
movement of uncontrolled industry and commerce was

made two hundred and fifty years ago, when Charles the First died for the "liberty of the people," as opposed to the "liberty" of their oppressors. Since then it has met with no formidable foe. It was able to do its worst in the nineteenth century, and the present age is its creation. (13.18:521)

This is a Royalism scarcely heard of in modern England— until the American T. S. Eliot came along and proclaimed himself a Royalist some years after this. The Cavalier/Roundhead opposition that Ludovici invoked when he entered the pages of *The New Age* as an art critic was no mere metaphor but a fundamental part of this critic's belief system. A profound hatred of modernity turns out to be a powerful element in some versions of Modernism, which meant, for certain critics and artists, that modernity could not be seen as beautiful or represented in a favorable light. This is why Ludovici was so disturbed by this exhibition of posters in which art explicitly served commerce—disturbed not because the works were so bad but because some of them were so good—and why he cited Huysmans, who had praised the posters of Jules Cheret as superior to much of the work in the salon—and, finally, why he felt melancholy even as he praised some of the advertising posters at this exhibition. These betrayers of art in the service of commerce should not have done it so well, and with so much gusto. But they did, and Ludovici acknowledged this and praised much of their work in this exhibition.

Some months later, in the course of an omnibus review of works at a number of galleries, Ludovici offered some observations that take us deeper into his understanding of the relationship between the state of society or culture and the state of art:

The graphic arts, to my mind, are dependent arts. When an age is animated by a great spirit, the graphic arts will be great by expressing the spirit of that age; when an age is animated by a pusillanimous spirit, or by none at all, they too will be poor in spirit or utterly devoid of it. The graphic artist does not create a state of affairs, or an order of existence, a scheme of life. A far greater artist does that, and he is the poet—or artist—legislator. It is the exuberant joy of the graphic artist over the order that the artist-legislator creates, and over the spirit that animates it, which impels the graphic artist to his work. (14.5:152)

This is a revealing—and a bit frightening—statement, because the "poet—or artist—legislator" strongly suggests the way that a figure like Hitler would be perceived just two decades after Ludovici was writing. What Walter Benjamin would describe as the fascist aestheticization of politics is anticipated here and justified as providing an order sadly lacking in modernity. Ludovici's thinking shows us why we need to understand fascism as a form of Modernism—as yet another critical response to what were perceived as the evils of modernity. If we really wish to understand what led Ezra Pound, for example, down the path toward treason, this is the place to start. For Pound, of course, was writing for *The New Age* at this time, almost every week. I am not suggesting that he learned his fascism from Ludovici but that Ludovici's writing allows us to see into the attitudes that led Pound in the direction that he took. Pound's hatred of what he called "usura" is not far from Ludovici's hatred of "commerce and industry." And the wish for a strong "poet—or artist—legislator" to restore order to a chaotic world was a common theme among the Modernists as well as among the ordinary people who would welcome their Führer when he arrived.

In the same article, responding to a request to explain what he liked in the work of Augustus John, Ludovici revealed another problematic aspect of the Modernist conundrum. "Shall I tell you why I like John? Because in the chaos of this abominable age, he not only seeks out the finest and healthiest type of man or woman, but seems to find joy only in the expression of that type" (14.5:153). There was a serious danger lurking here in that notion of "the finest and healthiest type of man or woman." A debate about eugenics was raging in *The New Age* and other journals at the time, and it is easy for us to see how the notion of an ideal type of human being would contribute to a politics of racial types. Ludovici himself finally produced (in 1938, under the pseudonym Cobbett) a tendentious book called *The Jews, and the Jews in England* in which he attempted to distinguish his own position from that of the Nazis and to make a sophisticated case for what amounts to racism without a "pure" concept of race. Ludovici's book on the Jews is now available online, courtesy of the white supremacist pages of Kevin Strom. My point here, however, is simply that the notion of ideal types of humans—and types that were less than ideal—was very much alive in Ludovici's writing and in the culture around him. Which, of course, makes it ironic that many of Augustus John's favorite subjects were Gypsies, whom the Nazis were going to lump with the Jews as inferior types to be eliminated in the name of Aryan purity. (In this connection I want to direct attention to Dan Stone's excellent book, *Breeding Superman: Nietzsche, Race, and Eugenics in Edwardian and Interwar Britain,* which has useful chapters on Ludovici and another *New Age* Nietzschean, Oscar Levy.)

Ludovici's next column was a fateful one. After wandering through some exhibitions, complaining about the mingling
of mediocre artists with their betters, he came to a show of
Jacob Epstein's work and wrote this notice of it:

> At the Twenty-one Gallery Jacob Epstein is exhibiting—
> both sculpture and drawings. To understand what I think
> of Jacob Epstein is not difficult. When the plastic arts can
> no longer interpret the external world in the terms of a
> great order or scheme of life, owing to the fact that all great
> schemes or orders are dead, they exalt the idiosyncrasy
> or individual angle of the isolated ego. But the only two
> factors in common between a plastic work of art and the
> people to whom it is supposed to appeal, have always been
> these: (1) the portion of the external world selected; and
> (2) the terms of the great order or scheme of life, shared
> by all, and revealed in the interpretation. Now, when the
> minor and non-value-creating ego is as isolated as he is
> today, the second factor falls out altogether, and leaves
> only the first. When, therefore, the first ceases to be pure
> transcriptism, the art has no interest whatsoever, save
> for cranks and people who have some reason of their own
> in abetting or supporting purposeless individualism à
> outrance. To these, the particular angle of vision of a
> minor personality has some value—to me it has none.
> (14.7:214–15)

For Ludovici, Epstein was merely an example of "purposeless
individualism" at work in a world that lacked any "great order
or scheme of life." This paragraph, as it happened, provoked a
powerful reply from another critic whose view of modernity
could also be called conservative: T. E. Hulme. In the next issue

of *The New Age*, Hulme, in an article called "Mr. Epstein and the Critics," savaged a number of critics who had written about Epstein's show and also tried to explain just what Epstein was doing. In the course of this he expressed a view of modernity that is not so different from the one frequently expressed by Anthony Ludovici:

> I do think that there is a certain general state of mind which has lasted from the Renaissance till now, with what is, in reality, very little variation. It is impossible to characterise it here, but it is perhaps enough to say that, taking at first the form of the "humanities," it has in its degeneracy taken the form of a belief in "Progress" and the rest of it. It was in its way a fairly consistent system, but is probably at the present moment breaking up. In this state of break-up, I think that it is quite natural for individuals here and there to hold a philosophy and to be moved by emotions which would have been unnatural in the period itself. To illustrate big things by small ones I feel, myself, a repugnance towards the *Weltanshauung* (as distinct from the technical part) of all philosophy since the Renaissance. In comparison with what I can vaguely call the religious attitude, it seems to me to be trivial. I am moved by Byzantine mosaic, not because it is quaint or exotic, but because it expresses an attitude I agree with. But the fate of the people who hold these views is to be found incomprehensible by the "progressives" and to be labelled reactionary; that is, while we arrive at such a *Weltanshauung* quite naturally, we are thought to be imitating the past. (14.8:251)

Hulme appeared to hold many of the values held by Ludovici. In particular, he was critical of the notion of progress

and nostalgic for the kind of Christian belief that animated
Byzantine iconic mosaics. But here is what he said when he
came to Ludovici's writing on Epstein, which he saved for last
in his discussion of the critics:

> I come now to the stupidest criticism of all, that of Mr.
> Ludovici. It would probably occur to anyone who read
> Mr. Ludovici's article that he was a charlatan, but I think
> it worth while confirming this impression by further evi-
> dence. His activities are not confined to art. I remember
> coming across his name some years ago as the author of a
> very comical little book on Nietzsche, which was sent me
> for review.
>
> I shall devote some space to him here then, not be-
> cause I consider him of the slightest importance, but be-
> cause I consider it a duty, a very pleasant duty and one
> very much neglected in this country, to expose charlatans
> when one sees them. (14.8:252)

After a longish paragraph of critical abuse on the subject of
Ludovici's understanding of Nietzsche, Hulme turned again to
Ludovici on Epstein:

> To deal definitely then with his criticism. He dismissed
> Mr. Epstein with the general principle "Great art can only
> appear when the artist is animated by the spirit of some
> great order or scheme of life." I agree with this. Experi-
> ence confirms it. We find that the more serious kind of art
> that one likes sprang out of organic societies like the In-
> dian, Egyptian, and Byzantine. The modern obviously
> imposes too great a strain on an artist, the double burden
> of not only expressing something, but of finding some-

thing in himself to be expressed. The more organic society effects an economy in this. Moreover, you might go so
far as to say that the imposition of definite forms does not
confine the artist but rather has the effect of intensifying
the individuality of his work (of Egyptian portraits). I
agree then with his general principle: we all agree. It is one
of those obvious platitudes which all educated people
take for granted, in conversation and in print. It seems almost too comic for belief, but I begin to suspect from Mr.
Ludovici's continued use of the word "I" in connection
with this principle, that he is under the extraordinary hal-
lucination that the principle is a personal discovery of his
own. Really, Mr. Ludo, you mustn't teach your grandmother to suck eggs in this way. (14.8:252)

This entire article is remarkable for its abusive, bantering tone,
which includes a threat of physical violence, and for the ad
hoministic intensity of the critique Hulme generated. For our
purposes, however, what is important is the agreement on the
general principle that living in an "organic" society is a great
advantage that modern artists do not enjoy. Having admitted
that, however, Hulme went on: "Admitting then, as I do, that
the principle is true, I fail to see how it enables Mr. Ludovici to
dismiss Mr. Epstein in the way he does, on *a priori* grounds.
The same general principle would enable us to dismiss every
artist since the Renaissance. Take two very definite examples,
Michelangelo and Blake, neither of whom expressed any general 'scheme of life' imposed on them by society, but 'exalted
the individual angle of vision of minor personalities'" (14.8:253).
And Hulme went on to show how badly, in his view, Ludovici
had gone wrong in looking at particular paintings by various
artists, with particular emphasis on Augustus John. But the last

word in this issue was given to Epstein himself, whose drawing
The Rock-Drill (Fig. 1), appeared on the final page of the issue.

In the course of his article, Hulme had said some things
about this drawing but noted that it was one that the public
and the critics had in general understood. He felt it important,
therefore, to explain what was happening in some of the works
that they hadn't understood, and to try to say why this should
be so. In this explanation lies the germ of his fuller defense of
Modernist experimentation in the arts. He is talking about an
image called *Generation*, in which this subject is represented in
a modern way:

> If a traditional symbol had been used they would have
> been quite prepared to admire it. They cannot understand
> that the genius and sincerity of an artist lies in extracting
> afresh, from outside reality, a new means of expression. It
> seems curious that the people who in poetry abominate
> cliché and know that Nature, as it were, presses in on
> the poet to be used as metaphor, cannot understand the
> same thing when it occurs plastically. They seem unable
> to understand that an artist who has something to say
> will continually "extract" from reality new methods of
> expression, and that these being personally felt will in-
> evitably lack prettiness and will differ from traditional
> clichés. (14.8:252)

Thus ended the year 1913, with the opening of the last
phase of the great debate we have been examining. The debate
continued, with Hulme and Ludovici as the main antagonists,
along with their supporters and detractors, but it also brought
others into the argument. One of those others was mentioned
by name only once, but his presence was powerfully felt. I am

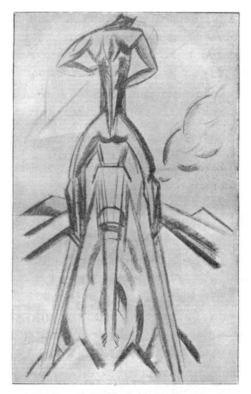

Fig. 1. Jacob Epstein, *The Rock-Drill*
(*NA* 14.8:256)

referring to Wilhelm Worringer, whose dissertation, *Abstraktion und Einfühlung* (Abstraction and empathy), had appeared in 1908 and made a profound impression on Hulme. In this book, which was not translated into English for several decades, Worringer made a case against empathy and in favor of abstraction, which, though the conduit of Hulme, had a major impact on British and American critical thought about Modernism in literature and art. (For an excellent discussion of this process, see Levenson, esp. 94–101.)

At this point Walter Sickert returned with images, and his fellow painter Charles Ginner entered the fray with a manifesto on behalf of Neo-Realism, which, along with Ludovici's reply to Hulme, were all in the first 1914 issue of *The New Age.* Ginner's article on Neo-Realism was the first piece on art in the pages of the issue that appeared on New Year's Day. Here is how his article began:

> All great painters by direct intercourse with Nature have extracted from her facts which others have not observed before, and interpreted them by methods which are personal and expressive of themselves—this is the great tradition of Realism. It can be traced in Europe down from Van Eyck and the early French primitives of the Ecole d'Avignon. It is carried through the dark period of the Poussins and Lebruns by Les Frères le Nain; in the eighteenth century by Chardin; in the nineteenth by Courbet and the Impressionists, and unbroken to this day by Cézanne and Van Gogh. Realism has produced the "Pieta" of the Ecole d'Avignon, the "Flemish Merchant and Lady" of Van Eyck, the old man and child of Ghirlandajo at the Louvre, "La Parabole des Aveugles" of Breughel (Le Vieux), the "Repos de Paysans" of Les Frères le Nain. Greco, Rembrandt, Millet, Courbet, Cézanne—all the great painters of the world have known that great art can only be created out of continued intercourse with nature. (14.9:271)

Ginner went on to elaborate his theory, pointing out that the great enemy of what he called "realism" was "academicism," and he accused most of the Post-Impressionist followers of Cézanne, Gauguin, and Van Gogh of just that, with Matisse being the most guilty party among them. He also criticized

Naturalism as another academic version of Realism—nature seen with "a dull and common eye," with "no personal vision, no individual temperament to express, no power of research" (14.9:272). Neo-Realism, for Ginner, was made up of nature plus the personality of the artist:

> Neo-Realism must be a deliberate and objective transposition of the object (man, woman, tree, apple, light, shade, movement, etc.) under observation, which has for certain specific reasons appealed to the artist's ideal or mood, for self-expression. When the artist is carried away by an intense desire to interpret an object or an agglomeration of objects, the only sure means at his disposal to find and express that unknown quantity in the object which raised his desire, mood, or ideal, and which united his inner self with the aforesaid unknown quantity, is a deliberate research, concise study and transposition. It is only this intimate relation between the artist and the object which can produce original and great work. Away from this we fall into unoriginal and monotonous Formula. (14.9:272)

Ginner claimed the Impressionists for Realism and argued that the Neo-Realists were their proper heirs, rather than the Post-Impressionists, who had merely made an academic formula out of what was alive in Impressionism, just as the Royal Academy had allowed Realism to degenerate into a formulaic Naturalism. Ginner's piece was immediately followed in the pages of the magazine by Walter Sickert's *Portrait of Enid Bagnold* (Fig. 2). This was the first of fourteen in a series called "Modern Drawings" edited by Sickert for *The New Age*.

The Neo-Realist label described Sickert fairly well, though, as we shall see, he was not comfortable with it. This crucial issue

Fig. 2. Walter Sickert, *Portrait of Miss Enid
Bagnold* (*NA* 14.9:273)

of the magazine also contained Ludovici's reply to Hulme. He
called the piece "An Open Letter to My Friends," but in it he
replied to Hulme. He objected to Hulme's tactics—as who
might not?—and he noted that Hulme seemed not to disagree
with his principles but only to point out that they were not
original and to argue with their application to Epstein's work.
He observed, however, that "the controversy is an important
one. These questions need open discussion" (14.9:279). His
way of justifying his case against Epstein, however, was a bit
peculiar. He accused Epstein of being a disciple of the Futur-

ists and then said, "I have listened to Marinetti," as if that explained his dismissal of Epstein as a "minor personality."

Finally, in the same issue, the cartoonist known as Tom Titt (Jan Junosza de Rosciszewski) offered, instead of his usual caricature of an individual, a piece of pseudo-Neo-Realist art called *Charing Cross Road: 11 P.M.* (Fig. 3). Meanwhile, of course, the controversy over Epstein's work raged on in the letters column of the magazine, with supporters and detractors of all concerned expressing themselves vigorously. The conclusion of a letter from Wyndham Lewis is one of the most interesting of these contributions. The subject in the following paragraph is, of course, Anthony Ludovici:

> He is obviously a fool it is worth no one's while to notice.
> But he suddenly threatens to engulf the entire superficies
> of one of the only good papers in the country with his
> gibberish, wildly and vacantly inflated, like some queer
> insect, in terror when attacked. May I use this occasion, as
> a great admirer of THE NEW AGE, to hope that for those
> "most sensitive men" (Nietzsche) some less ridiculous
> go-between may be found. His dismal shoddy rubbish is
> not even amusingly ridiculous. It is the grimest pig-wash
> vouchsafed at present to a public fed on husks. (14.10:319)

What we may learn from this, beyond Lewis's amusing opinion, is that British artists and critics were paying attention to what was going on in these pages. Immediately afterward both Hulme and Ludovici began contributing columns on art to the magazine, sometimes in the same issues. Asked by Orage himself, writing as R.H.C., to explain the social basis of his judgments, Ludovici replied by saying that it was "aristocratic" and that he wanted "superior men" to lead in "an

Fig. 3. Tom Titt, *Charing Cross Road: 11 P.M.*
(*NA* 14.9:288)

aristocratic order of society." He also inveighed against what
he called "the lie of equality, the lie of the rights of the individual conscience, and the lie of the rights of individual expression" (14.11:345–46).

In the same issue's letters column Ludovici tried to deal
with Wyndham Lewis by calling him a Futurist, as he had Epstein. This must certainly have had the virtue of annoying
Lewis, but it was not a strong defense of Ludovici's own position. Earlier in that issue Hulme had begun what was an-

nounced as a series of articles on Modern Art, promising an attempt "to define the characteristics of a new constructive geometric art which seems to me to be emerging at the present moment," while giving special attention to the problem of the word "new" (14.11:341).

I am afraid that my use of the word "new" here will arouse a certain prejudice in the minds of the kind of people that I am anxious to convince. I may say then that I use the word with no enthusiasm. I want to convince those people who regard the feeble romanticism which is always wriggling and vibrating to the stimulus of the word "new," with a certain amount of disgust, that the art which they incline to condemn as decadent is in reality the new order for which they are looking. It seems to me to be the genuine expression of abhorrence of slop and romanticism which has quite mistakenly sought refuge in the conception of a classical revival. By temperament I should adopt the classical attitude myself. My assertion then that a "new" art is being formed is not due to any desire on my part to perceive something "new," but is forced on me almost against my inclination by an honest observation of the facts themselves. (14.11:341)

If Hulme and Ludovici could have met to discuss the issue of Epstein in a way less fraught with personality and prejudice, these words might have helped that discussion along. Hulme proclaimed himself a Classicist who was opposed to the fetishization of the New that he associated with "feeble romanticism." But something genuinely New was happening in the arts, he insisted, which was being mistaken for decadence by people who shared his own values. It was his Classicism and detestation of "slop and romanticism," he implied, that should lend weight to his argument for "the new constructive geometric art." And here, at last, we come to the final stage of this long argument over the New and the Old, and the question of what Modernism in the arts really may be. Walter Sickert joined in this debate with a letter in the next issue, in which he took issue with Hulme on the quality of Roger Fry's painting, giving us his own views of some other Modernists in passing. Sickert thought Fry the artist was superior to Fry the critic and Fry the impresario:

> We must look at his canvases unbiased by the recklessness of his career as an impresario and the obscurantism of his criticism. As a critic he would have us take seriously Monsieur Picasso's tedious invention of the puzzle-conundrum-without-an-answer and the empty sillinesses of Monsieur Matisse. Himself has remained throughout a highly gifted and progressing painter on sane and normal lines. I do not profess to be able to explain this obvious incongruity, but there it is, staring us in the face, and it seems useless to deny it. (14.12:382)

Sickert's position was crystal clear. And he continued his visual argument in the series of drawings he edited for the magazine, which included *Leicester Square* (Fig. 4) by the author of the defense of Neo-Realism that we have already encountered, Charles Ginner. The cartoonist Tom Titt responded on the back page of the magazine with another parody of the work of the "street men" (Huntly Carter's term for artists who represented London street scenes—6.3:67), called *New Oxford Street and Holborn* (Fig. 5). Among other things, this exchange of drawings and criticisms should help us gain per-

Fig. 4. Charles Ginner, *Leicester Square*
(*NA* 14.12:369)

spective on Mrs. Dalloway's trip down Bond Street in the novel
that bears her name and the short sketch that preceded it in
Virginia Woolf's oeuvre, "Mrs. Dalloway in Bond Street."
Woolf, too, was finding beauty in the streets of what Sickert
had called, in the title of a drawing that had appeared earlier in
The New Age, Londra Benedetta (Blessed London, Fig. 6). And,
like her close friend Roger Fry and her sister Vanessa, Virginia
Woolf never adopted the extreme or geometric Modernism of
Joyce or Stein but remained something of a Post-Impressionist
to the end. Which is just one more reason why we need to see

Fig. 5. Tom Titt, *New Oxford Street
and Holborn* (*NA* 14.12:384)

the literature and art of Modernism in a way that does not exclude everything that is not extreme or abstract. Finally, in the
same issue, *The New Age*'s other cartoonist, Will Dyson, weighed
in with his own attack on Modernist geometricism with a cartoon called *Progress* (Fig. 7), in which a "Post-Elliptical Rhomboidist" denigrates a fellow artist as painting in the "old-
fashioned manner of last Thursday." Dyson's cartoon attacked
both the linking of Modernism to a progress gone mad in the
pursuit of innovation, and the geometrizing of art in particular. On the visual side, this is perhaps the most extraordinary

Fig. 6. Walter Sickert, *Londra Benedetta*
(*NA* 9.13:300)

issue of this extraordinary magazine, with Ginner's drawing,
Sickert's letter, and the two cartoons: one parodying Neo-
Realism and the other parodying Cubism, Futurism, and
Hulme's defense of "the new constructive geometric art" as
Post-Elliptical-Rhomboidism.

   This issue was followed by one with a typical Sickert
scene and another parodic cartoon by Tom Titt. As is so often
the case in Sickert's work, *The Music Lesson* (Fig. 8) seems to be
about a personal relationship that has reached some sort of

Fig. 7. Will Dyson, *Progress* (*NA* 14.12:376)

crisis. The pupil is not playing and has turned away from the
teacher, who is looking away from her. Is her shadowed face
blushing? Sickert's art has a narrative quality without being
merely illustrative or anecdotal. His puzzles are not geometrical but emotional, having more to do with what is represented
and less with how it is represented. And this is the crux of the
debate between what we should perhaps think of as the Radical
Modernists and the Conservative Modernists, or Geometrists
and Neo-Realists. On the back page of that issue Tom Titt
offered another cityscape, this one getting rather geometrical in

Fig. 8. Walter Sickert, *The Music Lesson*
(*NA* 14.13:401)

its drawing and a touch Futuristic in the rendering of its street signs and the movement of pedestrians—*St. Paul's Church-yard* (Fig. 9)—and he followed that in the next issue with a caricature of Ludovici himself (Fig. 10). The Futurist parody and the Ludovici cartoon demonstrate, if demonstration were needed, that the cartoonists were indeed paying attention to the artistic debate around them.

In the next issue T. E. Hulme began to develop his ideas about modern art in a more systematic way, offering three theses which he planned to illustrate in various ways:

Fig. 9. Tom Titt, *St. Paul's Churchyard*
(*NA* 14.13:416)

1. There are two kinds of art, geometrical or abstract, and
   vital and realistic art, which differ absolutely in kind
   from the other. They are not modifications of one and
   the same art, but pursue different aims and are created
   to satisfy a different desire of the mind.
2. Each of these arts springs from, and corresponds to a
   certain general attitude towards the world. You get long
   periods of time in which only one of these arts and its
   corresponding mental attitude prevails. The naturalistic art of Greece and the Renaissance corresponded to
   a certain rational humanistic attitude towards the uni-

Fig. 10. Tom Titt, *Anthony Ludovici*
(*NA* 14.14:448)

verse, and the geometrical has always gone with a different attitude of greater intensity than this.

3. The re-emergence of geometrical art at the present day
   may be the precursor of the re-emergence of the corresponding general attitude towards the world, and so
   of the final break up of the Renaissance. (14.15:467)

This is, without a doubt, the most important statement on
modern art made by Hulme anywhere. For our purposes it is
crucial, because it makes a distinction between Old and New

which manages to be both apparently evenhanded and yet invidious. Hulme divides all visual art into two modes, the geometrical and the real, or the abstract and the vital, with no necessary hierarchy putting one above the other—except that in every age one will be more suited to the spirit of the age itself, though he doesn't use that too Hegelian locution but merely refers to "a general attitude." He also loads the dice a bit by insisting that the geometrical has always had a "greater intensity" than the realistic. More important than this, however, is his claim that a major cultural shift may at last be taking place, so that the cultural presuppositions that have supported realistic art since the Renaissance may at last be yielding to something different, which will support geometrical art. Thus the artists who are reaching in that direction are attempting to help move the entire culture in this New direction, which is a healthy direction, because the humanistic impulse that drove the Renaissance is now exhausted if not sick. In this way, a New/Abstract/Healthy mode of art is opposed to an Old/Concrete/Sick mode. Clement Greenberg would not object to these combinations, presumably, but Ludovici and Lukács would combine the binaries in another way. The paradoxy of Modernist critical discourse is rooted in the alignment of the New with different combinations of the other features, and in the different relations of the elements in each binary to one another, as in the different possible relations between Old and New.

This formulation linked Hulme's claims with those made several years earlier by Huntly Carter about a "New Spirit" in art, though Hulme insisted on the geometrical as the carrier of this spirit in a way that Carter never did. And it ought to have aligned Hulme with Anthony Ludovici, except that Ludovici could not see abstract art as anything more than technical fiddling. But

Ludovici was quarreling with the editor of the magazine about Nietzsche, which was a dangerous thing to do, and losing his place as the journal's major spokesman on visual art. Walter Sickert, on the other hand, was a genuine representative of the realistic side of Hulme's distinction, both in his own work and in his attitude toward the abstract tendency in art. In Hulme's terms, however, if I am interpreting him correctly, Sickert was a genuine voice of the Old, which properly continued, though threatened by the "precursor[s]" of the New spirit or "attitude." As Hulme made his case, then, the new Geometrists should be given some allowance as precursors rather than masters of the New, and appreciated for the same reason—because they were both anticipating and bringing about a desirable change in modernity itself. And Neo-Realists like Sickert should be tolerated as honest practitioners of a dying mode of art.

In the course of this long, crucial essay, which should be read in its entirety, Hulme tackled Charles Ginner's position on Neo-Realism and brought the argument down to different responses to the work of Cézanne. For Ginner, Cézanne was a realist. For Hulme, there were in Cézanne's work the "elements which quite naturally develop into Cubism later" (14.15:468). Finally, Hulme extended the argument with Ginner to a disagreement about the artist's relation to "nature." Hulme's reasoning was straightforward and powerful:

> I admit that the artist cannot work without contact with, and continual research into nature, but one must make a distinction between this and the conclusion drawn from it that the work of art itself must be an interpretation of nature. The artist obviously cannot spin things out of his head, he cannot work from imagination in that sense. The whole thing springs from misconception of the na-

ture of artistic imagination. Two statements are confused:
(1) that the source of imagination must be nature, and
(2) the consequence illegitimately drawn from this, that
the resulting work must be realistic, and based on natural
forms. One can give an analogy in ordinary thought. The
reasoning activity is quite different in character from
any succession of images drawn from the senses, but yet
thought itself would be impossible without this sensual
stimulus. (14.15:469)

In the early phases of this debate, Walter Sickert had argued
that drawing was a kind of language, in which lines were like
words. Huntly Carter had also spoken of art as a language in
the pages of the magazine, as had Victor Reynolds. Hulme, in
comparing visual art to thought, was making a similar distinction (and following David Hume's distinction between impressions and ideas, we might note) between perceptions and
conceptions—between what the senses perceive and what the
mind conceives. But Sickert would not follow his notion of
drawing as a language to the point of allowing concepts as
much power in the production of art as Hulme would give
them—and that made all the difference in their positions.

Sickert's series of Modern Drawings calmly continued
in the next issue with a powerful landscape drawing by Fred
Richards of the *Temple of the Sibyl* at Hadrian's Villa in Tivoli
(Fig. 11). Sickert himself, however, remained as silent as any
sibyl, and Ludovici continued arguing with his editor about
Nietzsche, before taking on Darwin as well. But Sickert returned in the next issue with a drawing of his own and a review of Clive Bell's new book, *Art*. The drawing was called
Reconciliation (Fig. 12), but Sickert could not reconcile himself to Bell's view of Cézanne, though he liked other aspects of
the book:

Fig. 11. Fred Richards, *Temple of the Sibyl*
(*NA* 14.16:497)

Nor is the value of the book as an illuminant to thought on painting, henceforth impossible to ignore, sensibly lowered by the fact that it is written round a movement which is no movement or that the prophet has got hold of the wrong end of the wrong Messiah. I can see poor Cézanne's face at a "Cubist" exhibition! Never was a serious artist more shamelessly exploited than was Cézanne when his respectable name was made to cover the impudent theories of Matisse and Picasso, who, talented themselves, have invented an academic formula which is the salvation of all arrivistes without talent." (14.18:569)

Sickert conceded, at least, that Picasso and Matisse were "talented themselves" and confined himself to attacking the "aca-

Fig. 12. Walter Sickert, *Reconciliation*
(*NA* 14.18:561)

demic formula" they had invented, which was exploited by
"arrivistes without talent." This was not exactly a reconciliation with the views of Hulme, but Sickert's drawing shows that
he had reconciliation on his mind. Others were far from reconciled, and the letters column of *The New Age* continued to
receive "refutations" of Hulme's views.

　　Sickert himself returned to the debate in the next issue,
with a gently argued piece on the way artists work. The following passage is especially interesting:

We all know that picture of Moritz von Schwind, of the little German girl in plaits who throws open the casement of her bedroom to greet the sounds and scents of morning. The everlasting matutinal is enshrined in it once for all and for ever. No educated person can think of morning without thinking of that picture by Schwind, and Schwind wasn't labelled an anything-ist, but just a painter. His work required no treatise, and no abstrusely reasoned justifications. I once had the folly, in speaking to Monsieur Degas, to use the expression "a genius," of a painter of our acquaintance. "Ce n'est pas un genie," he said, "c'est un peintre." (14.20:631)

Von Schwind's *Morgenstunde* (Fig. 13), a painting which depends too much on its color to hold its own here, can easily be found on the Web, where it is still popular as a poster. The colorless image included here is meant only to give an idea of the arrangement of the painting. It is an example of what the Germans call *Fensterbilder,* pictures in which people are shown gazing out of windows—a popular motif among Romantic painters. This one shows a young woman, from the back, as she looks out a window at the mountains, with her unmade bed next to her. She is barefoot and on tiptoe, in the morning of the day and of her life, both of which she is rising to meet. What Sickert admired in this image, I believe, was a kind of universal experience, which he called "the everlasting matutinal," an image of a moment from an ordinary life that resonated with the feelings of many spectators and represented it with technical skill—a realistic treatment of a romantic moment, with the just-abandoned bed as important as the distant mountains. And he was asking, implicitly, whether the new geometric art advocated by T. E. Hulme could match this.

Fig. 13. Moritz von Schwind, *Morgenstunde* (Bayerische
Staatsgemäldesammlungen, Schack-Galerie Munich)

We can find Hulme's answer in the same issue of the
magazine, in the first of a new series he edited, which he called
"Contemporary Drawings." Here was the new geometrical
art with a vengeance, and Hulme could argue that it captured
powerfully a universal experience. The image is *A Dancer* (Fig.
14) by Henri Gaudier-Brzeska. If one were going to defend the
New geometrical art, this was a very strong card to play—an
image that captures the movement, grace, and power of dancing in a way that traditional Realism could not. In these two
images we have instances of the Old and the New, chosen by
their advocates. And the choices are very revealing. Sickert's
choice speaks to bourgeois life and bourgeois values, with a
comfortable room and a window opening on a romantic

mountain scene. The girl stands on her toes to greet the morning, and viewers are asked to share in or recall such moments
in their own lives. This is rather different from Sickert's own
work, which tends toward scenes of stress and trouble that
open fissures in the bourgeois world. Sickert himself is more
Modern than von Schwind. Hulme's choice is presented as
transcending time and place—representing the essence of
dancing, anticipating the famous lines Yeats added to "Among
School Children" more than a decade after Gaudier's death:
"How can we know the dancer from the dance?" But from our
present perspective it is as tied to time and history as von
Schwind's *Morgenstunde*. This is not just any dancer, it is a
nude dancer, performing a primitive dance like those in
Stravinsky's modern ballet *The Rite of Spring*. It represents not
the world of bourgeois comfort but the wilder world in which
Nina Hamnett would take off her clothes and dance with wild
abandon, as we shall see in Chapter 8. The technique of *A
Dancer* is aggressively Modernist, to be sure, but so, also, is the
subject matter. One of the things that offended the middle
classes in this kind of art was the absence of their world, which
had been replaced by a bohemia in which the artists themselves were the most important figures.

Hulme's offering says, "This is the New, deal with it."
Sickert's example was meant to convey, "This was the Old, let
the New try to equal it in interest." With Ludovici out of the
way, Sickert and Hulme then joined in the most crucial phase
of the debate over Modernism in visual art. Hulme himself returned to the debate with what was now the third in a series of
articles called "Modern Art." In this article he reviewed a show
of the London Group, which, as he explained, was "formed by
the amalgamation of the Camden Town Group and the Cubists" (14.21:661). This alliance between the Neo-Realists and
the Cubists was itself an attempt to transcend the developing

Fig. 14. Henri Gaudier-Brzeska, *A Dancer*
(*NA* 14.20:625)

paradoxy of Modernism, though it did not last for long after this show, the new paradigm being too strong for it. The most important part of Hulme's review, however, comes in his discussion of Cubism:

> It is possible, I think, to give an account of this movement, which will exhibit it as an understandable and coherent whole, closely allied to the general tendency of the

period, and thus containing possibilities of development. But this has now generated, a second movement based simply on the idea that abstract form, i.e., form without any representative content, can be an adequate means of expression. In this, instead of hard, structural work like Picasso's you get the much more scattered use of abstractions of artists like Kandinsky. It seems, judging by its development up to now, to be only a more or less amusing by-product of the first. Lacking the controlling sensibility, the feeling for mechanical structure, which makes use of abstractions a necessity, it seems rather dilettante. It so happens, however, that all explanations of the new movement as yet given, have been explanations of this second tendency only. In this way the real importance of the main tendency has been veiled. (14.21:661)

Here Hulme confronted, in the nascent form of some works by Kandinsky, the movement that became Abstract Expressionism and argued that it was the wrong direction for the New, and, furthermore, that it was distracting attention from the other, Older New, the Geometrical or Structural Abstraction, such as that of Picasso, which was Cubism proper. Hulme, that is, shared with the defenders of the Old a sense that art needs a connection to the Real, and he felt that pure abstraction loses that necessary connection. He also felt that Kandinsky's path was the way of the dilettante, and he went on to argue that the other kind of grounded abstraction from the Real aligned Cubism with the great movements of earlier art that preceded the Renaissance, adding that now, after drawing upon the primitive and archaic, the New Geometric art was starting to represent its own world more directly, drawing upon machines and mechanical objects for much of its material. He saw this as a healthy move, whereas he was suspicious of the Romanticism implied by Kandinsky's work.

British Vorticism was taking shape in these arguments of Hulme's, just as a nascent Imagism was learning from his poetry and his literary criticism. His career, like that of Gaudier, was ended by the war a short time after these essays. One would give a good deal to see where those two young men might have gone in art and thought after the war. Hulme ended this important essay by conceding that much of the work in the show he was reviewing was imperfect and experimental, admitting that only Jacob Epstein had gone beyond that stage. In the next issue Hulme explained just what he meant to do in the series of Contemporary Drawings he had begun with *A Dancer:*

> This series will include drawings by David Bomberg, Jacob Epstein, F. Etchells, Gaudier, C. F. Hamilton, P. Wyndham Lewis, C. R. W. Nevinson, Roberts, and E. Wadsworth. Most of them are members of the London Group, which is now holding an exhibition in the Goupil Gallery. Some of the drawings are Cubist, some are not. Perhaps the only quality they possess in common is that they are all abstract in character. The series includes everyone in England who is doing interesting work of this character. In view of the amount of capable work continually being produced it is difficult to realise that the only part of this which is important, that which is preparing the art of the next generation, may be the work of a relatively quite small group of artists. . . . Appended to each drawing will be a short note for the benefit of those who are baffled by the abstract character of the work. For this the editor, and not the artist, is alone responsible. You have before you a movement about which there is no crystallised opinion,

and consequently have the fun of making your own judgments about the work. You will have, moreover, the advantage of comparing these drawings with the not very
exhilarating work of the more traditional school—with
those, shall I say, in the series Mr. Sickert is editing?
(14.22:688)

Walter Sickert himself had a letter in that issue, but it was on a
different topic—the death of his friend Spencer Gore of pneu-
monia at the age of thirty-six, and the announcement that a
show of his works was being planned. We should note that,
though Gore, as an artist, was definitely on the Sickert side of
this dispute, Wyndham Lewis included two of his works in
the first issue of *Blast* when it came out in June of that year,
along with a number of examples of the geometric style more
typical of Vorticist art—another instance of the paradoxy of
Modernism.

　　In the next issue Sickert had a memorial piece on Gore,
which he called "A Perfect Modern" and used as a way of continuing the debate. He also included *Ethel* (Fig. 15), a drawing
by his student Mary Godwin, in his series of Modern Drawings. Godwin's drawing appears in the Table of Contents as
"Ethel: A Modern Drawing," echoing the title of Sickert's praise
of Gore. Clearly, at the center of this dispute was the issue of
what works of visual art had the right to be called "Modern,"
and both the New Representational art and the New Geometrical art were laying claim to that title. In our critical practice
we all too often award that disputed title to the geometrical,
erasing from view contemporary works in a more traditional
style, and the result is an impoverished Modernism, a Modernism with its paradoxy concealed.

　　In the next issue, Hulme countered with the third in his

Fig. 15. Mary Godwin, *Ethel*
(*NA* 14.23:721)

series of Contemporary Drawings, *A Study* (Fig. 16), by William
Roberts. Beneath the drawing Hulme's note appeared:

> This drawing contains four figures. I could point out the
> position of these figures in more detail, but I think such
> detailed indication misleading. No artist can create ab-
> stract form spontaneously; it is always generated, or, at
> least, suggested, by the consideration of some outside con-
> crete shapes. But such shapes are only interesting if you

Fig. 16. William Roberts, *A Study*
(*NA* 14.24:753)

want to explain the psychology of the process of composition in the artist's mind. The interest of the drawing itself depends on the forms it contains. The fact that such
forms were suggested by human figures is of no importance. (14.24:753)

In this note, if I have read him rightly, Hulme seems to deny the
importance of content altogether, taking abstraction a step further than he had in the past. Such a step intensified the break
between the two modes of art being practiced at that time and
embodied in his series of drawings and that of Sickert.

In the same issue, Ananda Coomaraswamy, the Indian art historian or philosopher of art, had a review of Clive Bell's book *Art*, which had been reviewed by Sickert six weeks earlier. It was an interesting and appreciative review of some length. For our purposes, however, the most interesting part is a short discussion of the contemporary situation, in which Coomaraswamy quotes Bell and seems to endorse his view, which is quite the opposite of that developed by Hulme:

> After the Post-Impressionists come the Futurists, Cubists, and the like. These are disposed of as a mere perversion of the main forward tendency, and they are condemned, as artists, because, "like the Royal Academicians, they use form, not to provoke aesthetic emotions, but to convey information and ideas—they aim at representing in line and colour the chaos of the mind at a particular moment." The Post-Impressionist tendency, on the other hand, is capable of endless development. (14.24:763).

For Bell (and apparently for Coomaraswamy) Post-Impressionism could claim the future because it could be developed endlessly, whereas the new geometric or abstract sorts of art were stuck in "the chaos of the mind at a particular moment." Bell's claim supported the kind of painting his wife, Vanessa, was doing, in contrast to that of the Cubists, and it could easily be extended to support the writing his wife's sister Virginia would do, in contrast to that of Joyce, for example, who was explicitly interested in the mental chaos of ordinary life. Neither Joyce nor Woolf, of course, actually presented such life chaotically, though Joyce's writing may well have seemed more chaotic initially. In 1914, however, Woolf had not written much, and Joyce's *Dubliners* was just finally getting published after a decade of difficulties. We are still some distance in time from the major works of these writers. Visual art, and the debates around it, were some distance ahead of verbal art at this moment, which makes these debates especially important for students of literary Modernism. The terminology of these debates about visual art, of course, will not transfer neatly into discussions of literary works, but literary critics may learn from them even so. It makes sense to see the later Joyce and much of Gertrude Stein in terms of a geometrical or abstract deconstruction and reconstruction of human life, and, at the same time, to see Woolf as, for the most part, developing a Post-Impressionistic form of literary narrative, which follows from the Impressionism of Conrad and Ford. What does not make sense, however, is to call one of these modes of textuality Modern and the other not.

In the next issue of *The New Age,* Sickert had a piece on "Drawing from the Cast," and what turned out to be the last in his series of Modern Drawings appeared: *The Doctor* (Fig. 17), by Sickert's pupil, associate, and lifelong friend, Sylvia Gosse, the daughter of the Victorian man of letters Edmund Gosse. Sickert soon continued the debate with a response to Charles Ginner's piece on Neo-Realism from several issues back, arguing that neither part of that term was useful. It is not good for artists to call themselves "New," he said, because that judgment should be left to posterity. And it is also a mistake to claim the name of "Realist," because the whole business of labels should be left to those "who have little else wherewith to cover their nakedness" (14.26:819). For most purposes, however, the term Neo-Realist describes the work of Sickert and the artists in his series better than any other critical term—especially if we understand Neo-Realism as pointing to an adaptation of Impressionist technique to an interior world in the double sense of situating characters in intimate spaces and in situations that

Fig. 17. Sylvia Gosse, *The Doctor*
(*NA* 14.25:785)

suggest their inner lives. We may need this concept to understand many of the verbal Modernists as well. What turned out
to be the last two items in Hulme's series of Contemporary
Drawings also appeared in that issue. One of the most interesting in this series, in my opinion, is a Cubist portrait of a
chauffeur (Fig. 18) by C. R. W. Nevinson, who was about to
weigh in on the critical side of this debate as well.

In the next issue of *The New Age* the editor mischievously
printed a translation of Marinetti's "Futurist Manifesto," followed immediately on the same page by a judicious review of

Fig. 18. C. R. W. Nevinson, *The Chauffeur*
(*NA* 14.26:814)

a show of the work of H. H. La Thangue, a founder of the New
English Art Club. The review was written by Walter Sickert,
who calmly went on in his way, praising the art and artists that
he liked—essentially those who had learned from the Impressionists and had avoided misinterpreting Cézanne and plung-
ing into the blind alley of Futurism, etc. In *The New Age* for
June 18, 1914, Nevinson responded to all this by printing a lecture he had given at the Doré Gallery called "Vital English Art."
The lecture was, among other things, a defense of Futurism.
Nevinson made a number of points that are important for our
purposes. One of these had to do with the relationship of
Modern to Primitive art.

The superb simplicity and intensity of the Primitives cannot be obtained by imitating their forms or technique nor
is it possible for an artist living to-day, travelling by tube,
by 'bus, by taxi, surrounded by steel construction hoard-
ings, petrol vapour and speed, how is it possible for that
artist to have the same emotions, thoughts or feelings as
an Egyptian, early Italian, or Byzantine. It is obviously impossible. So art must and always has represented the spirit
of its age.

That is why the Futurists claim to be the real Primitives, the Primitives of a new and modern sensibility; and
it is that which makes their work so vital, so intense,
though extremely complex.

In Europe there are roughly three modern schools that
in England are continually being confused with each other.
They all have one thing in common: they have abandoned representation of concrete forms or colours for
interpretation by means of abstract forms and colours,
the Cubists, such as Picasso, Metzenger, Léger, Gleizes,
Etchells, the Expressionists, such as Kandinsky, Wyndham-
Lewis, Wadsworth, etc., or Vorticists as I believe the latter
now like to be called, and the Futurists. (15.7:160)

Sickert had charged the Futurist painters with following
the dictates of a literary man, Marinetti. Nevinson answered
that charge by joining with Marinetti and taking responsibility, as an artist, for explaining the vitality of the three schools
of properly Modern art: Cubism, Expressionism (Vorticism),
and Futurism. Nevinson's argument, which is crucial for our
concerns, was based on the distinction between two forms of
representation, Concrete and Abstract, and two objects of representation, natural and mental. For him, only those modes of

art that tended toward abstraction were properly Modern. Pointing out that music does not imitate natural sounds but represents emotions powerfully, he argued that representational painting was inferior to abstraction, which could present mental states more directly:

> So in painting, by means of contrasts of abstract colour, form, lines, planes and dimensions that don't in the least imitate or represent natural forms, it is possible to create emotions infinitely more stimulating than those created by contemplating nature.
>
> Now this is the whole justification of all arts. Therefore representation in painting or sculpture is absurd.
>
> This had already been felt by Blake and Turner in England, by Cezanne, Van Gogh and Gauguin abroad, absolutely realised by Picasso and Kandinsky, but in the case of the two latter they seek form or colour for its own sake and are so able to produce an abstract emotion, and this is a very important movement, and the three paintings by Kandinsky at the Allied Artists are to my mind three of the finest modern pictures I have seen. (15.7:160)

In this passage, Nevinson distinguished himself from Hulme, who did not like Kandinsky's work, as we have seen, and he began to lay down the creed that a bit later on in the Modernist period we would come to know as Abstract Expressionism. Nevinson's view, as we shall see, also became the official view of New York's Museum of Modern Art. His lecture was detailed and eloquent, his main thrust being that art should be a tonic, not a drug, and that Futurism was capturing the spirit of modernity better than any other form of art, though he praised no other artist as highly as he did Kandinsky. This tack of Nevinson's, as it turned out, annoyed Wyndham Lewis, opening a fissure on the Abstract side of Modernism.

In the same issue Nevinson's lecture was parodied by one of the *New Age* regulars, writing as Charles Brookfarmer. And Sickert, in an article on "The Thickest Painters in London," also reacted to the Marinetti/Nevinson performance at the Doré, noting that these Futurists had "repealed" the Old Masters, and contemporaries like Gilman and Ginner, and saying that he expected them to be repealed themselves in the next week, a sentiment anticipated in Will Dyson's cartoon about the Post-Elliptical Rhomboidist and echoed in many places, including, as we shall see in Chapter 6, the fiction of Dornford Yates. Back in July, T. E. Hulme, in a long review of a show of David Bomberg's art, had tried to explain how abstract art was generated. It was a judicious review, rather than a piece of puffery, and concluded with the following paragraph:

> To sum up, then—in my notice of the London Group I said that I thought Mr. Bomberg was an artist of remarkable ability. This show certainly confirms that impression. It also adds something. It convinces me that his work has always been personal and independent—much more independent than that of most Cubists—and never reminiscent. If I am to qualify this, I should add that, as yet, his use of form satisfies a too purely sensuous or intellectual interest. It is not often used to intensify a more general emotion. I do not feel, then, the same absolute certainty about his work that I do about Epstein's. In Mr. Epstein's work the abstractions have been got at gradually, and always intensify, as abstractions, the general feeling of the whole work. But then Mr. Epstein is in a class by himself. I think that in this merely intellectual use of abstraction

Mr. Bomberg is achieving exactly what he sets out to achieve. But at the same time it is quite legitimate for me to point out why I prefer another use of abstraction. In any case, I think he will develop remarkably, and he is probably by this kind of work acquiring an intimate knowledge of form, which he will utilise in a different way later. (15.10:232)

Hulme is discriminating here between different sorts of abstraction, praising Epstein over Bomberg because his work intensifies a "more general emotion." We are back to what Sickert praised in von Schwind's *Morgenstunde,* and what we found in Gaudier's *Dancer.* There is something in the subjectivity of Expressionism that makes Hulme wary, as he was wary of Kandinsky as well. Those who favored Abstraction as the best mode for modern art were by no means entirely agreed about what Abstraction should be accomplishing. Hulme's Classicism led him to be suspicious of individualism and subjectivity as Romantic. On the literary side of Modernism, the Imagists, Ezra Pound, and, finally, T. S. Eliot would all share this suspicion.

Another thing that the apologists for the New Geometrism should have been concerned about was the sameness of their works. The work of Roberts and Bomberg, for example, is as hard to tell apart as the work of Picasso and Georges Braque in the early phase of Cubism. Very few artists could go the abstract route and remain as individual as Kandinsky, but Kandinsky's work blazes with power and originality from his Fauvish early landscapes to his later abstract Compositions, and his goal was not form itself but something deeper and more spiritual. David Bomberg was a talented artist, and Hulme was right both to praise him and to have some reservations, though he seems wrong, now, to have had reservations about Kandinsky. A work by Bomberg, called *Chinnereth* (Fig. 19), that Hulme reproduced as the second in his series of Contemporary Drawings, should be compared to *A Study* (Fig. 16) by Roberts. If the Neo-Realists were threatened by an appeal to emotion that was too direct and therefore sentimental, the Geometrists were threatened by an arid and repetitive formalism.

In the epigraph to this chapter, I quoted Ezra Pound, writing on art for *The New Age* as B. H. Dias, and pointing out the existence of such a figure as "the frenetic modernist" who will miss great drawing because the subject matter and style are not à la mode. Pound himself, of course, had a serious investment in the Old, and much of his work and T. S. Eliot's could be characterized as Neo-Realist, digging into the fissures of the modern psyche. By this time, of course, the first issue of the Vorticist journal *Blast* had appeared—in late June 1914—and this heated controversy in *The New Age* subsided. The guns of August were only a few weeks away, and the conflict of nations superseded the conflict of artists and critics. It is a good moment to stop this long chronicle and see what it has revealed about the paradoxy of Modernism. One thing we have certainly seen is that neither Old nor New was a simple term with a single meaning, but each was a complex signifier with submeanings within it that contributed to its paradoxical roles in discussions of Modernism. In that short period of five years that we have been considering (1910 through 1914, with emphasis on 1913–14), virtually everyone who addressed the issue of Old and New art agreed that a major cultural change had occurred.

Virginia Woolf, of course, made the definitive statement about this change with her famously hyperbolical assertion

Fig. 19. David Bomberg, *Chinnereth* (*NA* 14.22:689)

that "on or about December, 1910, human character changed" ("Mr. Bennett and Mrs. Brown," 96). Even so, for all those who felt that some break with the past was necessary, there was still the crucial choice of what part of the Old one was abandoning. It is one thing to break with Alma Tadema and another to break with Monet. Moreover, as we have seen in the discussions of Cézanne, he could be continued in more than one direction, and he himself could be seen as continuing the Impressionist line or breaking with it. There were Cubists, and Picasso is one of them, who were quite ambivalent about modernity, reacting to it with horror in some artworks and embracing it in others. And most of the Fauves, of course, fled the modern city, following Gauguin, and seeking "luxe, calme, et volupté." But the point is not to get every bird in the right pigeonhole but to point out the complexity of the Modernist aviary. If our goal is to understand Modernism and its relation to modernity, we shall need to consider the shadings and variations within and among the categories—the shifts, the ambiguities, the tensions within the work of individual artists and even within single works of art and literature. Joyce's *Ulysses,* to take a single obvious case, has elements of Neo-Realism and Abstraction, of Naturalism and Surrealism, in its construction—and these are part of the book's strength, not weaknesses or confusions. And we will find modernity itself represented with bitterness and fondness by an author who once tried to franchise a chain of cinemas in Ireland, to be called the Volta Theatres.

If we consider the work of the cartoonists we have seen in this chronicle, for example, we will find urban modernity represented in a traditional style by Tom Titt, in *Charing Cross Road,* but with a satiric or parodic intent. His London is not blessed. And in *St. Paul's Churchyard* he gave us images that echoed or parodied the Cubist style of Nevinson but seemed to accept and enjoy the communicative frenzy of modernity. Will Dyson, on the other hand, used a style that was less traditional to parody the whole contemporary rage for newness in *Progress.* Even the cartoons are not easily categorized, and they, too, are a part of Modernism in the arts. They may be "Low," but they are clearly engaged in a dialogue with the "High," and we need to hear the entire dialogue if we are to understand what Modernism was doing.

There are two more conclusions I wish to draw from this probe into the formation of Modernism in the visual arts. One has to do with the assumptions about modernity made by the apologists for the more radical forms of Modernist art. Every one of these critics agreed that Modernism was justified by a cultural break that was occurring in their world. And many of them hoped and believed that a New Order was coming to replace the disorder that was modernity. The New Geometrical art was to be supported by a New unified culture that would be equivalent to the Egyptian or the Byzantine in stability and profundity. This longing for a New Order was responsible for the welcome given to totalitarianism by certain artists, critics, and philosophers. But the political New Order turned out to be both disastrous and short-lived. And the move toward a New Geometrical art turned into abstract expressionism and played itself out, after producing some powerful and original work. Moreover, the political New Order, whether Fascist, Nazi, or Stalinist, hated the art that was supposed to be embodying its values and called for something more representational. The artists, in their turn, hated the New Order, though it took many of them some time to see through Stalinism, and some writers, like Pound, never abandoned their original receptive attitude toward Fascism.

Recently, as I was finishing revisions of this book, I revisited MoMA, in the week following its grand reopening—and this visit was a revelation to me. Going into the galleries three times in two days, looking at every Modernist work of painting and drawing that was on display, I realized for the first time that the notion of Modernism from which I had been trying for years to free myself had been created by my visits to MoMA from 1948 to the present. This struck me forcibly when I found, stuck in a tiny corner room, two paintings by Edward Hopper and one by Andrew Wyeth. Returning to the larger rooms, past the dozens of Picassos and Matisses on display, I found one work by Edgar Degas and one by Édouard Vuillard. There is a small room with Futurist works, but Vorticism is not repre-

sented—in fact, it is not even mentioned in Alfred Barr's famous diagram of modern art, which became the basis of his
founding curatorial practice at the museum.

Returning home, I checked MoMA's Web site, which,
among other things, offers a short discussion of "Modern Art
Despite Modernism" (emphasis in the display), from which
this is the key definition:

> A subset of modern art, modernism is the art that is es-
> sentially abstract, having radically detached itself from
> standard ideals of representation. Works from such van-
> guard movements as Expressionism, Cubism, Futurism,
> and Constructivism in the 1910s and 1920s, and Minimal-
> ism and Conceptualism in the 1960s and 1970s, appear as
> definitive forms of modernism on the walls of The Mu-
> seum of Modern Art and other public and private collec-
> tions. Nevertheless, the variety of representational art in
> the Museum's collection from the nineteenth century to
> the present attests to modern art being made to the pres-
> ent that is counter to classic modernism. In fact, an active
> anti-modernism initiated and has co-existed since the in-
> ception of the avant-garde agenda of Cézanne, Gauguin,
> Seurat, and van Gogh. Tradition-bound representations
> have consistently ignored or deliberately countered mod-
> ernism, to maintain earlier artistic ideals. Poised on the
> core of the modernist-antimodernist dichotomy is the
> plight of figuration. (<http://www.moma.org/exhibitions/
> 2000/madm/go.html>)

The "plight of figuration" is, apparently, to be modern without
being Modernist. But there is also the plight of being British.
MoMA admits to having one work by Gwen John and a couple

by Walter Sickert, but Wyndham Lewis and the Bloomsbury champions of Post-Impressionism—Roger Fry, Duncan Grant, and Vanessa Bell—whom Lewis detested, are impossible to find there on the walls or online. John and Sickert are at least discussed in the British section of "Modern Art *Despite* Modernism"—but mainly as leading toward the more abstract Francis Bacon and Lucien Freud. In the field of visual art, MoMA has led the way to the following accepted notions:

1. Modernism *equals* Abstraction—"is essentially abstract."
2. Modernism is mainly Parisian, with Continental off-shoots and American successors.
3. Figuration is a retrograde movement, going against the progressive tide that was flowing toward Abstract Impressionism.

To be a modern artist but not a Modernist is clearly an awkward situation. But this bit of paradoxy is as invidious as it is pervasive in the view of modern art put forward by this great and influential museum. The need to recognize this as a form of paradoxy is the first conclusion I want to draw here.

My second conclusion has to do with the art we have been considering. I find, personally, that the images which stay with me from those printed in *The New Age* come from both sides of the opposition between Representational and Abstract. I remember Gaudier's *Dancer,* Epstein's *Rock-Drill,* and Nevinson's *Chauffer,* but I have trouble recalling most of the other images from Hulme's sequence of Contemporary Drawings. And I remember Ginner's *Leicester Square* and Fred Richards's *Temple of the Sybil,* along with some of Sickert's own work. But I refuse to choose between von Schwind's *Morgen-*

stunde and Gaudier's *Dancer*. I have taken pleasure in both of these works and want each of them in my memory hoard. I also remember the cartoons by Tom Titt and Will Dyson. I want them there, too. And so, I am arguing, should you. The Neo-Realist tradition, which might have seemed eclipsed by the New Geometricists, was in fact continued by the *Neue Sachlichkeit* artists in Germany and is still alive and well today in the work of painters like Bacon, Freud and David Hockney, different as they are. As Post-Modernists, which we are now, whether we like it or not, we must sort out what Modernism was and what it should mean to us. In the chapters that follow, I shall take up some specific instances that I hope may serve as examples of the kind of sorting and sifting we should be doing.

3
Poetry and Rhetoric in the Modernist Montage

Paradise Lost *itself is a first-rate school in which to study montage and audio-visual relationships.*
—*Sergei Eisenstein*

The younger generation may have forgotten Binyon's sad youth, poisoned in the cradle by the abominable dogbiscuit of Milton's rhetoric.
—*Ezra Pound*

We make out of the quarrel with others, rhetoric, but of the quarrel with ourselves, poetry. Unlike the rhetoricians, who get a confident voice from remembering the crowd they have won or may win, we sing amid our uncertainty.
—*W. B. Yeats*

L ike High and Low or New and Old, the opposition between poetry and rhetoric is one of those key distinctions
used by Modernists to advocate the superiority of
their work to that of others. The way this invidious
distinction played out in Modernist discourse will emerge if
we look into the question of montage and its role in film and
poetry. It has been claimed that montage is the key device for
Modernism in the verbal as well as the visual arts, and this
chapter began its life as a contribution to a conference on just
that topic, in which my role was to join people mainly interested in film, adding something about montage in the verbal
arts to the general discussion. What I found, as I looked into the
matter, was another case of Modernist paradoxy, with major
Modernists firmly on both sides of a number of crucial issues.
But let us begin at the beginning, by looking at the dictionary.

There is—in English, at any rate—no such word as "montage," or there wasn't until recently. Neither the great *Oxford
English Dictionary* nor the second edition of *Webster's New
International Dictionary* included a definition of "montage,"
though this was remedied in later incarnations. The word,
then, is not native to our tongue. We have borrowed a French
word, *montage,* with a history in that language going back several centuries. Originally it had to do with bringing things up
from below, as the "*mont*" part indicates, but at some later date
it took on the meaning of putting parts together, as in those
complicated things that come to us with a little warning that
"some assembly is required." Assembly, putting-together,
montage—these are synonymous terms. So far, so good. But
"montage" comes to us with a special set of meanings derived
from its use in one sphere of cultural activity: film.

Putting a motion picture or a video together, which we
call editing, is called *montage* in French. So the term means

"editing." Why then do we need it at all in English, since we have another word that we use all the time that means the same thing? The answer to that question comes in the form of a single word: Eisenstein. Sergei Eisenstein, the brilliant Russian filmmaker, gave the word a special meaning—or, better, a series of special meanings—and these meanings have given the word "montage" a permanent currency in discussions not only of film but of Modernism in all the arts, and perhaps of Modernity itself. I shall be exploring these meanings, looking, in particular, at the way they intersect the Modernist opposition between poetry and rhetoric in the verbal arts. We will be coming to that intersection soon, led there by Sergei Eisenstein himself, who was surprisingly well versed in English poetry.

I propose to begin with what Eisenstein said about montage and then to consider the way certain poets and other writers combined images in literary texts, taking most of my examples from the Imagists and the Surrealists. As it happens, we have in literary criticism a venerable English word that refers to the combination of two concepts to make an emotional effect. The word is "metaphor," which, as the obsessive father in *My Big Fat Greek Wedding* would be quick to point out, is actually a Greek term. In ancient Greek, "metaphor" has, like "montage," a literal root in a notion of transportation of things from one place to another. As we shall see, Eisenstein himself gives us good reasons for connecting montage to metaphor, but neither of these terms is simple, and their meanings and uses diverge at certain crucial points.

In his first published article, in 1923, when he was still working in the theater and before he had directed a single film, Eisenstein was talking about theatrical production in terms of what he called a "montage of attractions" (230), by which he meant an assemblage or putting-together of theatrical effects to generate a particular emotional response from an audience. At this stage of his thought about montage he was drawing (as Peter Wollen pointed out long ago in *Signs and Meaning in Cinema*) upon two very different sources for conceptual support. One of these was the French theater of cruelty, the Grand Guignol, in which audiences were assaulted by realistic spectacles of brutality and torture. And the other was the work of the Russian behaviorist Ivan Pavlov, who could make a dog salivate by ringing a bell. Eisenstein wanted to dominate audiences the way Pavlov dominated dogs. When he moved to cinema from the stage, his montage concept was enriched by the work of his predecessors in that medium, Lev Kuleshov and Dziga Vertov, who had demonstrated a basic and crucial aspect of the cinematic process: namely, that audiences would connect any two sequential images in a narrative or conceptual way. The identical image of a face, coming after a scene of pain or pleasure, would be interpreted as a sad face or a happy face. The editor of cinematic images was thus in a position of great emotional power, and the montage or assemblage of cinematic shots in the editing process was the point at which this power could be exercised most efficiently. The later addition of sound to the process only increased that power.

A couple of millennia before Eisenstein, Aristotle was also interested in how emotional effects might be achieved in drama or in public speech through the organization of textual material. He found such structural devices as reversal and recognition crucial in dramatic performances, and he found such textual devices as metaphor, antithesis, and what he called "actualities" (*energeias*) crucial in effective public speaking. What the ancient Greek and the modern Russian had in common was a concern for the way that the emotions of audiences could be controlled by a textual performance. One of Aristotle's examples will show just how close they were in certain respects. He is writing about how an orator used a vivid metaphor in defending a general on trial for some crime. In this case the orator accused his auditors of forgetting what they owed to the great man, making his point by directing attention to a nearby statue erected in honor of the general in his days of glory. This is Aristotle's description of the crucial moment: "In defending Chabrias, Lycolon said: 'unawed even by that statue of bronze which there intercedes for him.' This was a metaphor for the moment, not permanent, but vivid; only while Chabrias is in danger can the statue be said to intercede for him; the lifeless monument of his service to the state becoming animate" (1411b, modified). The expressions translated by "that" and "there" (*that* statue . . . *there*) indicate that the speaker is directing the audience's attention to an actual statue erected in honor of the defendant. Pointing to it, the orator accuses his auditors of being unmoved by the intercession of this figure, which he has metaphorically energized for the occasion. Thus in the fourth century B.C. did Aristotle imagine a panning shot, in which the camera, matching the eyeline of a typical member of Lycolon's audience, shifts its gaze from the speaker to the statue, which seems to kneel in intercession for the accused. This is a blend of metaphor and "actuality," which brings us very close to what Eisenstein meant by montage. For the cinema gives us "actualities," in Aristotle's sense, automatically. It puts things before our eyes, immediately, as a sequence of images, which makes the combination of images—or montage—a crucial aspect of the poetics of film, and of all the other cultural fields that felt the influence of film from the 1890s on.

One of those other cultural fields was literature, and poetry in particular. It is no accident that one of the vital poetic movements of the early twentieth century in England and

America was called Imagism. Indeed, the combination of "images" in film and poetry is the ground upon which we may usefully compare the two. But the connection between film and poetry is a two-way street. Eisenstein himself was very much aware of poetry and poetics, and his essays are studded with references to literary texts and works of literary scholarship and criticism. His first book, published in English in 1942 as *The Film Sense*, begins with an essay that was called "Montage in 1938" when it originally appeared in a London magazine. The essay includes quotations from the English poets Samuel Taylor Coleridge, Robert Browning, and John Milton, from fiction writers Ambrose Bierce, Lewis Carroll, and Guy de Maupassant, from the Russian writers Aleksandr Pushkin, Lev Tolstoy, and Maxim Gorky, and even includes jokes recorded by Sigmund Freud. Eisenstein also mentions James Joyce as the greatest manipulator of what Lewis Carroll called the "portmanteau word"—a new word created by combining parts of old ones, which Eisenstein thought of as a verbal sort of montage. The range is impressive, but the intense focus on literature is the important thing for us to notice.

What is this filmmaker doing with all these literary texts? For the most part, he is showing us that, before cinema existed, these writers were thinking in sequences of images, and even attending to matters that must strike us, now, as highly cinematic—and doing so in order to achieve emotional effects. For instance, in discussing a passage from a Maupassant story, in which a tensely waiting character hears clocks striking from all over Paris, Eisenstein observes,

> The example from Maupassant can serve as a model for the most polished kind of montage scripting, where "12 o'clock" in sound is denoted by means of a whole series of

shots "from different camera angles": "distant," "nearer," "very far away." This striking of the clocks, recorded at various distances, is like the shooting of an object from various camera set-ups and repeated in a series of three different shot-pieces: "long shot," "medium shot," "distant shot." Moreover, the actual striking or, more correctly, the varied striking of the clocks is chosen not in the least for its virtue as a naturalistic detail of Paris at night. The primary effect of this conflicting striking of the clocks in Maupassant is the insistent stressing of the emotional image of the "fateful midnight hour," not the mere information that it is "12:00 A.M."

If his object had been merely to convey the information that it was then twelve o'clock at night, Maupassant would scarcely have resorted to such a polished piece of writing. Just as, without a carefully chosen creative-montage solution of this kind, he would never have achieved, by such simple means, so palpable an emotional effect. (21)

In selecting from the poets of the past, Eisenstein settles on John Milton, for reasons he carefully explains:

Paradise Lost itself is a first-rate school in which to study montage and audio-visual relationships. I shall quote several passages from different parts of it—firstly, because Pushkin in translation can never succeed in giving the English or American reader the direct delight in the peculiarities of his composition obtained by the Russian reader from such passages as those analyzed above. This the reader can successfully get from Milton. And secondly, because I doubt whether many of my British or American colleagues are in the habit of dipping often into

Paradise Lost, although there is much in it that is very instructive for the film-maker. (58)

Eisenstein then goes on to analyze some long passages from
Paradise Lost, showing how Milton anticipates a shooting script,
complete with camera set-ups and montage pieces or shots. Finally, Eisenstein brings his essay to a close by arguing that the
poet, the actor, and the director of a film share the same process of composition, which is best understood as a process of
montage, a process which he clearly understood as one that
put enormous power into the hands of the controller of that
process. In what may be the most important passage in this
essay, he defined the power of montage this way:

> The strength of montage resides in this, that it includes in
> the creative process the emotions and mind of the spec-
> tator. The spectator is compelled to proceed along that
> selfsame creative road that the author traveled in creating
> the image. The spectator not only sees the represented
> elements of the finished work, but also experiences the
> dynamic process of the emergence and assemblage of the
> image just as it was experienced by the author. And this is,
> obviously, the highest possible degree of approximation
> to transmitting visually the author's perceptions and in-
> tention in all their fullness, to transmitting them with
> "that strength of physical palpability" with which they
> arose before the author in his creative work and his cre-
> ative vision. (32)

What I find so crucial and so revealing in this passage is
the emphasis on textual power. Montage, in Eisenstein's view,
works in such a way that "the spectator is *compelled*" to experi-

ence what the author has experienced, and in the very way that the author has experienced it. Not allowed, not invited, but *compelled*. I associate this sort of insistence on authorial power with Modernism in all the arts, and especially with what we call High Modernism, the aesthetic developed by those writers and artists who dominated their fields in the first decades of the twentieth century—figures like Joyce and Picasso, and T. S. Eliot, whose description of what he called "the objective correlative" is very similar to Eisenstein on the function of montage: "The only way of expressing emotion in the form of art is by finding an 'objective correlative'; in other words, a set of objects, a situation, a chain of events which shall be the formula of that *particular* emotion; such that when the external facts, which must terminate in sensory experience, are given, the emotion is immediately evoked" (*Sacred Wood*, 100). The key words here are "formula" and "immediately"—words that connect the experience of art to behavioral science. Behind Eliot, as behind Eisenstein, Pavlov rears his ugly head. If the formula is right, the proper emotion will be evoked in the audience "immediately." This is the doctrine that Eliot and Ezra Pound were developing in the first decades of the twentieth century, deployed by Pound, in particular, under the banner of Imagism. It is a doctrine that is both like and unlike that of Eisenstein, in ways that should be relevant to our present concerns. For the sake of convenience I shall refer to the poetics of these British and American writers under the heading of Imagism, though Eliot himself never sailed under that banner, and those who did actually worked in various ways and had different notions of what they were doing. Nevertheless, articles and manifestos were produced in the name of Imagism that drew upon Eliot's thought as well as that of Ezra Pound, T. E. Hulme, Amy Lowell, Richard Aldington, Hilda Doolittle, and F. S. Flint.

The most obvious place where the Imagists diverged from Eisenstein was over the work of John Milton. For Pound and Eliot, Milton represented everything—or nearly everything—that a good poet should avoid. Moreover, Eliot, in particular, found Milton's poetry to be deficient in "visual imagination" (*On Poetry and Poets*, 139). This is ironic, to be sure, in light of Eisenstein's praise of Milton for describing the "heavenly battles with such strongly earthy detail that he was often the subject of serious attacks and reproaches" (58), but the two critics are not as far apart as we might think. Eliot thought that Milton was much better at sound than at visual imagery, and Eisenstein actually praised him most for what he called "the audio-visual distribution of images in his sound montage" (58). Eliot felt that Milton's visual images were vague and general rather than precise. But Eisenstein was not so concerned with description. After all, the camera took care of that. What he was looking for was set-ups and camera angles, things for the camera to record. Consider lines like these, quoted and discussed by Eisenstein:

> All in a moment through the gloom were seen
> Ten thousand Banners rise into the Air
> With Orient Colours waving: with them rose
> A Forrest huge of Spears: and thronging Helms
> Appear'd, and serried Shields in thick array
> Of depth immeasurable . . . (*Paradise Lost*, 1.544–49,
>   cited by Eisenstein, 59)

Eisenstein saw Milton as telling the camera what to shoot: first the banners, then the spears, then the helmets, and finally the thick array of shields. Eliot would claim that these descriptions do not show us anything. They may be the objective correlative of an emotion, but it is not a precise emotion, belonging to an individual poet. It is a mass scene, calculated to arouse a mass emotion. But is it poetry or rhetoric? And what, exactly, did these terms mean to the Modernist poets? As we might expect, they meant different things to different poets.

And this is a crucial distinction within the Modernist aesthetic. It is also the point at which the concerns of Eisenstein and the Imagists diverge most clearly. Ezra Pound despised Milton, observing that Laurence Binyon, a translator of Dante, had been "poisoned in the cradle by the abominable dogbiscuit of Milton's rhetoric" (*Literary Essays*, 201). And Pound's friend W. B. Yeats gave a definitive Modernist twist to the old distinction between rhetoric and poetry in a famous passage in *Per Amica Silentia Lunae:* "We make out of the quarrel with others, rhetoric, but of the quarrel with ourselves, poetry. Unlike the rhetoricians, who get a confident voice from remembering the crowd they have won or may win, we sing amid our uncertainty" (285). In the fate of these lines there is an important key to Modernist paradoxy. The first sentence is quoted everywhere, in print and on the Web. The second is ignored. But Yeats himself was making two points: one involving a binary opposition between quarreling with self or with others, and the second involving an opposition between certainty and uncertainty. Many of the Modernist poets who followed Yeats, including Eliot and the Imagists, did not accept uncertainty as their portion. They accepted the public/private opposition as crucial, but they thought that poetry should be hard and definite. There is nothing uncertain about an objective correlative. The Modernist poets all agreed, however, that common emotions and common thoughts were the stuff of rhetoric, while uncommon thoughts and emotions were the goal of poetry. Eisenstein, clearly a rhetorician, wanted powerful effects that would compel a mass audience to feel and believe what he wanted them to feel and believe. The Imagists, in contrast, less clearly, perhaps, but still rhetoricians, wanted to use combinations of images to compel individual readers to replicate the refined feelings experienced by that superior being, the poet. It is no accident that, for a time, their favorite magazine was called *The Egoist*. The common element here was control— power. Both modes aggrandized the power of the author, the collector and combiner of images, and diminished that of audiences, but Eisenstein wanted to control the emotions of a mass audience, whereas the Imagists disdained the mass audience and sought to refine the emotions of an elite group of readers. Looked at in this way, the rhetoric/poetry distinction is one not so much of persuasion versus meditation, as it is in Yeats's formulation, but of public persuasion versus private persuasion. Control over the responses of an audience is just as important in Eliot's "objective correlative" as in Eisenstein's "montage of attractions."

Poetry, then, is just rhetoric with those nasty connotations of mass audience and political effects removed. But something happened to the rhetoric of montage in Modernist poetry as the history of Modernism played out. Actually, two important things happened to this rhetoric, as we shall see. One of these is the movement of the Imagistic controlled montage from elite poetry to more popular forms of writing, and the other is a shift in the goals of poetry itself from the deliberate objective correlatives of the Imagists to the unconscious and anarchic montages of Surrealism.

There is no better introduction to the Imagist method of composition than some remarks of Ezra Pound's about how he came to write one of his poems:

Three years ago in Paris I got out of a "metro" train at La Concorde, and saw suddenly a beautiful face, and then another and another, and then a beautiful child's face, and then another beautiful woman, and I tried all day to find words for what this had meant to me, and I could not find any words that seemed to me worthy, or as lovely as that sudden emotion. And that evening, as I went home along the Rue Raynouard, I was still trying and I found suddenly the expression. I do not mean that I found words, but there came an equation . . . not in speech but in little splotches of colour. (*Memoir of Gaudier-Brzeska*, 86–87)

This is the poem Pound was able to write after he found the "equation."

In a Station of the Metro

The apparition of these faces in the crowd:
Petals on a wet, black bough. (*Personae*, 109)

That's it. Just a title and two lines of free verse. It is the perfect Imagist poem, one of the few, along with some short poems by T. E. Hulme and H.D., that actually adhere closely to the doctrine. It is also, of course, a montage of two images, superimposed, and it is an excellent example of what Eliot would later call the objective correlative: "the formula of that *particular* emotion; such that when the external facts, which must terminate in sensory experience, are given, the emotion is immediately evoked." From the Imagist point of view, such a combination of images was a superior method because it eliminated all figures of speech as such—no rhetoric, just the two

visual images, the faces in the crowd and the petals on the
bough. Unless, of course, montage—the combination of images—is itself a rhetorical device. True, we don't have the machinery of figural speech here. This is not technically a simile, a
metaphor, or even a symbol—just two images juxtaposed,
though the use of a colon at the end of the first line is surely a
sign of equivalence. But it works exactly like a simile, and the
reader must treat it as one in order to understand it. The faces
are *like* petals on a bough. The figure of speech may be repressed here, but the repressed, as we know, always returns.

As it happens, Pound's discussion of how he came to
write this poem, when it was published in the *Fortnightly Review*, attracted the attention of the redoubtable editor of *The
New Age*, A. R. Orage, who expressed admiration for the poetry in Pound's new *Cathay* volume but thought his theory of
Imagism was pretentious if not absurd.

> Imagism . . . at last takes on a meaning for me. I feel about
> it what M. Jourdain felt about prose: it is a very old trick
> disguised as a modern invention. Let me take one of Mr.
> Pound's examples. Arriving in Paris one day he was struck
> on his first walk by the number of beautiful women and
> children that he saw. He desired to set down his impres-
> sion, and this is how, after dozens of attempts, he scored
> a success:

> *The apparitions* [sic] *of these faces in the crowd:*
> *Petals, on a wet, black bough.*

> The image here, you are to understand, is Mr. Pound's
> imaginative equivalent for the scene of which he was a
> sensitive witness; and we ought further to conclude that
> it is the perfect image. But is it? On the contrary, I could

invent a score of other images of quite equal equivalence. So could anybody. Meredith was perpetually doing such things: his "dainty rogue in porcelain" is the most familiar instance. Shelley was prolific in them. The Japanese have made their only literary art of such bon-bons. What of these, for instance, as other images for the same scene: white wheeling gulls upon a muddy weedstrewn beach; war medals on a ragged waistcoat; patches of blue in a sky of smokecoloured clouds; oases in a sand-storm; flaming orchids growing upon a gooseberry bush; mistletoe on bare trees snow-clad; iridescence upon corpses; a robin's song on a dark autumn day. Had enough? I could go on ad infinitum. But I should not set up as an Imagist, but only as a journalist, on the strength of them! (*NA* 15.19:449)

Orage obliterated the distinction between poetry and rhetoric, arguing that many images might function as the formula for that "*particular* emotion," and that finding one of them would not necessarily elevate the finder above the level of journalism. I think it would be interesting (in a class, for instance) to offer Orage's examples and discuss them as alternatives to Pound's. We might find that Pound's image is indeed more appropriate for his purpose—but we would also, I believe, have to admit that Pound's obvious need to provide a prose explanation for his poem in a journalistic setting is itself revealing, since it has now become attached to the poem as a kind of footnote. In any case, the concern with the particular, unique emotion drives the literary montage farther and farther away from common feelings and deeper into feelings that are uncommon, feelings that cannot even be represented by images of actualities or possibilities. The quest for the particular, in the end, leads to the peculiar, as we saw, even in Orage's mocking examples. And the peculiar, ultimately, frees the reader to have a unique response. Let us look, then, you and I, at more examples of the Modernist way of combining images:

> *Let us go then, you and I,*
> *When the evening is spread out against the sky*
> *Like a patient etherized upon a table . . .*

This is a simile, with the word "like" boldly present at the beginning of the third line. But in what sense is it an "image"? Can we "see" the evening in the form of a patient about to be operated on? Not really, I should say. To visualize it too precisely would be to vulgarize it—imagine a scene from hospital soap opera superimposed upon a sunset. Eliot's evening and sky, in this image, are as vague as anything in Milton, though the hospitalized patient comes out of a register of colloquial experience and language that Milton would never have employed. Still, we can certainly feel the emotion of the speaker, for whom the image of a patient—helpless, unconscious, awaiting some ominous medical encounter—gives the evening and the visit upon which we are invited to join the speaker an air of dull foreboding. As in Pound's poem, this is a combination of two elements, bringing the "evening" and the etherized patient together, in an attempt to provide the formula of a particular emotion. These words, of course, are from the opening lines of Eliot's "Love Song of J. Alfred Prufrock," published first in *The Egoist* in 1917 (*Complete Poems,* 3).

Here is a similar combination of images to consider: "It was twilight, and the lights were coming on in the houses. The mountains lay like great veiled women against the green east. Some random stars began to nail up the edges of the evening."

This is prose, rather than verse, and it begins with a simple image of lights coming on in houses and then offers us two sentences, each of which contains a combination of images, the first in the form of a simile and the second in the form of a metaphor. It is not so easy to tie these images into the formula for a particular emotion, but the veiled women of the east and the nailing up of edges suggest some sort of theatrical setting, in which nature is providing a slightly ominous though alluring space for the events to come. This image occurs in chapter 23 of a novel called *Find a Victim,* written by Ross Macdonald and first published in 1954 (142). I introduce a montage from a work of detective fiction from the 1950s in order to show how the literary montage unites the work of High and Low Modernists over a span of nearly fifty years. A bit farther on in the same book, the narrator, Lew Archer, contemplating an automobile wreck, experiences a different kind of sensation: "A thousand feet below, it was still burning brightly. Among the faint odors of burning oil and alcohol I could smell Okinawa again" (157). A Proustian moment, here, in which a particular aroma induces an involuntary memory, though we have traveled some distance from Marcel's tea cakes. It is also a powerful objective correlative. Ross Macdonald had a Ph.D. in English, to be sure, but I could find equally interesting combinations of images in the work of other writers whose schooling did not extend so far—such as Raymond Chandler or Dashiell Hammett, though Chandler took exception to this "literary" quality in Macdonald's early work. But my point is that the elite rhetoric of Eliot and Proust was readily absorbed into a supposedly Low and "popular" mode of writing.

Keeping Prufrock's and Archer's evenings in mind, let us look at an image of morning from another source: "Day unfolded like a white tablecloth" [Le jour s'est déplié comme une

nappe blanche]. Simpler than the montages of Eliot and Macdonald, this image of dawn as a promise of order and civility
comes from the work of the Surrealist Pierre Reverdy, and was
used by André Breton (*Manifestoes,* 36; *Manifestes,* 51) in one
of his manifestos to illustrate the unpremeditated juxtaposition of images in Surrealistic writing. For Breton, Reverdy provided the most convenient description of Surrealistic image
making. Writing about his own awakening to Surrealist possibilities, Breton described it in this way, quoting Reverdy's essay
from the March 1918 issue of *Nord-Sud*:

In those days, a man at least as boring as I, Pierre Reverdy,
was writing:

The image is a pure creation of the mind.
It cannot be born from a comparison but from a
juxtaposition of two more or less distant realities.
The more the relationship between the two juxtaposed realities is distant and true, the stronger the
image will be—the greater its emotional power and
poetic reality. (20)

[A la même époque, un homme pour le moins aussi en-
nuyeux que moi, Pierre Reverdy, écrivait:

L'image est une création pure de l'esprit.
Elle ne peut naître d'une comparaison mais du
rapprochement de deux réalités plus ou moins
éloignées.
Plus les rapports des deux réalités rappprochées
seront lointains et justes, plus l'image sera forte—
plus elle aura de puissance émotive et de réalité
poétique.] (31)

A number of things about this formulation and Breton's use of it are important for our present concerns. What Reverdy means by an "image" is actually a montage—an image composed of two elements that he calls "realities" but that I would prefer to think of as concepts or images, as in the morning and the tablecloth in his own expression or the evening and the etherized patient in Eliot's. As Breton develops Reverdy's principles of Surrealist montage, he insists that the combination of "realities" cannot be conscious, cannot be a matter of "comparison," or any reasoned or reasonable relationship. The new combined "image" must be generated unconsciously. Breton puts it this way:

> We are . . . obliged to admit that the two terms of the image are not deduced one from the other by the mind for the specific purpose of producing the spark, that they are the simultaneous products of the activity I call Surrealist, reason's role being limited to taking note of, and appreciating, the luminous phenomenon. (37)

> [Force est donc bien d'admettre que les deux termes de l'image ne sont pas déduits l'un de l'autre par l'esprit *en vue* de l'étincelle à produire, qu'ils sont produits simultanés de l'activité que j'appelle surréaliste, la raison se bornant à constater, et à apprécier le phénomène lumineux.] (510)

This is not so far from Ezra Pound's description of how he arrived at the verbal formula for his Metro poem, though Pound insisted that the stimulus for his poem was an actual, conscious experience, even if the process of composition was not. But in fact, Pound never tells us about his actual process of composition, the choosing of words and putting them on the page. He tells us only about arriving at an "equation" in the form of splotches of color, which enabled him, at some point, presumably later that evening, to sit down and find the right words for his poem. But the words are very important, and more than one critic has pointed out that the word "apparition" does a lot of work in the poem—work that the more obvious word, "appearance," could never have done. "Apparition" adds connotations of the supernatural to the denotation of appearance. It turns those faces into what Breton would call "a luminous phenomenon." And if the word "apparition" is not rhetoric, I do not know what is. If you try to make a haiku (or Japanese bon-bon, as Orage would say) out of Pound's poem—and it's a useful exercise, I recommend it—you will find that the first thing you do is drop the word "apparition." Pound is, in fact, an extremely rhetorical poet, in the sense of quarreling with others rather than with himself. Consider, for example, the second poem in *Hugh Selwyn Mauberley:*

The age demanded an image
Of its accelerated grimace,
Something for the modern stage,
Not, at any rate, an Attic grace;

Not, not certainly, the obscure reveries
Of the inward gaze;
Better mendacities
Than the classics in paraphrase!

The "age demanded" chiefly a mould in plaster
Made with no loss of time,
A prose kinema, not, assuredly, alabaster
Or the "sculpture" of rhyme. (Personae, 188)

Here Pound gains some distance from himself through the persona of his speaker—a speaker who is not exactly like him but shares many of his values. And this whole poem is an attack on modernity and the kind of art it demands, a cinematic art to match its accelerated pace, which disdains the inward gaze of the poet and the alabaster image of the sculptor, preferring a "prose kinema," to "the 'sculpture' of rhyme." Even Pound's rhymes are part of his argument here, and it is definitely an argument in favor of itself, a work of self-promotion. Nor is there a single concrete image in it. Pound has rejected Imagism and moved on to something else. These are not, emphatically, "the obscure reveries/Of the inward gaze," or singing "amid our uncertainty." So has Pound given in to the age, providing it with what it wants? He has certainly turned his gaze outward and become rhetorical, but he is rejecting Modern mendacities and embracing the Old. For him it must be either old wine in new bottles or new wine in old ones, because new wine in new bottles, it seems, is poisonous. We may say that by embracing the Old in this slightly exaggerated manner he is distancing himself from his persona, Mauberley—but not very far.

My point here is that Imagism and the objective correlative for the private emotion were very difficult to sustain in a modernity driven by those forces Pound described so eloquently in his bitter little poem. For him, as for many others, the answer to Modernism's disintegrating power became Fascism's promise of integration. For others the answer lay in going deeper into the private, in search of an unconscious that might be collective. And the path to that unconscious was paved with impossible images: "Great isosceles wasps flew up from below. The pretty dawn of evening preceded me, its eyes on the heaven of my eyes, without turning round. Thus do

ships lie down in the silver storm" (53) [De bas en haut s'en-
volaient de grandes guêpes isocèles. La jolie aurore du soir me
précédait, les yeux au ciel de mes yeux sans retourner. Ainsi les
navires se couchent dans la tempête d'argent]. This is André
Breton himself, writing in *Soluble Fish* (*Poisson soluble*, 29).
The required Surrealist distance is achieved here by combining
things that are contradictory or come from totally different
registers of experience, dawn with evening, isosceles not with
triangle but with wasp, and a "Thus" that implies connection
where none is obvious. These are images that resist combination, resist interpretation, mock meaning. A notion like "the
pretty dawn of evening" does not make sense, nor does it control the response of a reader to align it with the feelings of the
poet. Rather, it forces the reader to stop thinking and start
dreaming—or perhaps to think in a more flexible way, closer
to dreamwork. The "dawn of evening" may refer to twilight, its
eyes the stars, which are in heaven, even if "my eyes" are not.
Connections can be made between these images, but not by
reason or logic, only by following associative links. And if we
make them thus, imaginatively, they are ours, not the poet's,
though he has provided the stimulus. We are a long way, here,
from the objective correlative—and from the montage of attractions. A long way from Pavlov, and closer to Rorschach. If
there is a politics that really belongs to Surrealism, it is Anarchism, which was detested by Communists and Fascists alike.

Surrealism never really captured the imagination of
poets in the English language, but one major writer came
close enough to it to change the possibilities of English poetry forever. I am referring to Gertrude Stein, who had gone
beyond (or around) Imagism as early as 1911, when she wrote
Tender Buttons, which was first published in New York in
1914. This text (Is it a poem?) was republished in *transition*

in 1928, taking its proper place between Imagism and the
L=A=N=G=U=A=G=E poetry of recent years. *Tender Buttons* has lasted well, continuing to draw clever interpreters like
William H. Gass, but resisting interpretive closure mightily. It
is a text that teaches well, but dethrones the teacher from the
role of New Critical Explicator, requiring the instructor to join
the students and Stein herself in playing with the possible
meanings of the words and the images they generate. When
Stein says, at the beginning of the third section of the text, "Act
so that there is no use in a centre" (63), she may well be giving
us a clue to her own anarchic view of how to use her words.

When this chapter was a lecture, I ended it with a paragraph from *Tender Buttons,* letting Stein have the last word. I
will end this chapter with that same paragraph, but this time,
since a book is a book is a book, I shall have to say what I think
it means and tie that into my larger argument: "To consider a
lecture, to consider it well is so anxious and so much a char-
ity and really supposing there is grain and if a stubble every
stubble is urgent, will there not be a chance of legality. The
sound is sickened and the price is purchased and golden what
is golden, a clergyman, a single tax, a currency and an inner
chamber" (75). We must always take her literally, to begin with.
She will drive us off the literal when she wants us to move. She
invites us to think about lectures, and how we should attend to
them. She asks us to be charitable, to think of the lecturer's
anxiety and match it by being anxious to get something out of
it: to suppose that it contains grain, or food for thought, and,
if it doesn't, to take even the stubble seriously—in short to
consider it well. And, if we do, we may find it worthy—or at
least not fraudulent ("legality"). What sort of things are lectures about? Currency, the single tax—topics dear to many
Modernists, including Pound. The most puzzling passage is

also the most attractive in many ways: "The sound is sickened and the price is purchased and golden what is golden . . . " I have no clear idea of what it means, but, as so often with Stein, that is not the same as having no idea at all or being certain that she is talking nonsense or playing Dada-ish sound games. She may be suggesting that lectures do not sound good, the way music in the same hall might sound. She may be suggesting that, if we have paid to be there, we can't get our money back. And she may be suggesting that there may be something that will repay our attention after all, if not with information about currency, perhaps with something for our "inner chamber," our interior lives. Or she may not. The words guide our interpretation, to some extent, but they do not control it, and they do not want to control it. This is not paradoxy, not a set of pseudo-oppositions in need of deconstruction. This is something else, undeconstructible, emerging from Modernism, leading toward the future.

The rhetoric/poetry opposition, on the other hand, is clearly a case of Modernist paradoxy: a binary opposition that covers complexity with a facade of simple clarity. As we have seen, for Yeats himself, who gave the opposition its most telling expression, it involved an opposition between certainty and uncertainty. And it was framed in terms of quarrelling—with oneself or with others. But poets are not always quarrelling, and neither are rhetoricians. Both, on the other hand, are often persuading, and using figures of speech in their persuasive efforts. Pound, for example, is trying to persuade us that faces in a subway station can be as beautiful as flowers, and he stretches things a bit by bringing in his "wet, black bough," for which there is no analogy in the Metro station, and pumping up the atmosphere with the word "apparition." The poet's aim— that we should learn to see human beauty in the midst of

Modernity—is laudable. But to claim that this is not rhetoric simply makes no sense. And, of course, it is also poetry. But there are, in fact, many kinds of rhetoric and many kinds of poetry. Even the private/public distinction will not finally preserve this binary opposition. For there is indeed public poetry, designed to move large groups of people, and there is private rhetoric, as in the language of a wooer to a beloved—the kind of language that animates a poem like "To His Coy Mistress." So perhaps we should see poetry as a special form of rhetoric—until it gives up its wish to control the emotions of readers, as the Surrealists and Gertrude Stein seem to do. And we should certainly learn from this glance at the Modernist montage that Modernism included both public and private persuasion, and that it ranged from trying to control responses as completely as possible all the way to giving readers the maximum amount of freedom and responsibility for the meanings of texts.

4

Hard and Soft:
Joyce and Others

Strauss has gone further than he has ever gone, further in
several directions. He has concentrated more agony into
music than he has ever done, as the subject of course requires.
He has written into it more tenderness, more beauty
(I had almost said sentiment, but I don't want to be
misunderstood) *than he has ever done in anything before.*
And this is the great and startling surprise of the opera.
—Herbert Hughes (emphasis added)

My epigraph comes from a review of a London performance of Richard Strauss's opera *Elektra* that appeared in *The New Age* in March 1910. During this year, and those immediately following it, the journal became the central battleground in England for debates over the direction that literature and the arts should take to meet the demands of modernity. What art, what music, what kinds of writing might be adequate to express the thoughts and feelings of the new age that so many people felt was coming into being around them at this time? These questions were debated with wit, passion, sincerity, and great critical acumen in the pages of this magazine, and it is clear that the same debates were going on at many levels of English culture and society, in the popular press and the learned quarterlies, as well as in this "Weekly Review of Politics, Literature, and Art."

Herbert Hughes's contribution to those debates interests me on a number of scores, but especially because of what it reveals through that word that is simultaneously offered and withdrawn in the parenthesis: "sentiment." The reviewer wants to make a claim for the tenderness and beauty of Strauss's aggressively modernist music, but he feels that the natural word for that combination—"sentiment"—is no longer natural. It may be misunderstood, so he avoids it. But it still seems right enough so that he has to utter it, if only to withdraw it at once. I want to read this hesitation as symptomatic of that shift in the critical climate that we know as the emergence of Modernism. It is easier to read it in that way now, when we may at last be able to position ourselves outside the discourse of Modernism itself. It was harder a few decades ago, as I believe the following anecdote will illustrate. In 1958 I began working on James Joyce, having been given his newly acquired papers at Cornell University to sift through and catalogue. As I did this research and began to publish my work, I met a number of the pioneers of Joyce studies, including Richard Ellmann, who took me under his wing, William Noon, with whom I quarreled but made it up before he died, Richard M. Kain, who collaborated with me on *The Workshop of Daedalus,* and Clive Hart, whom I knew primarily as a *Finnegans Wake* scholar.

Well, shortly after I moved to the University of Iowa in 1964, Clive Hart wrote me about a problem he was having with a little essay he had written about Joyce's sentimentality. As I remember the matter, he was having trouble placing this essay and asked whether I had any ideas about who might be interested in it. I have retained the impression that the Joyce industry, such as it was in those days, did not want to hear about Joyce's sentimentality, and Clive was looking for someplace outside the pale, where his essay might be published. (I asked Tom Staley, founding editor of the *James Joyce Quarterly,* whether Hart had sent him the essay, and Staley said that he hadn't, and that if he had, the *JJQ* would have published it.) Anyway, Clive sent me a copy, which I liked a lot. I took it down the hall to Curt Zimansky, the editor of the *Philological Quarterly,* explained the situation and recommended the manuscript. Curt liked it, too, and published it in the October 1967 issue of *PQ.* On this occasion, I want to return to the question of Joyce's sentimentality, and, indeed, to the question of sentimentality within Modernism, as it is now possible to do, but I want to begin by giving Hart full credit for opening up this discussion when it was much harder to do so. Let me begin, then, by returning to the opening paragraph of Clive Hart's essay, "James Joyce's Sentimentality":

> I believe that Joyce's works exhibit a great deal of sentimentality, and while I do not think that this is a damning criticism, it seems to me that the Joycean modes of sentimentality require closer and more careful scrutiny than they have hitherto received. In this article I shall try to indicate some of the directions which such an investigation might profitably take. (516)

Hart went on to define "sentimentality," indicating a debt to I. A. Richards, and offering us four overlapping points of identification that can be reduced to a demand for emotion not justified by the subject matter and a certain indulgence in emotion for its own sake. I'm willing to follow such thinkers as Hart and Richards here and accept that definition, to start with, though I want to diminish if not reject the pejorative implications. Hart went on to say that modern critics considered sentimental attitudes "inherently immature and debilitating, despite the fact that they characterize some of the world's most outstanding literature" (516), and he added that "fear of sentimentality seems to be responsible for preventing critics who are otherwise sympathetic towards Joyce from admitting its presence in his works" (516).

I could not have agreed more. When I began my own serious work on Joyce in 1958, I read through all the works (a second or third reading for most of them), with the help of the available guide books and Herbert Gorman's biography (which was all the biography we had then), and I concentrated on the works close to the material in the Cornell collection, which is to say *Dubliners* and the various versions of what became *A Portrait of the Artist as a Young Man*. Doing this, I found myself in trouble because I could not make my reading of the autobiographical fictions match those of the great critics, who saw Stephen as the victim of a pitiless irony, while I saw him as, in some ways, the beneficiary of authorial tenderness, which is to say as much sentimentalized as ironized. The Modernist critics, from Richards through all the New Critics, had an almost pathological fear of sentimentality. But there are signs that scholars of Modernism are at last getting over that fear, and this is important, for there are things about Modernism that are not visible clearly without a proper appreciation of the sentimental.

This statement of mine may need some justification, so, let me start by reminding you that one of the "men of 1914," Wyndham Lewis, has remained largely unreadable, despite serious critical efforts on his behalf, mainly because his fiction is totally lacking in sentiment. Long narratives require an emotional investment in the characters. They require other things as well. Dorothy Richardson has not lasted well either, though she has plenty of sentiment. What she lacks is suspense, narrative drive. The old Victorian formula, put into words, apparently, by Charles Reade—make 'em laugh, make 'em cry, make 'em wait—calls for comedy, sentiment, and suspense. I would say that a long narrative needs at least two of these—suspense and one of the others—and many of the best have all three in abundance.

One of the signs that sentiment is at last getting serious attention may be found in a recent issue of *Literary Imagination,* the Review of the Association of Literary Scholars and Critics. There the poet and critic James Longenbach has an essay called "Randall Jarrell's Legacy." Which might have had the adjective "Sentimental" placed before "Legacy," for Jarrell's sentimentality is what the essay is about. Longenbach begins by quoting a remark Jarrell made about John Crowe Ransom, which he then applies to Jarrell himself: "'He was writing in an age in which the most natural feeling of tenderness, happiness, or sorrow was likely to be called sentimental; consequently he needed a self-protective rhetoric as the most brutal or violent of poets did not'" (358). And Longenbach adds this telling comment a few pages later: "If Jarrell tried to protect himself by surrounding the tender-minded poems with the ramparts of a tough-minded criticism, the beauty of the strategy is that it failed. Today as fifty years ago, the charge of sentimentality hovers over the poems" (360–61). Longenbach, I want to emphasize, does not refute the charge. Rather, he embraces it. "Jarrell," he concludes, "preferred to remain vulnerable to his own poems, and it was a risk that he continues to pay for today" (367). We are meant to conclude, however, that it is we, we readers, who really pay, if we allow our fear of sentiment to blind us to the richness and beauty of these poems.

In the past decade or so we have seen a strong surge of interest in sentimental writing, especially in American literature, in books like Jane Tompkins's *Sensational Designs* and Suzanne Clark's *Sentimental Modernism* and Talia Schaffer's *The Forgotten Female Aesthetes*. And just as I was writing the first version of this chapter, I came across Laura Jane Ress's book *Tender Consciousness: Sentimental Sensibility in the Emerging Artist—Sterne, Yeats, Joyce, and Proust,* which argues for a connection between these modern writers and the sentimentalism of Laurence Sterne. But Clive Hart wrote his essay long before this rethinking of the sentimental had begun, which means that he was ahead of the curve, but also that he was still, to some extent, operating within the Modernist view of sentimentality as a dangerous weakness. This is how he began his discussion of Joyce's writing:

Joyce was a poor critic. He had not read widely enough in the main stream of English literature to be an accurate judge of writing. He was out of touch with the work of his contemporaries and wrote, despite his surface brilliance, in an unsophisticated, even naive manner. This is most obvious in his poetry, which is almost uniformly of a mediocre undergraduate standard and cannot be retrieved from triviality by critical gymnastics such as those of Professor Tindall. When Joyce is over-emotional toward his subject, as in the case of parts of "Anna Livia," he reveals some of the sentimentality of the proletarian writer who gives undue emphasis to the cultivation of "feeling" for his subject. (516–17)

I'm inclined to agree about most of the poetry, but I like those sentimental rushes Joyce gives us in the closing passages of "The Dead," *A Portrait, Ulysses,* and *Finnegans Wake.* And Hart himself, after acknowledging these problems, goes on to argue that "fear of such sentimentality on the part of the reader is . . . often inhibiting and limiting. The tendency toward emotional naiveté is not always a bad thing, as I shall go on to show" (518). And go on he does, pointing in a very useful way to what he calls Joyce's "double-dealing"—a mixture of the sentimental and various antidotes, including especially obscenity. I strongly recommend a return to Hart's essay. In fact, I urged the *JJQ* to reprint it now, for a new generation of students and scholars of Joyce, and they have done so. But Clive drew most of his illustrations from the *Wake,* and I want to draw mine from *Ulysses.*

I would not wish to argue that literary critics or readers in general have been blind to the richness and beauty of this text. Having celebrated the hundredth anniversary of Bloomsday, we are all familiar with Joyce's dazzling interior monologues, his ingenious Homeric parallels, his elaborate scaffolding of colors, organs, and literary styles. These are extraordinary displays of linguistic virtuosity, exceeded only by those of his next book. But these are not responsible, in my opinion, for the durability of the work, which has depended on something quite different: the powerful concoction of laughter, tears, and narrative suspense without which that scaffolding would have collapsed long ago. The laughter, I suppose, we can take for granted now. The Broadway performance of *Ulysses in Night-*

town demonstrated more than three decades ago that Leopold Bloom is one of the great comic characters in our literature—if the issue had ever been in doubt. But we have been less ready, or less willing, to acknowledge that sentiment and suspense are important qualities in this book. Yet the book, as Cyril Connolly insisted long ago, is a novel that has "remorse" as its "central emotion."

Yes, indeed, *Ulysses* is a novel, and emotions—though not just remorse—are central to its power to attract and hold readers. I find that students still want to read this book, and, if it isn't in the curriculum, they will seek out faculty to help guide them through it. At Brown University, I know young teachers who have led high school students through some chapters in summer school, or have taken first-year students in our lowest-level writing course through the entire book. This is possible partly because the book has celebrity status, to be sure, but there is more at work here—something to do with the basic pleasures of emotional involvement and narrative suspense. But how much suspense can there be in a story that lasts only for a single day? Well, it depends on the day, doesn't it, and on how the day is positioned. Graham Swift has reminded us recently in his Booker Prize–winning novel *Last Orders* that one day is enough, if you bring the past and the future properly into the frame, and the splendid film made from that novel reinforces the point.

As readers of *Ulysses* know very well, June 16, 1904, turns out to be a busy day for our central characters, from start to finish. Moreover, beyond this single day stretch a past of momentous events, recent and distant, and a future that is being shaped even as these hours pass. A lot has gone on, is going on, and will go on. To the extent that we make emotional investments in these characters, these narratives are suspenseful. To recover the emotional elements in Joyce's novel, I ask you to think of it, at least momentarily, as a continuation of Victorian fiction. This is a story of two households, the houses of Bloom and Dedalus, haunted by death and troubled by economic and emotional turmoil. We learn, before we finish the book, how they got that way, and we are given evidence about what will become of them. Stephen has left home to live in the Martello tower. On this day he leaves the tower, intending not to return, having given up his key. Will he find a home with the Blooms? Apparently not. At the end of the book, he is on a trajectory out and away from home, repeating, perhaps as farce, his earlier departure for Paris, burdened not only with remorse over his mother's death but also with a terrible sense that he is abandoning his siblings to a wretched fate. Where will he go? What will he do? Will he really abandon all his sisters?

Bloom departs in the morning, also keyless, his bed about to be usurped by the bill-sticker Boylan, but he returns at evening to resume his place, his trajectory a circle, of which Molly is the beginning and the end. What will happen the next morning in the Bloom household? We are left in suspense about this, for he has requested more service and respect than he is used to getting from Molly. And what of Molly? Is her future to be a parade of Boylans? All this suspense is not resolved in the novel. The future is in question. But the very urgency of the questions is a measure of the long-term suspense that has been generated.

There is also a good deal of short-term suspense in the book, as in Bloom's adventure with the Citizen or Stephen's discourse in the library, not to mention how these two will get through the land of Circe and past the army of the conquerors. And there is plenty of sentiment as well. What Cary Nelson says of modern poetry ("There is more commonplace sentiment in many modern poets than English professors like to admit" [100]) is equally true of modern fiction. In *Ulysses* the sentiment is frequently mocked, as in the manifestation of Rudy near the end of "Circe," dressed and behaving according to Bloom's unconscious desires. But it can't be mocked if it isn't there to begin with. Joyce's novel is as full of emotion as it is of irony—and sometimes the irony is emotional, too. Given the size and density of the book, it seems absurd to illustrate this with a short selection or two, but I must try. The chapter known as "Wandering Rocks" will serve for this purpose, for it is there that we see most fully the situation of the Dedalus household and Stephen's reaction to it. This is a chapter broken into episodes of apparently aimless wandering by a variety of Dubliners, crisscrossed by the stroll of Father Conmee and the Viceregal procession, representing the two powers that together control the destinies of this subject people: Rome and London, or Christ and Caesar, as Joyce liked to think of them. But among the wanderings we are given three scenes involving the Dedalus family directly and another in which Buck Mulligan and Haines discuss Stephen. Taken together, these scenes are as full of emotion as one could wish.

In the first of these scenes (226), we see three of the Dedalus girls at home, where Maggie is boiling shirts and cooking some soup provided by Sister Mary Patrick. Katey and Boody enter the kitchen and ask Maggie whether she has been able to pawn some of Stephen's books. She hasn't. Dilly, who is absent, has gone to meet "Our father who art not in heaven," according to Boody, who is breaking bread into her soup in an unconscious parody of the Mass that contrasts with Buck Mulligan's conscious parody in the opening pages of the novel. Boody is reprimanded by her sister: "Boody! For shame!" (227). For shame, indeed. It is a touching moment, in which only the toughness of the girls counteracts the sentimental potential of the scene—or heightens it. This prepares us to see Dilly, in a later episode, confronting her father, brushing aside his patriarchal criticism of her posture and staring down his pretense of having got no money that day. She extorts a shilling and tuppence from him, causing him to wonder out loud, "Was it the little nuns taught you to be so saucy"—those same little nuns who are keeping the girls from starvation with gifts of bread and soup. The father's selfishness and sarcasm—"An insolent pack of little bitches since your poor mother died"—do not scare off this daughter, who is visibly being toughened by what she has to do, and Simon walks away, muttering about "The little nuns! Nice little things" (238–39). Joycean irony, here, is not working to undercut Joycean sentiment but to reinforce it. The irony and the sentiment are taking us in the same emotional direction.

In the third family episode Stephen notices "Dilly's high shoulders and shabby dress" at a bookstall. He is looking at a charm that, if repeated three times, will "win a woman's love"—something of which he is very much in need. Shutting his book so she will not catch him looking at it, Stephen asks Dilly what she is doing there, thinking of how, when "she crouched feeding the fire with broken boots," he lay in bed and told her about Paris. He asks her what she has:

—I bought it from the other cart for a penny, Dilly said, laughing nervously. Is it any good.

My eyes they say she has. Do others see me so? Quick, far and daring. Shadow of my mind.

He took the coverless book from her hand. Chardenal's French primer.

—What did you buy that for? He asked. To learn
French?

She nodded, reddening and closing tight her lips.

Show no surprise. Quite natural.

—Here, Stephen said. It's all right. Mind Maggie doesn't
pawn it on you. I suppose all my books are gone.

—Some, Dilly said. We had to.

She is drowning. Agenbite. Save her. Agenbite. All
against us. She will drown me with her, eyes and hair.
Lank coils of seaweed hair around me, my heart, my soul.
Salt green death.

We.

Agenbite of inwit. Inwit's agenbite.

Misery! Misery! (243)

This is one of the novel's most emotional moments. Its power
is based on the previous two episodes and what we have
learned from them about the situation of the Dedalus girls
and their relationship with their father. Stephen's gentleness is
particularly striking coming after his father's brutal sarcasm.
Dilly's vulnerability is all too apparent now, though she hid it
when confronting Simon. And Stephen reads it in her blush
and her tight lips. "Show no surprise," he admonishes himself.
"Quite natural." For this is the sister who most resembles him,
the one he told about Paris, which has led her to spend a precious penny on a French grammar. Stephen's recognition of the
resemblance, his acceptance of responsibility, is all compressed
into that single two-letter paragraph: "We."

But accepting familial responsibility frightens Stephen.
He would like to avoid it. At the end of *A Portrait of the Artist
as a Young Man,* he was talking bravely about flying by the nets

spread to entrap him. Now he is thinking about drowning with the other members of his sinking family. Like his namesake's son Icarus, first he flew, now he may drown. He seems to have a choice between letting his sisters drown and drowning with them. This is why the word "We"—that simple word—is so frightening to him. The final chorus of "Misery! Misery!" undoubtedly exaggerates and mocks Stephen's emotion to preserve the text against the charge of sentimentality, pushing the excessive emotion on to the character, away from the author—another form of Joycean "double-dealing." But the emotion is there, and it is one of those aspects of Stephen's character that enables us to make an emotional investment in him rather than merely regard him with ironic detachment. He is very different, for example, from the artist figures Wyndham Lewis gave us in *Tarr,* whose major emotions are boredom and annoyance, various forms of ennui. If Joyce had been as unsentimental as Lewis, Bloomsday would not be an international event.

Not that Joyce avoided irony in *Ulysses*—but when he waxes ironic in "Wandering Rocks" it is often at the expense of those characters he is teaching us to despise. For example, the scene of Haines and Mulligan stuffing themselves with mélanges, plus "scones and butter and some cakes as well," sends our thoughts back to the bread and soup consumed by the Dedalus girls, even as Mulligan is mocking Stephen for the benefit of Haines. Follow the food in this passage, as Joyce's language turns the sweets to a bitter irony in the service of sentiment.

[Haines] sank two lumps of sugar deftly longwise through the whipped cream. Buck Mulligan slit a steaming scone in two and plastered butter over its smoking pith. He bit off a soft piece hungrily

—Ten years, he said, chewing and laughing. He is going to write something in ten years.

—Seems a long way off, Haines said, thoughtfully lifting his spoon. Still, I shouldn't wonder if he did after all.

He tasted a spoonful from the creamy cone of his cup.

—This is the real Irish cream I take it, he said with forbearance. I don't want to be imposed on. (249)

Joyce's hatred of Oliver Gogarty shines through this portrait of him in the guise of Malachi Mulligan, but we need not know anything about Joyce's life to recognize the emotion being poured into these teacups and spread on these scones. Real Irish cream, indeed! But this irony is deployed to improve our opinion of Stephen, by making his mocker unattractive. Even Haines seems to withdraw from Mulligan a bit at the end of this exchange.

Now nothing I have said here will come as news to Joyceans, whether professional or amateur. We (if I may consider myself one of them) have known all along that *Ulysses* asks for and rewards the same kind of emotional investments we regularly make in novels with less exalted aspirations than this. But we may be less ready to acknowledge that we would like to know whether any of those girls avoid drowning in Dublin, and whether Stephen will indeed escape and write something by 1914. Many readers, I want to suggest, including perhaps some otherwise distinguished scholars, have a sufficient investment in these matters to be tempted to use the events of the author's life to fill in the stories of his characters. Joyce did write something in ten years, and he got some of his siblings out of Dublin and into less desperate situations. But my point is not that we should—or should not—read in this way, but only that some of us want to because we have been moved, engaged, made to laugh, cry, and wait in the traditional manner. And these emotions have much to do with the durability of this masterpiece of High Modernism.

Clive Hart suggested that "the propensity to deal with sentimental subjects in a sentimental way distinguishes Joyce from many of his more hard-boiled contemporaries, such as Eliot and Pound" (518). But I am not so sure about that. I think much of the strength of Eliot and Pound in their best work comes from a similar propensity. In his essay on Jarrell, James Longenbach made this point cleverly by quoting the following lines from Eliot's "Love Song of J. Alfred Prufrock":

> *But though I have wept and fasted, wept and prayed,*
> *Though I have seen my head brought in upon a platter,*
> *I am no prophet.*
> *I have seen the moment of my greatness flicker,*
> *And I have seen the eternal Footman hold my coat,*
> *And in short, I was afraid.* (359)

What the clever critic has done here is simply to suppress the asides Eliot put in the poem. Longenbach has done this so as to allow us to contemplate the poem's sentimentality without its protective coating of irony. As he puts it, "I want us to hear that Eliot used irony not simply to distance himself from overpowering emotion but to allow those emotions into the poem" (359). Here are the same lines, with the asides:

> *But though I wept and fasted, wept and prayed,*
> *Though I have seen my head [grown slightly bald] brought*
> *in upon a platter,*
> *I am no prophet—and here's no great matter;*
> *I have seen the moment of my greatness flicker,*

And I have seen the eternal Footman hold my coat, and
  snicker,
And in short, I was afraid. (*Complete Poems,* brackets in
  original)

We might add that Ezra Pound, in some of his most admirable poetry, is no more hard-boiled than Joyce or Eliot,
whether we think of his imagist couplet on the beautiful faces
he saw in a Metro station in Paris or of "The River-Merchant's
Wife: a Letter" from *Cathay.* Consider, for instance these lines
from that poem:

At fourteen I married My Lord you.
I never laughed, being bashful.
Lowering my head, I looked at the wall.
Called to, a thousand times, I never looked back.

At fifteen I stopped scowling,
I desired my dust to be mingled with yours
Forever and forever and forever. (*Personae,* 130)

Using the voice of a sixteen-year-old girl from a culture distant
from his own in time and space, Pound was able to give us a
poem about love that is pure emotion. I did not have to suppress any phrases in quoting this, and could have used the entire poem, which is emotionally consistent throughout. To
write with such direct feeling in his own voice may have been
impossible for him, though he spoke to us later with genuine
emotion in the anguished "Pisan Cantos." Sentiment, I wish to
conclude, has been an integral part of Modernism for a long
time, and the question, for the greatest Modernists, has always
been not how to avoid it but how to include it, protect it, and

enhance it. And at this, Joyce was very good indeed, a writer whose sentimental prose has moved and sustained us all these many years.

Before leaving Joyce, I want to look at a few lines from the closing section of *Finnegans Wake*

> And it's old and old it's sad and old it's sad and weary I go back to you, my cold father, my cold mad father, my cold mad feary father, till the near sight of the mere size of him, the moyles and moyles of it, moananoaning, makes me seasilt saltsick and I rush my only, into your arms. I see them rising! Save me from those therrible prongs! Two more. Onetwo moremens more. So. Avelaval. My leaves have drifted from me. All. But one clings still. I'll bear it on me. To remind me of. Lff! So soft this morning, ours. Yes. Carry me along taddy, like you done through the toy fair! (*FW* 627–28)

We are dealing here with a humanized version of the water cycle, with the part of the cycle where a river comes down to the sea. In this case it is the river Liffey, passing through Dublin and on out to the Irish Sea, where the Irish equivalent to Neptune, the god Mananan, awaits the return of his daughter, Anna Livia Plurabelle. The old, weary river goddess is becoming youthful again. This is a scene of recognition, reversal, and renewal—full of the Aristotelian virtues, and Joyce's own wit and sentiment, supporting one another. And the voice sings its hail and farewell (ave atque vale) in river language, so that it sounds like "alluvial," as it deposits its burden of seasilt and saltsick in the arms of its cold mad feary father. The allusive burden of this prose is enormous, too—equaled only by the emotional burdens of age and youth, love and fear, death and rebirth. This is something very like Nietzsche's Eternal Return, accepted with a kind of Nietzschean joy. The "Yes" uttered by this voice connects this passage to the end of Molly Bloom's soliloquy in *Ulysses,* to the "Welcome, O life!" at the end of *A Portrait,* and to the descent of the snow at the end of "The Dead" in *Dubliners,* borrowed from that archsentimentalist Bret Harte. Affirmation, acceptance, joy in the process that unites death and life. That is what Joyce gives us, and that is what we love in his work, and in the work of the other Modernists we still admire and enjoy.

We need not look far to find the sentimental at work in that other "Man of 1914," Ford Madox Hueffer, who dropped his German name after the war and became Ford Madox Ford. In the first issue of *Blast* we find the beginning of a work of fiction by Hueffer called "The Saddest Story." The title alone suggests sentiment, of course, and it is there in the fiction, which was never continued in *Blast,* since the journal itself scarcely continued, but was ultimately completed and published as the novel we know as *The Good Soldier.* This novel, which has proved to be the only truly durable work in Ford's extensive body of writing, is a tour de force of sentiment controlled by irony, supported by Ford's masterful use of an unreliable narrator. These features are apparent even in the segment featured in *Blast,* in which the narrator Dowell begins to tell us about his protagonist, Captain Edward Ashburnham:

> And yet, I must add that Edward was a great reader—he would pass hours lost in novels of a sentimental type— novels in which typewriter girls married Marquises, and governesses, Earls. And in his books, as a rule, the course of true love ran as smooth as buttered honey. And he was fond of poetry of a certain type—and he could even read

a hopelessly sad love story. I have seen his eyes fill with
tears at reading a hopeless parting. And he loved, with a
sentimental yearning, all children, puppies, and the feeble
generally. (94)

Even Dowell tries to take an ironic distance from this archsentimentalist, who loves "children, puppies, and the feeble generally." But Dowell also insists that the story he is telling is "The
Saddest Story," and Ford supported him in that position by
wanting that title for his book and only reluctantly accepting
his publisher's attempt to cash in on the war by calling it *The
Good Soldier* when it was published in 1915.

This "saddest story" mixes sentiment and irony, comedy
and pathos in a dazzling way, and I do not wish to suggest that
the sentiment triumphs over the irony. I do want to claim,
however, that the sentiment is what makes the irony possible,
and that without it this would be just another dreary exercise
in supposedly Classical Hardness. While we are looking at
Blast, we should notice that Ford's fictional episode was followed in the journal by a story written by Rebecca West, which
is about a husband who tries to drown his wife and then kill
himself by turning on the gas in a sealed room; he fails as a
murderer because the wife is too strong and healthy for him,
and fails as a suicide because his frugal wife, whom he thought
he had killed, has come home and turned off the gas, as she always does at nighttime. This story, called "Indissoluble Matrimony," has its own blend of irony, comedy, and sentiment,
which is not the same as that of Ford's novel, being closer to
naturalism or Thomas Hardy's brand of tragic irony, but it il-
lustrates perfectly well the principle that sentiment is essential
to success, even in the heart of the Vortex. Wyndham Lewis's
play *The Enemy of the Stars*, which is the longest work of prose

in the first number of *Blast*, is an excellent example of Modernism without sentiment. It was scarcely readable then, and has sunk like a stone since.

In the visual arts the closest counterpart to James Joyce is undoubtedly Pablo Picasso, whose work offers the same relentless migration of styles, based on the same command of a vast stylistic repertory from the masters of the past, and the same awareness of contemporary materials, both High and Low. And we can find in the work of Picasso's early Rose and Blue periods the same kinds of unconcealed sentimentalism that we recognize in Joyce's early poetry and prose. But what of the major works? Is it there, too? I would say that it is. As I have argued elsewhere (see "In the Brothel of Modernism," in *In Search of James Joyce*, 178–207), the brothel episodes represented in Joyce's "Circe" chapter of *Ulysses* and Picasso's *Demoiselles d'Avignon* have much in common in their presentation of the brothel as a place of terrifying transformations, though Picasso erased from the later versions of this painting the young men who were present in the earliest sketches.

For Picasso, however, the turn to the brothel represents a hardening or toughening of his view of the denizens of the underworld—a move from pink and blue to harder colors, and from sentimentalized representations of the human form to brutalized images, borrowed from cultures that Picasso saw as both savage and creative. We can see something similar in Joyce's shift from the prostitute represented in *A Portrait*, with a doll on her bed, to Bella Cohen in *Ulysses*. These changes are driven by a fear of softness in artists who know they are soft and are seeking some means to escape their own sentimentalism. Those to whom hardness comes naturally are seldom as interesting as those for whom it is a cloak for an inner softness. And that is part of the paradoxy of Modernism.

Part II
Paradoxes

In this part, I propose several paradoxical categories as a means of counteracting the paradoxy of Modernism—Durable Fluff, Iridescent Mediocrity, and Formulaic Creativity—paying considerable attention to individual writers and texts as a way of indicating what we lose if we accept as modern literary art only works that match the categories generated by the paradoxies that have been crucial to the critical discourse of Modernism.

5
Durable Fluff:
The Importance of
Not Being Earnest

According to the Wall Street Journal, *when asked by*
an audience member to assign a "light and funny"
book, the serious, teacherly Oprah replied,
"I don't read anything light and funny."
—R. Mark Hall

Oh! it is absurd to have a hard and fast rule about what one
should read and what one shouldn't. More than half of
modern culture depends on what one shouldn't read.
—Algernon Moncrieff

The first of my two epigraphs is from an article in
College English on "The 'Oprahfication' of Literacy."
The second comes, of course, from the first scene of one
of the lightest and funniest texts in our literary her-

itage: *The Importance of Being Earnest.* Among those things one shouldn't read, those things that Oprah wouldn't read, are a group of texts that belong to the category that I want to call "durable fluff." I am using this paradoxical expression in an attempt to name a phenomenon that fascinates me: the way certain texts that are "light and funny"—totally lacking in what Matthew Arnold called "high seriousness"—manage to survive and find audiences at least as well as others that are intended to be masterpieces of profundity. The works I am interested in are all "light and bright and sparkling"—a phrase used by Jane Austen to disparage her own work, though how seriously she made that charge against *Pride and Prejudice* we shall never know. Perhaps she did not know herself. Wit will do that to you, and that is one of its sources of pleasure—a certain tantalizing suspension of meaning. The supreme example of durable fluff, of course, is Oscar Wilde's play itself, which was recently released once again as a film and continues to play on stages all across the country in amateur and professional theaters. Even in the film *Spider-Man 2*, Peter Parker's girlfriend is starring in a stage production of Wilde's play—and the film is all about whether the earnest young Peter will continue to play the role of Spider-Man.

It is my intention in this chapter to discuss *The Importance of Being Earnest* as an exemplar of a certain element in literature—nothing so grand as a genre, perhaps, but a bright thread running through the textual tapestry that constitutes our literature and is therefore important in understanding that part of our literary heritage. There are two main problems in trying to discuss durable fluff. One is that the sources of its durability are mysterious. The other is that discussions of things that are light and bright and sparkling are all too often heavy, dull, and boring. I can promise neither to solve the mystery nor to avoid ponderosity, but I shall try not to be too earnest in attempting a solution.

Let us begin, then, by looking more closely at the title of Wilde's play. In most editions there is a subtitle, "A Trivial Comedy for Serious People." Wilde's combination of the words "trivial" and "serious" here offers us a clue to the nature of the sort of text we are considering. Like "durable fluff" and other phrases we may encounter, referring to similar literary works, it offers us a paradox as the key to our puzzle. Let us explore some of its ramifications. It suggests, perhaps, that serious people may need the relief of a trivial comedy to mitigate the burden of their gravity. "Serious," of course, is a synonym for "earnest," which connects the subtitle to the title. And the title is deliberately misleading in a way that is almost too bright and comic to be labeled "irony"—a word weighted for us by the gravity of its use in New Critical exegeses and its own metallic connotations. The play is not about the importance of being earnest but about the importance of being *called* Ernest, the importance of having the *name* Ernest attached to one, however the attachment is achieved: some are born "Ernest," some achieve Ernest-ness, and some have Ernest-ness thrust upon them—as Shakespeare almost said.

Well, here we are, still bogged down on the title, loading it with explicatory footnotes, being just the serious sort of people for whom this trivial comedy was designed. The justification for this, I would argue, is that by taking the play seriously we are following Wilde's advice; we may thus come to understand why he said it was intended for such invincibly serious people as ourselves, and, ultimately, to see what it is that has made this particular piece of fluff so durable. The difference between the words "earnest" and "Ernest," of course, is almost exactly the same as the one Jacques Derrida made so much of, between the French words "*différence*," and "*différance*," the difference created by the letters *a* and *e* appearing in words that are pronounced exactly the same. Derrida, however, had to invent his own new word, *différance* with an *a*, while Wilde found his difference already present in the language, which makes Wilde the wittier of the two—but then we knew that already, didn't we? I bring Derrida on stage in this cameo part mainly to show that Wilde, in the title of his play, was pointing to exactly the same kind of linguistic slippage that the French philosopher was fond of describing. Wilde took the very word that described the heart of Victorian culture, a culture of earnestness, if there ever was one, and showed that it was just a signifier that might be attached to different signifieds. And he took the proper name, or what Derrida would call the "signature," and showed that it, too, was not really proper, not the identifier of a unique individual, but a word that could be attached to different referents, by different means: some are born Ernest, etc.

The young women in the play, who will love only men named Ernest, feel that way because the connotations of the adjective, for them, have leaked into the supposedly blank referential indicator of the proper name. The play, which was first performed at the height of the Victorian era, in 1895, two years before Queen Victoria's Diamond Jubilee, can be read—in fact, begs to be read—as a deconstructive drama, in which language and other behavioral conventions are shown to make it quite impossible to be earnest at all, especially about the serious matters of birth, death, love, money, and marriage. The last words of the play remind us of this, and neatly echo the play's subtitle and title:

LADY BRACKNELL: My nephew, you seem to be displaying
signs of triviality.

JACK: On the contrary, Aunt Augusta, I've now realised for
the first time in my life the vital Importance of Being
Earnest. (329)

Accused of triviality, the gentleman replies by quoting the title
of the play in which he is a character, with the word "Earnest"
spelled like the adjective but capitalized like the proper name
which he has just determined is probably his own. The text of
the play itself, however, assigns Ernest's speech to the character
named Jack, though only the reader of the text will see that.
The spectator will probably hear Ernest, though the text says
Earnest. Part of Wilde's technique, I am suggesting, and part of
his meaning, has to do with a kind of linguistic suspense, or
suspension of closure, which prevents us from settling our interpretation, even of little matters.

For instance, in that same final scene, when Jack wants to
leave in search of his natal handbag, he and Gwendolen exchange the following words:

JACK: I must retire to my room for a moment. Gwendolen, wait here for me.

GWENDOLEN: If you are not too long, I will wait here for
you all my life. (320)

Gwendolen takes away and gives her promise in the same sentence. If Jack does not take too long, she will wait all her life.
But if he does take too long—what then? The wit here is a wit
of performative logic, of a contradiction being uttered as if it
were not one, resulting in a suspension of meaning. We might
call it dialogical suspense. And suspense itself becomes a topic

in this scene's dialogue. Lady Bracknell wants closure. Gwendolen does not. After Jack rushes off, they have the following exchange:

> LADY BRACKNELL: I wish he would arrive at some conclusion.
> GWENDOLEN: This suspense is terrible. I hope it will last.
> (321)

The Honorable Gwendolen is a mistress of paradox. Wilde's women are as witty as his men, though Lady Bracknell seems less aware of her wit than Gwendolen. In the present case, the paradox seems both intentional and meaningful. Gwendolen speaks here not only for herself but for the audience, or for audiences in general, who love the state of being in suspense. This is one of a number of metafictional moments in this text, in which the nature of narrative and dramatic texts is illuminated by the dialogue.

Some of these moments revolve around the figure of Miss Prism, the governess who left baby Jack (or Ernest) in a handbag at Victoria Station, making him a Victorian in more ways than one. When the perambulator that should have contained the baby was recovered, it was found to hold what Lady Bracknell describes as "the manuscript of a three-volume novel of more than usually revolting sentimentality." What she means by this phrase may be explained by what Miss Prism had earlier told Cecily about her novel. Their conversation went this way:

> MISS PRISM: Memory, my dear Cecily, is the diary that we all carry about with us.

CECILY: Yes, but it usually chronicles the things that have
never happened, and couldn't possibly have happened.
I believe that Memory is responsible for nearly all the
three-volume novels that Mudie sends us.

MISS PRISM: Do not speak slightingly of the three-volume
novel, Cecily. I wrote one myself in earlier days.

CECILY: Did you really, Miss Prism? How wonderfully
clever you are! I hope it did not end happily? I don't like
novels that end happily. They depress me so much.

MISS PRISM: The good ended happily, and the bad unhappily. That is what Fiction means.

CECILY: I suppose so. But it seems very unfair. And was
your novel ever published? (224–25)

Miss Prism's novel was never published, and apparently was
read only by Lady Bracknell, whose literary standards are not
so different from those of Cecily. For Miss Prism fiction means
that the good end happily and the bad unhappily. For Lady
Bracknell, this constitutes revolting sentimentality. Cecily's position is more complex. On the one hand she blames memory
for the events chronicled in these novels. But on the other, she
finds happy endings depressing and "unfair." However, Cecily
is herself a fictional character in a play which has a distinctly
happy ending. Wilde himself, of course, famously wondered
how anyone could read Dickens on the death of Little Nell
without laughing, which may lead us to believe that the views
of literary art offered by Lady Bracknell and Cecily are close to
his own. But Wilde also wrote "De Profundis" and "The Ballad
of Reading Gaol"—two works dripping with sentiment. For
Lady Bracknell, Cecily, and the others, of course, the ending of
The Importance of Being Earnest is not fiction but life, and

therefore, perhaps, exempt from accusations of repellent sentimentality. For Wilde, however, and for us, it is a work of dramatic fiction, and therefore open to just that critical response.

But would it be a just critical response? We want to say, I imagine, that Wilde's happy ending is not sentimental because it is not serious. Yet in reading the play or in watching it, do we not make some emotional commitment to these puppets and their affairs? Do we not *want* that happy ending? I believe that Wilde gives us what we want, which is what Miss Prism calls fiction, and absolves us from the charge of being sentimentalists by allowing us to wrap our emotions in the cool texture of his paradoxes. Concerning ourselves emotionally with these events and characters would be ridiculous, we tell ourselves, because they are so unreal. Above all, they are too witty to be true. And, thus absolved, we go right ahead and take pleasure when the good are rewarded—and the not-so-good are rewarded, too, there being no really bad persons in this world.

The plot, such as it is, is absurd, but in a metafictional way. It is based on devices noted by Aristotle in his treatise on poetic drama, such as reversal and recognition, combined with such elements of three-decker novels (and fictional romance in general) as the marriage plot in which well-mated couples are kept apart by difficulties but united in the end. The pedigree for this sort of plotting goes all the way back to the ancient Greek romances, but it received a powerful impetus in English literature from the romantic comedies of Shakespeare—plays like *Twelfth Night*, in which the happy endings are leavened with comedy and framed by the titles and subtitles of the plays (such as *As You Like It* or *What You Will*) that tell the audience that they are only getting this kind of stuff because they like it. They do like it, of course, or rather, *we* like it, but we know that we shouldn't, because the critical Lady Bracknells (and Oprahs) of this world keep telling us we shouldn't, and even the playwrights pass the blame right on to us.

As I pointed out in Chapter 1, our notions of High and Low, of serious and trivial, originate with Aristotle, where they are mixed with notions of social position. Critical terms like "noble" and "base," High and Low, Good and Bad have ever since mixed social and aesthetic qualities, sometimes concealing the one behind the other. Matthew Arnold's famous concept of "high seriousness" is thoroughly Aristotelian and privileges the same set of works, with the addition of a few others like those of Dante and Shakespeare. But Shakespeare, as I have already hinted, resists and challenges those categories and those criteria. Among other things, he initiates the thread of durable fluff that I am trying to identify in English literature— which connects some of his work to *The Importance of Being Earnest.*

I hope you will bear with me if I digress briefly at this point to illustrate what I mean by looking at just one of his plays. The play called *Twelfth Night or What You Will* dramatizes the story of two siblings, a young brother and sister of very similar appearance, who survive the same shipwreck and land on the coast of Illyria, each supposing the other to have drowned. When the sister decides, for safety's sake, to assume a male persona, the stage is set for a comedy of mistaken identities and mistaken genders. This is very much a play about appearances and realities. It is also a play about love, about money, about pleasure, and about the social hierarchy. As the play opens, the Duke Orsino is wallowing in a hopeless love for the Countess Olivia, who will not listen to his emissaries because she is herself wallowing in hopeless love for her dead brother. Love, then, is quickly ironized as an emotion that has more to do with the self-indulgence of the lover than with the supposed object of the emotion. That, at least, is one kind of love presented to us by the playwright. The entrance of the shipwrecked Viola into this field of emotions changes the dynamic. Hearing from the Captain, who has been shipwrecked with her, of the Duke's situation, she describes her plan to the Captain this way:

> *I prithee, and I'll pay thee bounteously,*
> *Conceal me what I am, and be my aid*
> *For such disguise as haply shall become*
> *The form of my intent. I'll serve this Duke.*
> *Thou shall present me as an eunuch to him.*
> *It may be worth thy pains, for I can sing,*
> *And speak to him in many sorts of music,*
> *That will allow me very worth his service. (act 1, scene 2)*

We should notice several things about this speech. One is that money is exchanged for a service. The play attends to the exchange of money to a startling degree. Another is that Viola thinks of a disguise as enabling her to "become the form of my intent," an idea realized. But the most important is the nature of her disguise. She proposes to don male clothing as a member of a third sex, "an eunuch," as she says, who can "sing, and speak to him in many sorts of music." This status will account for her feminine voice and manner, while allowing her to count as a man for other purposes.

Singing eunuchs, the famous castrati, had just been officially approved by the pope to sing in the churches of Rome a year or so before Shakespeare's play was first performed at Elizabeth's court to amuse the queen and, possibly, a visitor from Italy named Duke Orsino. Shakespeare's play was timely as well as timeless. And it is mainly about people Aristotle would have considered *spoudaios* or noble, but behaving in ways that were all too *phaulos* or common. This mixture is quintessentially Shakespearean, though it has roots in ancient comedy, and is a key to the kind of literature that I am calling durable fluff. I am suggesting that a crucial element in durable fluff is the perception that social structures and roles are performative rather than innate. The perception that life consists not so much of destinies as of roles is at the heart of this sort of comedy. Tragedy and high epic narrative are all about fate—heroes driven by fate to Italy, like Aeneas (*Italiam fato profugus*, as Virgil put it), and star-crossed lovers, like Romeo and Juliet. But comedy functions in another world. We value both modes, I would say, because they are *not* the mode of our actual world— and we should value them equally. Our lives are not really controlled by fate or the stars, nor can we change our situations as freely and easily as the characters in comedy. We live somewhere in the midst of these possibilities. We need the comedies, I am suggesting, to remind us of our freedom, as well as to amuse us with the gift of laughter.

One of the things that makes certain pieces of literary fluff durable, then, is their representation of people readily changing social positions or genders or emotional commitments— or transcending the limits normally taken to be those of a social position or gender or a strong emotion like love. We like to see these possibilities represented, and even pushed to the limits of believability, which may be why Pierre de Marivaux's play *Le Triomphe de l'amour*, first performed in 1732, has been brought back to us in 2001 as a film by Clare Peploe and Bernardo Bertolucci, with Ben Kingsley in a comic role. The film follows the play fairly closely, with the exception that at odd moments we catch a disconcerting glimpse of a grandstand with spectators in casual modern clothing, watching these figures in period costumes as they go about their business—and their business has much to do with transcending limits, especially those of gender and emotional commitment.

The story concerns a princess who has glimpsed and fallen immediately in love with a young man, whose proper rank she has, through no fault of her own, usurped. The problem is that the young man has been raised for a decade by a philosopher who has taught him to despise all women and, in particular, the one who has usurped his right to the throne. The princess proposes to deal with this situation by playing the role of a young nobleman on the grand tour who just happens to arrive at the scene of the young man's instruction, accompanied by her maid, who also dons manly attire. To make a complicated story simple, she does what she has proposed, interacting with some servants who aid her, and in the process causes the philosopher (played by Kingsley), and his sister (played hilariously by Fiona Shaw), and the young man himself—all—to fall "in love" with her, as either a woman or a man. This is all accomplished through the witty dialogue that came to be called "Marivaudage." For our purposes, what is most interesting is that both gender and love are treated as performance—and at the same time regarded as absolute—by the characters themselves. For us, of course, it is all performance, as those metafictional glimpses of the modern audience remind us. (Some reviewers, by the way, found them very disturbing and thought they ruined the film. I, of course, thought they were exactly right.)

The famous Shakespearean line "all the world's a stage," as you no doubt remember, comes from a piece of durable fluff called *As You Like It*, and we can take it as the guiding principle of this kind of writing, which is frequently associated with the theater or with writers who have had some theatrical connection, like Henry Fielding and Max Beerbohm, who were masters of it—as was Jane Austen, whose novels have adapted beautifully to stage and screen, though she had no theatrical connection herself and treated the theater severely in *Mansfield Park*. So role playing, and the playing on stage of characters who are role playing, lie at the fluffy heart of the durable texts I am discussing. The thought of fluffy hearts should serve to bring us back to Wilde's play about earnestness.

What is the status of love in *The Importance of Being Earnest*? In their first conversation in the play Algernon and Jack discuss love and marriage. Jack means to marry, and Algernon tries to talk him out of the project, praising flirtation but denigrating marriage, observing finally that "Divorces are made in Heaven." Like Duke Orsino's, Algernon's first appearance is accompanied by music, but it is not the "food of love." He has been playing the piano, as he says, inaccurately but with passion: "As far as the piano is concerned, sentiment is my forte. I keep science for Life." As it turns out, however, he will become sentimental over Cecily. It is the women who keep science for life. Cecily and Gwendolen have agendas. They will love only men named Ernest. The standards of the time, for them, have been reduced to Ernestness. Lady Bracknell, of course, has her own brand of "science," and standards more severe than mere earnestness. When Jack proposes to Gwendolen, he is quizzed by Lady Bracknell:

LADY BRACKNELL: I have always been of opinion that a man who desires to get married should know either everything or nothing. Which do you know?
JACK: [After some hesitation.] I know nothing, Lady Bracknell.
LADY BRACKNELL: I am pleased to hear it. I do not approve of anything that tampers with natural ignorance. Ignorance is like a delicate exotic fruit; touch it and the

bloom is gone. The whole theory of modern education is radically unsound. Fortunately in England, at any rate, education produces no effect whatsoever. If it did, it would prove a serious danger to the upper classes, and probably lead to acts of violence in Grosvenor Square. (199–200)

The Oscar Wilde who wrote *The Soul of Man Under Socialism* gleams faintly through Lady Bracknell's words. Then she quickly moves on to more serious matters, asking Jack about his income, which is satisfactory, because it is in investments and not in land, land having become undesirable because of changes in the tax structure. The interrogation moves on to property. Jack has property in the country, but Gwendolen, as Lady Bracknell points out, is a simple girl, who cannot be expected to live there. Fortunately, Jack also has property in the city, on Belgrave Square. Lady Bracknell asks him what number; he says "149"; and the conversation continues as follows:

LADY BRACKNELL: [Shaking her head.] The unfashionable side. I thought there was something. However, that could easily be altered.

JACK: Do you mean the fashion, or the side?

LADY BRACKNELL: [Sternly.] Both, if necessary, I presume. What are your politics?

JACK: Well, I am afraid I really have none. I am a Liberal Unionist.

LADY BRACKNELL: Oh, they count as Tories. They dine with us. Or come in the evening, at any rate. Now to minor matters. Are your parents living? (201–2)

Money and social position first, family second, in Lady Bracknell's catechism. And love just isn't in the running.

Moreover, in her world, political affairs are reduced to who is invited to dinner, or, in a nicely graduated scale of values, who is invited to come after dinner is over. These people are all titled or of "gentle" birth, thus *spoudaios*, in Aristotle's terminology, but they do not act noble at all. They are either too frivolous or too concerned with money and position for that. Aristocratic pride has dwindled into something very like snobbery. In Wilde's world, servants are still in their place, but they are not firmly fixed there. And they are as snobbish as their "betters":

ALGERNON: Oh! . . . by the way, Lane, I see from your book that on Thursday night, when Lord Shoreman and Mr. Worthing were dining with me, eight bottles of champagne are entered as having been consumed.

LANE: Yes, sir; eight bottles and a pint.

ALGERNON: Why is it that at a bachelor's establishment the servants invariably drink the champagne? I ask merely for information.

LANE: I attribute it to the superior quality of the wine, sir. I have often observed that in married households the champagne is rarely of a first-rate brand.

ALGERNON: Good heavens! Is marriage so demoralising as that?

LANE: I believe it IS a very pleasant state, sir. I have had very little experience of it myself up to the present. I have only been married once. That was in consequence of a misunderstanding between myself and a young person.

ALGERNON: [Languidly.] I don't know that I am much interested in your family life, Lane.

LANE: No, sir; it is not a very interesting subject. I never think of it myself.

ALGERNON: Very natural, I am sure. That will do, Lane,
thank you. (164–65)

Algernon's charge that Lane is drinking his wine is answered by Lane's explanation that it is good wine. Lane's report
on his conjugal experience is rebuffed as uninteresting, thus
keeping him in his place, but Lane is equal to that, agreeing
that it is, and topping Algernon by saying that *he* never thinks
of it himself. In short, he is as much of a snob as Algernon himself. At a later moment he gets in a jab at his master in public.
This comes when Lady Bracknell asks for the cucumber sandwiches Algernon had promised her. Algernon, who has eaten
them all himself, professes to be astounded at their absence,
and the following dialogue occurs:

ALGERNON: [Picking up empty plate in horror.] Good
heavens! Lane! Why are there no cucumber sand-
wiches? I ordered them specially.
LANE: [Gravely.] There were no cucumbers in the market
this morning, sir. I went down twice.
ALGERNON: No cucumbers!
LANE: No, sir. Not even for ready money.
ALGERNON: That will do, Lane, thank you. (186)

Exit Lane, having conveyed that Algernon's credit is not good
at the market even as he supports his master's imposture about
the reason for the absence of the sandwiches, giving his fiction
plausibility by adding the gratuitous detail of a second trip. In
this play, as in *Twelfth Night*, part of the wit depends upon the
ability of servants to talk back to their masters and mistresses.
The aristocracy is getting lighter and lighter, more *phaulos* and
less *spoudaios*, driven by fashion, snobbery, and economic im-

peratives. But the servant class is staying the course, and Jeeves is just around the corner.

You may be wondering whether all this has brought us any closer to solving the mystery of fluffy durability, or what keeps these trivial texts alive. I must confess that I have been wondering the same thing myself. It has something to do with the language, of course, and especially with language as it is used in speech—something to do with dialogue. The usual name for this sort of thing is irony, which I have been avoiding because of its weighty connotations, but it is time to admit, perhaps, that it is irony that puts the durability into fluff in the case of Wilde, as in the case of Jane Austen. Wilde's ironies operate at two levels: that of his paradoxical dialogue, and that of his absurd parody of the romantic plot with its happy ending. It is Wilde, whom we should perhaps think of as Mister Prism, who has appropriated the machinery of the Victorian three-decker and the Hellenistic romance for his own purposes in constructing this text.

Let me try to be more precise. Wilde's witty dialogue functions to make the characters more attractive to the audience. It's hard not to like people who are so amusing. Their ironic speeches function to generate an emotional flow toward them. And the ironies of the plot put them in situations that use this emotional flow to make the audience invest in the happy ending Mister Prism intends to provide. Irony and sentiment serve one another in this text at the level of speech and the level of action. And something similar happens in the comedies of Shakespeare and Marivaux. In all these cases, as well, this combination of irony and sentiment generates a dividend of thought, thus making the investment pay off in a manner that even Lady Bracknell would have to approve. And it is a dividend of an especially theatrical sort, it seems to me.

As I noted earlier, many of those writers most successful with this kind of comedy were either playwrights or had some connection with the theater. In attending to comic dialogue, we must be aware of the speaker and whoever is addressed and have some sense of the different ways in which they understand the words being uttered. The way Cecily takes her tongs and drops four lumps of sugar into Gwendolen's tea cup after hearing that Gwendolen takes none (because sugar is out of fashion) is funny because we understand that this really is an emotional tempest in a literal cup of tea. Wilde's wit functions even without his words, once he has established the relationships among his characters. But the wit is not purely verbal, in any case. We are getting a view of the social world here, as in this quite astonishing speech of Gwendolen's on the subject of her father, Lord Bracknell:

> GWENDOLEN: Outside the family circle, papa, I am glad to say, is entirely unknown. I think that is quite as it should be. The home seems to me to be the proper sphere for the man. And certainly once a man begins to neglect his domestic duties he becomes painfully effeminate, does he not? And I don't like that. It makes men so very attractive. (267)

There is a kind of feminist gender reversal at work here, in the opening lines of this speech, culminating in the observation that "the home seems to me to be the proper sphere for the man." This is amusing, especially coming from Gwendolen, who is very far from appearing as a "new woman" or a heroine out of an Ibsen play. But that is a gentle reversal. I doubt that anyone expected the turn that occurs in the speech after that— the suggestion that a neglect of domestic duties makes a man painfully effeminate. The opposite—that a neglect of domestic duties makes a woman too masculine—would be a commonplace, but Wilde's rigorous extension of this logic startles us. That is, if the home is truly the proper sphere for the male gender, a neglect of it would indeed suggest a slippage in the masculinity of the neglector. The total effect of this is to question the connection between gender and spheres in all cases. But the final turn of the speech transcends logic and reaches a higher plane of wit—and perhaps of truth as well. Speaking of "painfully effeminate" men, Gwendolen concludes, "I don't like that. It makes men so very attractive." Attractive to whom, one may ask. We do not know whether Gwendolen is concerned about their attractiveness to men or to women—or just attractiveness in general, which is a field she likes to dominate. But there is plenty of evidence that effeminate men are attractive to women. We can certainly find this in life, if we look for it, and we can find it on the stage as well—in plays like *Twelfth Night,* for example, and in operas like Beethoven's *Fidelio.*

Wilde's "trivial comedy" has been kept alive by a wit that operates on a number of levels. One of these is at the level of the dialogue itself, where we encounter a pleasurable suspension of meaning in statements that are paradoxical or counterintuitive. A second level is in the way that some of the things said in dialogue encourage us to see the world freshly, to rethink our presuppositions, to become more lively ourselves. And there is a third level, in which we become aware not only of the amount of life captured in this supremely artificial text but also of the amount of artifice and performance that goes into our experience of life itself. We live in a world of fragile social constructions, a trivial world, in that sense. And that is a major reason why a trivial play can speak to us in such a profoundly earnest way. Perhaps, then, after all, it *is* important to be earnest.

6

Iridescent Mediocrity:
Dornford Yates and Others

The more books we read, the sooner we perceive that the true function of a writer is to produce a masterpiece and that no other task is of any consequence. Obvious though this should be, how few writers will admit it, or having made the admission, will be prepared to lay aside the piece of iridescent mediocrity on which they have embarked!

Sometimes, at great garden parties, literary luncheons, or in the quiet of an exclusive gunroom, a laugh rings out. The sad, formal faces for a moment relax and a smaller group is formed within the larger. They are admirers of Dornford Yates who have found out each other. We are badly organized, we know little about our hero, but we appreciate fine writing when we come across it, and a wit that is ageless united to a courtesy that is extinct.

There is, as you will have noticed, a striking contradiction between these two views. The first seems to set out the official program of High Modernism, while the second praises the work of a writer who never approached canonization in the Modernist pantheon. In fact, that gorgeous phrase "iridescent mediocrity" in the first statement might seem a particularly apt description of "the *Berry* volumes of Dornford Yates," which are the subject of the second. The first of these pronouncements was made by Cyril Connolly. It is from the opening paragraph of his extended literary meditation, *The Unquiet Grave.* The second statement, as it happens, was also made by Connolly, at about the same time. It appeared in an essay called "The Novel-Addict's Cupboard," collected in *The Condemned Playground.* Clearly Connolly was a master of negative capability, holding two conflicting ideas in mind with consummate ease. Even the titles of these two books stand in eerie opposition to one another. But I bring these two passages together not to embarrass the shade of Connolly, who has, no doubt, greater things to atone for, but to point out something about the literature and doctrine of High Modernism itself.

Connolly, we may need to remind ourselves, was one of the few writers of his time to understand what James Joyce's *Ulysses* was all about. His essay "The Position of Joyce," written in 1929 and collected in the same volume as the remarks on Dornford Yates, is an eloquent argument for all of Joyce's work, including the experimental *Work in Progress.* In this essay, Connolly makes a very persuasive case for *Ulysses* as a novel in which the central emotion is "remorse." He really did understand both Joyce in particular and Modernism in general. His remark on the necessity of producing masterpieces is quintessentially Modernist. It describes what Joyce, Eliot, Ford, and

Pound, for example, all thought they were doing. And Connolly, who edited one of the best literary magazines of the forties, *Horizon,* fully sympathized with the projects of those High Modernist writers and others who shared their aspirations.

How does it happen, then, that a person so committed to the High Modernist enterprise should single out for special praise a writer like Dornford Yates (the pen name of C. W. Mercer)? For Yates is not only a writer of modest ambitions, he is truculently Anti-High-Modernist in his views, which are aired in a number of his works, usually in connection with the visual arts. In a story from *The Brother of Daphne,* Yates's protagonist, Berry Pleydell, has just seen the tide make off with his clothing while he was bathing and asks to be left alone: "But leave us here in peace. I have almost evolved a post-futurist picture which will revolutionize the artistic world. I shall call it 'The Passing of a Bathe: a Fantasy.' It will present to the minds of all who have not seen it, what they would have rejected for lunch if they had. To get the true effect, no one must see it" (68). The hostility of Yates to Modern Geometrist art began early and lasted long. This passage from "Clothes and the Man" first appeared in the *Windsor Magazine* in summer of 1913 (where the story was called "There Is a Tide"), and Berry was already talking about "post-futurist" art—implying a very short future for futurism itself. In this he was prophetic. But his words also point to the "post-age" that we have just been living through, which he seems to anticipate here. The title of Berry's imaginary painting may allude to the various bathers of Cézanne or to the derivative images of Post-Impressionist painters like Duncan Grant, and the tone is that of the many critics who responded with hostility to the London Post-Impressionist shows of 1910 and 1912. But that last line, "To get the true effect, no one must see it," seems to anticipate and parody a host of Modernist performances from Dada to John Cage. Indeed, the very idea of trying to "revolutionize" the art world mocks the sententious blending of political and aesthetic matters that we recognize as avant-gardism. At the same time, the ultimate title of the story, "Clothes and the Man," alludes playfully to the opening phrase of Virgil's *Aeneid* (*Arma virumque cano*), borrowed by George Bernard Shaw in 1894 for his play *Arms and the Man,* while the magazine title merely alludes to Shakespeare.

My point here is that in endorsing Yates, Connolly had chosen a writer who was not only on the Low (or light) side of High (or heavy) Modernism but on the wrong side as well—opposed to the work most ardently championed by T. E. Hulme, Wyndham Lewis, and Ezra Pound. So what can we suppose led Connolly to this praise of him? The passage itself contains more clues. The name of Yates is introduced by the eruption of a laugh that transforms the "sad, formal faces" of people attending "great garden parties" or "literary luncheons." The faces relax; a more intimate group is formed. The "admirers" are sharing their pleasure in his work. Yates is not a serious writer—and this is seen as a good thing. But he is not exactly Low, either. We can learn something about the actualities of the Great Divide by looking at cases like his. Who read Yates? And why did they read him? Can such a writer possibly be Modern?

We can start by looking more closely at Connolly's praise of Yates: "Sometimes, at great garden parties, literary luncheons, or in the quiet of an exclusive gunroom, a laugh rings out." Connolly gives us three places—or sorts of places—where admirers of Yates may encounter one another: (1) "great garden parties" suggests affluence at least and social eminence as well. You need a great garden for such a party, and that means a garden both large and well kept. Unseen gardeners lurk in the background here. One visualizes an assemblage of very well-dressed people, with servants passing among them holding trays of hors d'oeuvres and drinks; (2) "literary luncheons"—a hint of solemn stuffiness, here, associated with High literature; (3) "the quiet of an exclusive gunroom"—here we have a landed estate, no doubt, with a host, perhaps in evening clothes, or dressed for shooting, talking informally with other men. These groups are not the "peasants who settled in the cities as proletariat and petty bourgeois" and, learning to read and write, became the market for kitsch, as Clement Greenberg described them (10). Rather, they are social and cultural leaders, drawn to the work of Yates for reasons we shall consider.

Connolly continues: "The sad, formal faces for a moment relax and a smaller group is formed within the larger." There are two things to be noted here. One is the relaxation of the "sad, formal faces," and the other is the formation of an exclusive group within the larger group, which is already exclusive in a social (garden party, gunroom) or intellectual (literary luncheon) way. The discussion of Yates brings pleasure to "sad, formal faces" by giving them a topic of conversation superior to the ordinary chat of garden parties, gunrooms, or literary luncheons. And it brings them something else that may be found in Connolly's charming expression of praise for the work of Yates: "wit that is ageless united to a courtesy that is extinct." What I admire in this phrase (beyond its appropriateness to Yates) is not merely its elegant syntax, but the way that the syntax balances against each other and thus emphasizes the words "ageless" and "extinct"—suggesting that the admirable quality of Yates's work derives from an oxymoronic or paradoxical combination of something durable with something perishable, so that we may admire Yates's writing both for its freshness and for its staleness, for its strength and for its weakness. It is surely a combination of qualities similar to those noted by Connolly that has kept the work of P. G. Wodehouse in print for more than half a century with little or no support from academic critics and curricula: something fresh and ageless united to something charmingly dated. Not to mention the great progenitor of so many works of this sort, *The Importance of Being Earnest,* a piece of durable fluff that we have already considered.

Now we cannot accept Connolly's casual remarks as evidence about who actually read the Berry volumes of Dornford Yates, but we can use them as evidence of where this shrewd literary editor saw the books as having their appeal. They appealed to a class that was not comfortable with the changes modernity had brought to their world and liked to be reminded of the things they believed they were losing. Members of this class subscribed to *The Windsor Magazine: An Illustrated Monthly for Men and Women.* The title tells it all, with "Windsor" suggesting Tory allegiances, and "Illustrated" pointing to one of the journal's sources of popular appeal. In the volume in which "There Is a Tide" first appeared, we can find features on the following artists: Anna Lea Merritt, Ford Madox Brown, G. H. Boughton, R.A., Sir John Everett Millais, Bart, P.R.A., and Sir John Gilbert, R.A., along with individual images by artists like Dante Gabriel Rossetti. The Pre-Raphaelite Brotherhood and the Royal Academy were alive and well in these pages, even as the Neo-Realists and the Geometrists were fighting bitterly over their corpses in the pages of *The New Age.* For this is the world of the "middlebrows," so despised by Virginia Woolf and her Bloomsbury friends: "The middlebrow is the man, or woman, of middlebred intelligence who ambles and saunters now on this side of the hedge, now on that, in pursuit of no single object, neither art itself nor life itself, but both mixed indistinguishably, and rather nastily, with money, fame, power, or prestige" (155). This essay was written as a letter to the *New Statesman*, but never sent. Leonard Woolf published it after Virginia's death. I think Virginia never sent it because she was not happy with it. But Woolf is always interesting. In this case, she is probably right in recognizing a middlebrow level of intellectual activity, which she understands as an attempt to educate lowbrows: "It is very kind of the middlebrows to teach them culture" (158), she ironizes. Woolf sees this attempt as ridiculous, since the middlebrows themselves play no active part in culture, being totally dependent on the creative achievements of highbrows. Her highbrows were devoted to the mind and her lowbrows to the body, and, she argued, they needed each other. She wanted to see her world in terms of High and Low, with the middle excluded, because the middle consisted of uncreative parasites—critics and teachers rather than artists and thinkers. Where I think she is wrong— as so many Modernists were wrong—is in refusing to recognize a middle level of creative work and thought, and, even worse, in refusing to recognize the existence of middlebrow readers who were a significant part of her own audience and the audience for middlebrow writers as well.

There was a lot of fiction in the *Windsor Magazine,* amid the articles on famous pianists, cricket bowlers, and "The Wordsworth Country," and a lot of "verse" as well. Some of the fiction was written by writers still remembered, such as Wodehouse, Edgar Wallace, and H. Rider Haggard, and some by writers long forgotten, like Albert Kinross and Charles G. D. Roberts. Scarcely one of the poets is still read today, apart from Kipling, but I would argue that students of the period should read even them if we are to understand the climate of expectations in which the works of poets like Yeats, Pound, and Eliot appeared. Seeing what the middlebrow reader was really reading would also help us decode Virginia Woolf's conjuring trick in turning writers like H. G. Wells and Arnold Bennett into despised Edwardians while she and her friends were breaking new ground as Georgians. For Wells and Bennett were actually Neo-Realists, like Walter Sickert in visual art, and Wells's novel *Tono-Bungay* was serialized not in the *Windsor Magazine* but in Ford Madox Hueffer's aggressively Modernist *English Review*. What the middlebrow reader was actually consuming, along with articles on such matters as "Curiosities of Church Architecture," were mainly fictions of romance and adventure, and Dornford Yates was a master of these modes.

The Berry books began as very light literature indeed, little stories of romantic episodes, collected in *The Brother of Daphne* in 1914—a final echo of *la belle époque*. But the second volume containing stories in this series, *The Courts of Idleness,* did not appear until 1920. In the middle of that volume, which is set in the spring of 1914, a group of characters with other names, but in other respects much like those of the Berry books, are vacationing on an island called Rih, which resembles Madeira. At a certain point in a story of romance, "For Better or for Worse," a sound is heard that the female characters believe is the hoot of a steamship but the male characters hear as the noise of a big piece of artillery. By the end of that story one of the men has died in the war, and in the next story, "Interlude," other gallant young men die. Among the stories that follow are some from before the war, but the others trace Berry and his companions, under their own names, from his wartime assignment in Egypt back to England after the war— an England that is both changed and the same. The rest of the Berry books chronicle that bittersweet sameness in difference, the persistence of Edwardian England in Georgian times and after. They are, in some respects, like the novels and memoirs of Siegfried Sassoon (*Memoirs of a Fox-Hunting Man,* for example, or *The Weald of Youth*), and their real center of interest is the clash between the old values and the new world in which they were fighting a gallant but losing battle—a war after the War. These are certainly Modernist topics. Ford Madox Ford's *Parade's End,* for example, shares many of these sentiments. But are they Modernist in other ways as well? Let us look more closely at the text.

The Berry books follow the fortunes of five people, belonging to two intermarried and interrelated families, right up to the next war, after which Yates published some volumes that were cast in the mode of reminiscence about those earlier days. These people own an ancestral home, White Ladies, in Hampshire on the edge of the New Forest, and many of the episodes are set there or in the surrounding countryside and villages. The setting is not accidental, for this is a part of England designated by William the Conqueror as a game preserve, and it continues to boast of its ancient lineage on its Web pages today. The return of the family to White Ladies after the Great War, in which all three of the men had served and two were wounded, is chronicled in the first story of *Berry and Co.* The family attend their local church service, where Berry is asked to read the lesson. As he reads, and the choir sings, his brother-in-law, called Boy, gazes around the old church:

> Doors and windows were open as wide as they could be set, and the little church was flooded with light and fresh warm air, that coaxed the edge from the chill of thick stone walls and pillars, and made the frozen pavements cool and refreshing. Mustiness was clean gone, swept from her frequent haunts by the sweet breath of Nature. The "dim, religious light" of Milton's ordering was this day displaced

by Summer's honest smile, simpler maybe, but no less reverent. And, when the singing stilled, you overheard the ceaseless sleepy murmur of that country choir of birds, beasts, and insects that keeps its contented symphony for summer days in which you can find no fault. My impious eye wandered affectionately over familiar friends—the old oak pews, almost chin-high, the Spanish organ, the reluctant gift of a proud galleon wrecked on the snarling coast ten miles away, the old "three-decker," with its dull crimson cushions and the fringed cloths that hung so stiffly. A shaft of sunlight beat full on an old black hatchment, making known the faded quarterings, while, underneath, a slender panel of brass, but two years old, showed that the teaching of its grim forbear had not been vain. (13–14)

What passages like this offered the English reader of 1921 was a comforting evocation of English history and an English cultural heritage embedded in a post-Romantic appreciation of nature—not transcendental so much as political. It does this, however, by means of a distinctly Modernist technique—the montage—in which images are blended or superimposed to produce a complex meaning that invites the interpretive activity of the reader. This is a mode of what Andreas Huyssen called "suggestive intertextuality" in establishing his criteria for reconsidering modern texts. The New Forest itself has come to church here, where it meets a phrase from Milton's "Il Penseroso" and an organ left over from the Spanish Armada's defeat in Elizabethan times. The intertexts here are the "dim religious light"—a phrase from Milton's poem that takes us back to the age of Cromwell and the Protestant heritage of England—and a musical instrument salvaged from the wreckage of the Armada at another great and decisive moment in English history.

And all this is seen by the "impious eye" of a demobilized soldier recognizing architectural features of the building as "familiar friends." The "old 'three-decker,'" by the way, here refers to a feature of English church architecture deplored by advanced thinkers as early as the middle of the nineteenth century: "In the midst of the church stands . . . the offensive structure of pulpit, reading-desk, and clerk's desk: In fact, a regular old three-decker in full sail westward" (*Christian Remembrancer*, July 1852, 92). But this is not simply a piece of outmoded architecture. The metaphor of a "three-decker" ties the pulpit and the two desks below it to the organ and the three-decked galleons that sailed in the time of the Armada, just as the little brass panel ties those local dead in the Great War to their illustrious predecessor, whose escutcheon hangs above the modern panel. But there is more. The "three-decker" also refers to a kind of writing celebrated by Kipling in a poem that likens the old three-volume novel, the three-decker, to a sailing ship outmoded by the coming of steam. Here are a few stanzas from Kipling's poem:

> *No moral doubt assailed us, so when the port we neared,*
> *The villain had his flogging at the gangway, and we*
> *   cheered.*
> *'Twas fiddle in the forc's'le—'twas garlands on the mast,*
> *For every one got married, and I went ashore at last.*
>
> *I left 'em all in couples a-kissing on the decks.*
> *I left the lovers loving and the parents signing cheques.*
> *In endless English comfort by county-folk caressed,*
> *I left the old three-decker at the Islands of the Blest!*

That route is barred to steamers: you'll never lift again
Our purple-painted headlands or the lordly keeps of
 Spain.
They're just beyond your skyline, howe'er so far you cruise
In a ram-you-damn-you liner with a brace of bucking
 screws. (1.17–28)

Dornford Yates did not write three-decker novels. His Berry books are collections of linked stories, each one with an ending of its own, but they consciously preserve the values Kipling ascribed to the old novels—the happy endings, the villains punished, the lovers loving, and, above all, the "endless English comfort by county-folk caressed."

All this, to be sure, is not avant-gardist Modernism. It seems the very opposite, but that is perhaps too simple a conclusion about the work of Yates, for he is reacting to some of the same things that drove the High Modernists to their avant-gardist heights, and he is, as I have already pointed out, using adroitly the Modernist devices of montage and suggestive intertextuality. But Yates deploys his intertextual montage to connect the past to the present, insisting on continuity where many Modernists often insisted on rupture, and he keeps his language within the reading range of the common reader—a common reader, to be sure, who knows the history of England and is familiar with its literature—and this may be a better definition of middlebrow than the snobbish dismissal provided by Virginia Woolf.

The narratives collected in these volumes are often about White Ladies and the quasi-feudal relationship of the Berry family to the local villagers. Sometimes the old house is invaded by thieves, or the family portraits are threatened by unscrupulous relatives, or an ancient right-of-way is jeopardized by a newly rich landowner. But these stories are comic idylls, that end as happily as any three-decker novel. In the larger scheme of things, however, the family is unable to hold on to White Ladies and must give up their ancestral home, building a new one called Gracedieu, in the French Pyrenees. Throughout all their adventures, they are served in a semifeudal way by loyal retainers, in the mode of Lord Peter Wimsey's man Bunter or P. G. Wodehouse's Jeeves, though Berry and his family are by no means as inept as Bertie Wooster.

We may read a writer like Yates simply for the pleasures his texts afford, and which Cyril Connolly has already described for us as "wit that is ageless united to a courtesy that is extinct," but that may not be enough to justify a place for him in any curriculum of academic study. For students of modern culture, then, I want to suggest that we can learn something important about that culture by examining the attitudes toward class and gender that are expressed in Yates's work, along with his representations of the quintessentially modern object, the automobile. Take, for example, an episode in a story called "Jill's Education Is Improved," from *Berry and Co.* The family group has been traveling from London to Oxford so that Jill might become acquainted with the town where Berry, Jonah, and Boy were educated while she was still quite young. En route they have a flat tire, which is being changed by Jonah and Berry, allowing Boy and the ladies to go for a stroll down the road, where they meet an old man working as a stonebreaker on the road. When the strollers learn that he has worked on the road for seventy years, as his father did before him, they ask him about his memories:

> "I've seen the coaches, m'm, and I've seen the motors, an' they can't neither of them do without the road, m'm. As

it was in the beginnin', so it ever shall be. Soon I'll pass, but the road'll go on, an' others'll break for 'er. For she must needs be patched, you know, m'm, she must needs be patched. . . . "

We gave him money, and he rose and uncovered and pulled his white forelock with the antique courtesy of his class. As we turned away, I pinched Daphne's arm.

"I'll bet no man's ever done that to you before."

She shook her head, smiling.

"I don't think so. It was very nice of him."

"What would you call him?" said Jill. "A stonebreaker?"

I raised my eyebrows.

"I suppose so. Or roadman."

"I know," said Agatha softly. "He's a Gentleman of the Road."

"Good for you," said I. "The title never became a highwayman one half so well." (117, ellipsis in original)

Written in 1920, and set, presumably, in that period as well, this story offers us a glimpse of a kind of feudal nostalgia that was important to conservative thought in Britain at that time—and may still be an aspect of that thought. Like the passage in which we saw Boy musing in church just after the war, this one, too, has some historical reach, as the stonebreaker recalls his father showing him the coaches that passed on the road, with the coachmen who would wave to the two of them as they flew by. And he seems as firmly rooted in his class position as any feudal peasant might have been. With the classes so solidly in position, however, they can treat one another with courtesy and respect—the "gentleman of the road" tugging his forelock in the ancient salute, after being listened to attentively and given some money for his trouble and his tale. This England may be no more real than the visions of America in Norman Rockwell's covers for the *Saturday Evening Post*, but it is an England that had considerable power in the British imagination of its day—which was the day of modernity and Modernism.

Nostalgia, then, is a driving force in the Berry books, along with a kind of benevolent Tory view of the world. But this is not to be mistaken for snobbery. One story, for example, is about a dispute over the attempt of a landlord to close an ancient right-of-way through his property. Here is the background given in the story:

> The first Lord Withyham had been a rivetter when he was seventeen. He had risen by sheer merit to become the honoured chairman of one of the shipping lines. Never was a peerage more deservedly bestowed. And then he died, and his son, the present Withyham, reigned in his stead. But his was a spirit of another sort. It was said that his mother had spoiled him. Be that as it may, he was not even a shadow of what his father had been. The man was proud of his title, ashamed of his birth. He set no store by work, but much by his dignity. (*Berry Scene*, 47)

This is not exactly a feudal view of the world, and in no sense a snobbish one. There is no objection here to the rise of a manual laborer to a peerage. Quite the contrary. But there is an objection, and it is developed in the story, to a man who has inherited a title without the code of behavior that should accompany it, and who abuses his rank and wealth to bully his neighbors, whether they are well-to-do or poor. He tries, for example, to force one of them to sell him some land he had been renting:

"I'd have let his lordship have it, if only he'd spoken me

fair. But he couldn't do that. We're only farmer stock, and
he's a lord. But he's a stranger, sir, and we've been here for
a hundred and fifty years. An' he talked to me as if I was
one of his gardeners. 'I'm buying those meadows,' he says.
'I don't want another lease. I'm telling my lawyers so, and
you'll hear from them.' Well, that's not neighbourly, sir,
an' when his lawyers wrote, I said they was not for sale.
An' then he writes to me, an' talks about impertinent con-
duct. . . . An' now he shuts Romany Lane. . . . He don't
know behaviour, sir, and that's the truth." (49)

These books are all about manners—in the full sense of that
word. About codes of behavior that enable people to "get along"
with one another, despite differences in wealth, education, and
social position. And that is part of what Cyril Connolly meant,
no doubt, when he referred to "courtesy that is extinct"—
because the books are about the extinction of courtesy under
the regime of modernity, a regime described this way in another story from the same volume:

> But even within our gates we could not feel secure. Un-
> certainty's lease was running; and Pleasure, Uncertainty's
> steward, was calling the tune. People were grasping at the
> present, because they had no idea what the future might
> hold. They lived for the moment—often from hand to
> mouth. High and low gambled like madmen. Expenses
> were continually rising, while income was going down.
> The best was still to be had—at a fearful price. But crafts-
> manship was dying. The silversmith could not live; though
> he beat his vessels out in the sweat of his face, he could not
> earn a quarter of what the machinist made. . . . The old
> world was giving way to a less substantial structure, whose

motive power was so huge that it seemed as though its
engines would shake everyone from his seat. (226)

The image here of modernity as a great engine, shaking
its denizens from their places and driving them to various
kinds of desperate gamble, is a powerful one, and it helps to
explain the motivation of those writers and artists who resisted it and refused to align themselves with this devastating new
machinery. It explains also the hostility of critics like Anthony
Ludovici—and of many ordinary people—to such developments as Futurism, which seemed to embrace the deadly machinery of modernity and produced manifestos that derided
tradition, thus allying themselves with Uncertainty. As Boy
puts it in one story, "We all disliked 'modernist' painting; but
Berry's comments upon it were the most embarrassing" (*Berry
Scene*, 132). This observation comes during a trip to a gallery in
which Modernism seems to be represented by a mixture of
Surrealism and Abstract Expressionism. In this story a friend
of the Berry group, Lady Morayne, actually relieves Berry of
his role as most embarrassing critic. She remembers playing a
game with her mother in which she sold "berries and pebbles
and pips" as actual "goods":

> "But this is no game. Adults are offering adults rubbish
> tricked out as art. Frames such as these have been set
> about old masters. Famous works have been hung in this
> gallery. And now these antics, which would offend a ma-
> niac—these contemptible scrawls that no pavement
> artist would dare to perpetrate—are displayed with hon-
> our and actually offered for sale. And not in vain. Because
> they are here, people are going to buy them. If they were

offered horse dung, they would refuse, But I'd rather have
a shovel of horse dung than ten of these." (135)

This was written, no doubt, around the time when Clement
Greenberg was contrasting Modernist art with kitsch and arguing that the wealthy classes were not supporting Modernist
art properly because they had been lured away from its austere
virtues by the easy pleasures of kitsch. But it is entirely possible
that Yates, and not Greenberg, has it right, here—namely, that
the cultivated upper classes just plain hated abstract art, and
Surrealism as well. They hated it, as we can learn from Yates,
precisely because it represented a break with tradition, because
it embraced the social engine of modernity, and refused to
represent the beauties of the world they knew and loved—and
felt they were losing.

What they loved can be found in passages like this one,
in which Boy is describing a portion of the road from White
Ladies to the town of Brooch, on a morning when "the way was
as it had been before my father was born." He continues:

Three miles I will remember as being the fairest of all.
Here Nature and Husbandry seemed to go hand in hand:
wild rose and honeysuckle tricked out the wayside hedge,
elms guarded lovers' stiles, and oak and ash and chestnut
held up a ragged canopy for passers-by. Now and again an
aged, five-barred gate hung like a window-sill, to offer
such a landscape as Thomson sang and Constable loved
to paint, and once the road curled down to a little ford,
where the stream ran clear upon gravel, murmuring out
of a thicket and into a meadow's arms, and turning sweet-
ness to fragrance down all its length. (*Berry Scene*, 13)

Loving the land itself, and its history, they loved the poet and the painter who had held the land up for their examination in words and pigments, in ways that made its beauties manifest and gave them permanence. Which makes all the more offensive the words of an art snob to this group about one of their family paintings: "'Detestable as I find them, there is a section of the public that likes these things. They don't look at the work; the name is enough for them. They can't understand that Gainsborough couldn't paint because Gainsborough couldn't see'" (228). There is more, but this is surely enough to make the point that we can learn a good deal about the values of the upper and middle classes in England between the wars by reading the fiction of Dornford Yates. We can also learn something—and this is at least as important—about the manner in which those values were held.

As we have noted, there are echoes of a feudal value system in the conservative thought of a writer like Yates. These echoes, however, are not simply presented with solemnity. They are offered with something between a smile and a wink. For the greatest and most perfect exemplars of the feudal form of service in these books are not the humans but the dogs, who are also treated as family members. Among these are Nobby, a Sealyham terrier, and The Bold, a diminutive Chinese creature of royal canine blood who inspires respect in humans and other canines as well. One passage devoted to Nobby will illustrate this. The episode begins with a culinary crisis: "Three weeks had passed since the mistress of our kitchen, who had reigned uninterruptedly for seven years, had been knocked down by a taxi and sustained a broken leg" (166). We might pause to note that even the kitchen is seen in feudal, almost regal, terms, but our attention here must be on Nobby. He has been in disgrace over some canine misbehavior, but he is restored to his position on the occasion of Daphne's placing an advertisement for a temporary cook in the newspapers. Berry immediately imagines a flood of candidates for the job descending upon the household and prepares Nobby for the occasion in the following terms:

"Nobby, my lad, come here."
    Signifying his delight at this restoration to favour by an unusually elaborate rotary movement of his tail, the terrier emerged from his cover and humbled himself at his patron's feet. The latter picked him up and set him upon his knee.
    "My lad," he said, "this is going to be a momentous day. Cooks, meet to be bitten, are due to arrive in myriads. Be ruthless. Spare neither the matron nor the maid. What did Mr. Henry say in 1415?—

> *This day is called the feast of Sealyham:*
> *She that outlives this day, and comes safe home,*
> *Will sit with caution when this day is named,*
> *And shudder at the name of Sealyham.*
> *She that shall live this day, and see old age,*
> *Will yearly on the razzle feast her neighbors,*
> *And say, 'To-morrow is Saint Sealyham':*
> *Then will she strip her hose and show her scars,*
> *And say, 'These wounds I had on Nobby's day.'*
> *Old cooks forget; yet all shall be forgot,*
> *But she'll remember with a flood of talk*
> *What feats you did that day."* (173)

King Henry V did not actually say that in 1415, of course, but Shakespeare gave him a speech about St. Crispin's day that ran much along those lines, which Berry is adapting here for the amusement of himself and those around him. Old (and young)

readers forget, too. For their benefit, I will supply the relevant
part of King Henry's speech:

> *This day is called the feast of Crispian:*
> *He that outlives this day and comes safe home,*
> *Will stand a tip-toe when this day is namd,*
> *And rouse him at the name of Crispian.*
> *He that shall live this day and see old age*
> *Will yearly on the vigil feast his neighbours*
> *And say, "To-morrow is Saint Crispian."*
> *Then he will strip his sleeve and show his scars,*
> *And say "These wounds I had on Crispin's day."*
> *Old men forget, yet all shall be forgot,*
> *But he'll remember with advantages*
> *What feats he did that day. . . . (King Henry V,*
> *act 4, scene 3)*

There is an important clue for us here, in the method
employed by Yates. The feudal world is evoked, but in a spirit
of pastiche that is not exactly parody. Shakespeare is so deeply
embedded in this culture that both Berry the performer and
Yates the author can rely on audiences who will enjoy this
adaptation of those lofty lines of military rhetoric to the spectacle of a yappy terrier nipping at the heels of a herd of cooks,
lured to the household by modern advertising. It is not mock-
ery, because nothing is being mocked—neither Shakespeare,
nor royal rhetoric, nor even the behavior of terriers. Berry is,
among other things, exaggerating his own apprehensions of
the flood to be unleashed by a few words in the help-wanted
column of a paper. He is having fun, partly at his own expense,
and this is the key to his character, upon which the whole series of Berry volumes may be said to rest. We have to assume

that Berry knows his Shakespeare, and we have, I believe, to admire the way he (and Yates) have supplied just the right variations (such as "sit with caution" in place of "stand a tip-toe") in adapting the Shakespearian intertext for this occasion. Berry is both witty himself and the cause of wit in others.

This is a Modernism that dislikes modernity and has adopted a style that is full of allusions to just those authors whom Wordsworth felt were being "driven into neglect" by "idle and extravagant stories" in 1800. The Berry books are certainly idle, and perhaps even extravagant, but they assume that what Wordsworth called "the invaluable works of our elder writers" are a part of their heritage and that of their readers. The Jeeves books, too, are riddled with allusions to Shakespeare—whose works are a possession of Jeeves, though Bertie's grasp of them is shaky. But P. G. Wodehouse assumes that his readers share Jeeves's knowledge rather than Bertie's ignorance. And Wodehouse, too, wrote sometimes for the *Windsor Magazine*. This is a Light Modernism that insists on its connection with the canonical masters of English literature, and it has been written for an audience that knows the work of those masters and can appreciate the various montages, pastiches, and outright misappropriations of the elder writers by the authors and characters of these modern texts. But the Berry books are modern in other ways as well. Consider, for example, the following instance.

As we have already noted, many of Yates's works follow the fortunes and adventures of the second generation of a pair of intermarried families, the Pleydells and the Mansells. These books fall into two main categories, adventures of a type similar to Anthony Hope's *Prisoner of Zenda* involving Jonathan Mansell (known in the family as Jonah), and comic romances involving the other family members with Jonah as a minor char-

acter. The first adventure novels are narrated by one William
Chandos, but Jonah is the leader of the adventurous group. The
other books, for which comic romances is a convenient though
not strictly accurate designation, are narrated by Jonah's cousin
Boy Pleydell. You need to know these things, I am afraid, to
understand what happens in the story called "Letters Patent."

Before we get to that story, however, I must tell you about
those first two adventure novels narrated by William Chandos.
In the earliest of these, *Blind Corner*, Jonah and his friends
snatch a treasure from the hands of a nasty British criminal in
the Austrian Alps. In the second, *Perishable Goods*, the wife of
Boy Pleydell, from the other series of books, is kidnapped and
held for ransom by the same criminal, in the same part of the
world. As Boy is laid up with a broken leg, it is Jonah, with his
own group of adventurous companions, to the rescue. There is
a complicating factor in this novel, however, in the shape of a
romantic attraction between Adèle, Boy Pleydell's wife, and
Jonah Mansell, his cousin. When Jonah is seriously wounded
in the struggle with Adèle's captors and is lying near to death,
Adèle's love for him cannot be concealed. At the end of the
novel, however, the lovers agree to return to their former lives
and pretend that their love never happened, thus enacting what
Connolly called "courtesy that is extinct." These are books
dominated by adventure and romance, love and honor: formulas of behavior and formulas of fiction. Hence their "mediocrity." Which brings us to "Letters Patent." Here are the opening paragraphs of the story:

"Oh he mustn't die," said Adèle. "Don't make him die."
    "Of course he must die," said Berry. "In great agony. I'll
help you with that bit."

"I'm not sure I oughtn't to," said Jonah. "Besides, I rather fancy that chapel. Make a magnificent tomb."

"I won't hear of it," said my sister. "Think of the shock to Adèle."

"As a matter of fact," said I, "it's all over. I've passed the proofs."

There was an electric silence.

In a sudden burst of ambition, I had written a book. Requiring a resourceful hero, I had looked to my cousin Jonah, to fill the rôle. This he had so much adorned that my wife, my sister and her husband had all demanded as of right to appear in "my next." "All is vanity." When, like a fool, I consented, I cut my own throat. From that time on neither plot, nor style, nor construction—least of all my life was my own. (*Maiden Stakes*, 295)

The rest of the story has to do with a critical letter Boy received after the book's publication and with a bet on a horse race. We need not concern ourselves with the bet. But these opening paragraphs point to something especially interesting. They are, of course, metafictional, which one would not expect, perhaps, from a popular writer in 1931, but that is the least of their interest. They have a special claim on us because they are metafictional in a particular way. They offer us the "same" characters operating at two different levels, as fictional personages in *Perishable Goods* and as "real" people in this story from *Maiden Stakes*—as when the "real" Jonah, speaking of the "fictional" Jonah's possible death, says "I'm not sure I oughtn't to"—a curious phrase, in which the first "I" refers to the "real" and the second to the "fictional" Jonah. In this conversation, the "real" characters expose the entire composition of a romantic adventure as a highly artificial and arbitrary process, with a result that should not be confused with "real life"— which is, of course, the life being lived by the fictional characters in the collection of comic romances called *Maiden Stakes.*

I think Yates, like his contemporary Graham Greene, may be trying to establish a distinction between the levels of artificiality in the two kinds of books he is writing, but in doing so, he has reminded us that they are, indeed, only levels of artificiality, and that the formulas of fiction are indeed fictional. We had thought of Dornford Yates as the author of *Blind Corner* and *Perishable Goods,* and of William Chandos as the narrator of those novels. But now we learn that Boy Pleydell is the author, which makes Yates, perhaps, a meta-author. That "Yates" is merely a pen name for C. W. Mercer opens up another level of unreality. On the other hand, the fact that Mercer put a good deal of his actual life into Yates's fiction reminds us that the real and the unreal flow in both directions in these works. (See Richard Usborne's *Clubland Heroes* for the biographical details.) The very distinction between real life and fiction is called into question, however lightly, in these books.

The writers enshrined in the High Modernist canon were also, of course, concerned about the relations between the real and the fictional. Let us attend to one of them in the process of distinguishing Modernist fiction from the superficial trivialities of supposedly realistic writing—here called "the literature of description":

How could the literature of description possibly have any value, when it is only beneath the surface of the little things which such a literature describes that reality has its hidden existence. . . . Gradually, thanks to its preservation by our memory, the chain of all those inaccurate expressions in which there survives nothing of what we have really experienced comes to constitute for us our thought, our life, our "reality," and this lie is all that can be reproduced by the art that styles itself "true to life," an art that is as simple as life, without beauty, a mere vain tedious duplication of what our eyes see and our intellect records, so vain and so tedious that one wonders where the writer who devotes himself to it can have found the joyous and impulsive spark that was capable of setting him in motion and making him advance in his task.

I want to pause for a moment and contemplate the rich theoretical implications of this statement. We can see it, I believe, as not far from the position taken by Virginia Woolf in *Mr. Bennett and Mrs. Brown,* in which she attacked the attention given to external details in the fiction of her Edwardian predecessors on behalf of a turn to a deeper, interior reality in the work of the writers she called "Georgian," which ultimately, of course, included her own work. In the passage we are considering, the "literature of description" plays the role of Woolf's Edwardians—that is, it offers a false, external reality. But Woolf, in the final version of her essay, avoided any attempt to claim success for the Georgians. She asked her readers to "tolerate the spasmodic, the obscure, the fragmentary, the failure" (119), as her Georgians groped for an appropriately new way to cope with the changed character of modern life. But the other writer, whom you have no doubt recognized as Marcel Proust (*Time Regained,* 297–98), had a different solution.

For Proust, groping was over. He knew what the novelist must do, and he (if he is like his narrator, Marcel) would do it. Of course, as the writer Proust, he had already done it, since this discussion of narrative theory comes late in the last vol-

ume of his major work. What had to be done, as he explained
at length, involved the capturing of two orders of time: (1) the
absolute essence that lies at the heart of a moment, a place, or
a character, accessible only to involuntary memory or its artistic equivalent, and (2) the workings of temporality that mod-
ify moments, places, and characters, making of every human
being a multiple entity, which only literature can capture.

Proust is the enemy of mediocrity—let me not try to
suggest anything different. He is consciously and deliberately
engaged in the production of a masterpiece of Modernism.
And this means, as he tells us over and over, that his goal is
"truth" rather than entertainment. Still, his enemies are not
the aesthetes and dilettantes but naturalists like the Goncourt
brothers, who claim to be putting slices of life under their mag-
nifying glasses. Moreover, there are aspects of Proust's masterpiece that resonate with the efforts of less powerful writers to
achieve iridescence for their mediocre productions. I find such
an aspect in the following text, also from the last volume of the
Recherche: "In this book in which there is not a single incident
which is not fictitious, not a single character who is a real person in disguise, in which everything has been invented by me
in accordance with the requirements of my theme, I owe it to
the credit of my country to say that only the millionaire cousins
of Françoise who came out of retirement to help their niece
when she was left without support, only they are real people
who exist" (225).

This is a singular moment, in which our narrator, Marcel, speaks as the author, Proust, to tell us that everything in
this book is fictional, except for certain millionaires, whom he
goes on to name a few lines later—and that these "real people
who exist" are relatives of the invented character, Françoise,
who exists only fictitiously, to serve the author's theme (*ma dé-*

monstration). The word "cousins" (*parents*) is doing heavy duty here, uniting beings from two incompatible orders of existence. Something has to give, and not only in this instance. We know that the characters in this novel are often intimately and intricately linked with real people who existed. Have we not just heard the real Proust speaking of his book as existing, virtually complete, through the mouth or pen of the fictional narrator Marcel, who has yet to begin writing *his* book—which is nevertheless the same book? This reminds me very much of the situation in "Letters Patent," where the characters who were fictional in one book are now real and commenting on the writing of the other. Which does not turn Dornford Yates into Proust, to be sure—Yates being less serious though also less clumsy in his metafictional moment—but the two moments taken together show that Proust and Yates share a certain Modernist perspectivism as well as an aesthetic interest in joy and beauty.

Yates, like Proust, is turning away from the materialistic naturalism that Modernist writers and critics tended to see as their major opponent, the part of the Old they needed to deny or suppress in order to be New. But there were different ways of making that turn, and different directions in which to move. One of those directions was that of comedy or comic romance, and Yates developed his own version of that mode of writing. Many of the critics we considered in Chapter 1, I am sure, would be quick to label that mode of writing and the works of Yates—and Wodehouse—in particular, as kitsch. Let us pause and consider the notions of kitsch and mediocrity before looking a little more deeply into the shallows inhabited by Dornford Yates.

To begin with, let us return, for a moment, to what Matei Calinescu said about kitsch: "To understand the nature of

kitsch we should, then, analyze the particular hedonism char-
acteristic of middle-class mentality. Its primary feature is
perhaps that it is a middle-of-the-road hedonism, perfectly
illustrated by the 'principle of mediocrity' that always obtains
in kitsch (this all-pervading mediocrity is easier to notice in
the more elaborate and exaggeratedly complicated forms of
kitsch)" (244). I love the way that academic critics always assume that the middle class is elsewhere, and that they are outside of it, or rather above it, looking down. But Calinescu is
onto something here. The reason that the kind of writing I am
discussing is a form of Modernism is to be found in its relation
to the "terrible and incomprehensible boredom" which does
indeed haunt modern life. But the attack on the mediocre hedonism of the middle class is even more revealing, because it
reveals a Puritanism at the heart of the High Modernist aesthetic. You would think that the terror and boredom of modern life might justify a little pleasure, but, no, fun will be ex-
posed and rooted out wherever it lurks. Watch out, Possum,
they're coming to get you! I must admit, then, that my "iridescent mediocrity" is another person's kitsch, and my argument
is that we should look more closely—and more kindly—at
works that offer us textual pleasure mixed with the sort of
frailty that I am willing to call mediocrity.

Hostility to mediocrity, as we have seen, is often mixed
with hostility toward the middle class, the dreadful bourgeoisie, the middlebrows, the Philistines. And here (full disclo-
sure) I must admit that I belong to that abhorrent group. My
parents, both of them, worked their way up from the working
class, through the petty bourgeoisie, to a precarious position in
the middle class—and that was their gift to me. If I ever seemed
to despise that gift, I must apologize now, when it is too late,
and say, "Thanks, Mom and Dad. I know who I am, now, and

I accept the gifts you gave me, along with the responsibilities that go with them." Which means accepting mediocrity as my own portion of life, as Robinson Crusoe's father tried in vain to get his son to do. It takes a while for sons to learn to listen. But what, exactly, is mediocrity, anyway? It has not always meant what it seems to mean today. I shall try, then, to restore something of its earlier meaning to the word "mediocrity," as referring to balance or measure, a modest avoidance of excess. Mediocrity, in this sense, can refer to the work of art or literature that resists or rejects certain grand ambitions in order to accept the more menial task of providing pleasure for those who attend to it. This is the kind of work, as we have seen, produced and defended by Walter Sickert and his fellows nearly a century ago. Literary work of this sort, I shall argue, when it rises to a certain level of lightness or brightness, may be quite properly be called iridescent. E. M. Forster, as it happens, used that adjective as I am using it in discussing Max Beerbohm's *Zuleika Dobson:* "Has not a passage like this . . . a beauty unattainable by serious literature? It is so funny and charming, so iridescent yet so profound" (118). I agree with Forster, of course, but I want also to insist on the mediocrity of the work I am discussing, in the process of arguing that "iridescent mediocrity" is a valuable mode of modern fiction. We should note that Forster distinguished this kind of work from serious literature—but not simply as something lower. For him it was higher in certain respects, reaching iridescence because it is light enough to get there, but also establishing its own connection with the beautiful and the profound. But we should look at the passage in Beerbohm that led Forster to this conclusion. The Duke is on his way to drown himself for love, and is walking through Oxford, where the permanence of the buildings threatens to trivialize his death:

Aye, by all minerals we are mocked. Vegetables, yearly de-
ciduous, are far more sympathetic. The lilac and labur-
num, making lovely now the railed pathway to Christ
Church meadow, were all a-swaying and nodding to the
Duke as he passed by. "Adieu, adieu, your Grace," they
were whispering. "We are very sorry for you, very sorry
indeed. We never dared suppose you would predecease
us. We think your death a very great tragedy. Adieu! Perhaps we shall meet in another world—that is, if the
members of the animal kingdom have immortal souls, as
we have."

The Duke was little versed in their language; yet, as he
passed between these gently garrulous blooms, he caught
at the least the drift of their salutation, and smiled a vague
but courteous acknowledgment, to the right and the left
alternatively, creating a very favorable impression. (70–71)

Beerbohm used the license of the fantasist to give his
flowers language and theology, along with a keen social sense
that enables them to appreciate the Duke's good manners.
They speak in whispers, as flowers may seem to do, when the
wind moves through them, and their first words, "Adieu,
adieu, your Grace," suit that whispered language very well.
Their religious condescension—so confident of their own ultimate immortality—mixes wonderfully with their keen sense
of protocol, so that they are impressed in turn by the social
condescension of the Duke as he courteously acknowledges
their good intentions without quite comprehending their actual message. The lightness of Beerbohm's touch, and his delicate modulations from mortality to propriety, combined with
the elegant precision of his language, justify Forster's claims
about iridescence and profundity.

Now I would not wish to claim that Dornford Yates is in Beerbohm's league as a writer. Few are. His work has perhaps less iridescence in it and more mediocrity. But I do want to argue that they are playing the same game, producing writing that turns away from the realistic and distances itself from modernity in order to criticize it. In Beerbohm's case the turn took him to fantasy and parody. In the case of Yates it took him toward romantic comedy. A number of other writers during the period that includes Beerbohm and Yates made a similar turn. I'm thinking of Katherine Mansfield's cousin Elizabeth von Arnim, for example, of Ada Leverson, whom Oscar Wilde called "The Sphynx," of Yates's own cousin, Hector H. Munro, who wrote as Saki, and, of course, of P. G. Wodehouse himself. All these used comedy, in modes ranging from bitter to bland, as a way of presenting worlds that were both like and unlike the world they lived in—different enough to provide more pleasure than pain, but like enough to generate a critical perspective on modernity. The iridescent part of their achievement, if it be admitted, needs no defense, but the mediocrity does. So I shall conclude this discussion of Yates by looking, as he might suggest himself, into the traditional meaning of this word now used so often with casual abusiveness.

Here I shall require some help from "Dictionary Johnson" himself, who had no qualms about being a magazine journalist and writing to earn money:

Among many parallels which men of imagination have drawn between the natural and moral state of the world, it has been observed that happiness, as well as virtue, consists in mediocrity; that to avoid every extreme is necessary, even to him who has no other care than to pass through the present state with ease and safety; and that

the middle path is the road of security, on either side of
which are not only the pitfalls of vice, but the precipices
of ruin.

Thus the maxim of Cleobulus the Lindian, métron
äriston, Mediocrity is best, has been long considered as an
universal principle, extended through the whole compass
of life and nature. The experience of every age seems to
have given it new confirmation, and to shew that nothing,
however precious or alluring, is pursued with propriety,
or enjoyed with safety, beyond certain limits. (38)

Remembering lines like these, no doubt, Johnson's great ad-
mirer Jane Austen condemned her own novel *Pride and Prejudice* as "too light and bright and sparkling," which has not prevented it from being the favorite of most of her readers. For
many of us, there may be no such thing as *too* light and bright
and sparkling, and we would not give up *Pride and Prejudice* for
three more *Mansfield Parks*. But what, after all, can "light and
bright and sparkling" mean if not "iridescent"? Perhaps, then,
I may conclude this brief excursus by modifying the golden
phrase of Cleobulus the Lindian and saying, "iridescent mediocrity is best"—or, if not best, at least worthy of our attention
as readers, and as students of modern literature and culture.

7
Formulaic Creativity: Simenon's Maigret Novels

*Simenon est un grand romancier, le plus grand peut-être
et le plus vraiment romancier que nous avons
en littérature française aujourd'hui.
(Simenon is a great novelist, perhaps the greatest and the
most truly a novelist that we have in French literature today.)*
—André Gide, Les Cahiers du nord *(all translations from
the French in this chapter and the next two
are my own, except as noted)*

*We were getting a little far down into the book bag but there
were still some hidden values mixed in with the required
reading and there were twenty volumes of Simenon in French
that I had not read. If you are to be rained in while camped in
Africa there is nothing better than Simenon and with him I did*

*not care how long it rained. You draw perhaps three good
Simenons out of each five but an addict can read the bad
ones when it rains and I . . . would read happily, transferring
all my problems to Maigret, bearing with him in his
encounters with idiocy and the Quai des Orfèvres.*
—*Ernest Hemingway,* True at First Light *(spelling corrected)*

*I now prefer Claret to Burgundy and I prefer
Inspector Maigret to Arsène Lupin.*
—*T. S. Eliot's response to a question about "the two most
important changes in his life" in the Fiftieth Anniversary
Report of the Harvard Class of 1910*

Or consider the Pendu de St. Pholien *or the* Ombre Chinoise
*of M. Georges Simenon. . . . It is Dostoevsky . . . and
Dostoevsky,* corsé, *constructed, economized and filled
with the poetry of pity . . .*
—*Ford Madox Ford,* The March of Literature, *titles corrected,
first ellipsis mine, others Ford's*—corsé *means
full-bodied, spiced up*

B ack in Chapter 1, I raised the question of literary formulas, suggesting that many excellent writers had
worked with formulas of one kind or another, mentioning Jane Austen in passing. This, of course, was in

the context of High Modernist denigration of formulaic writing as inevitably inferior and Low, which, like the automatic association of literary Lowness with social Lowness so frequently made by critics, is simply an error that prevents us from understanding the way literature actually works. It is time, now, for me to return to the question of formulaic writing and try to justify my claim that good writing can be formulaic, and that a notion of Modernism that excludes formulaic fiction would be impoverished. As my major example, I wanted a writer whose work fell within the chronological boundaries of Modernism and was clearly formulaic, but also good enough to have captured not only my own interest but that of my betters. In the vast body of work of Georges Simenon, the seventy-five Maigret novels seemed to provide the best combination of literary quality and formulaic construction for my purposes.

I considered writing about Chesterton's Father Brown stories, which were admired by Borges, but they seem to me less interesting and durable than Simenon's work. I might also have chosen the fiction of Raymond Chandler or Dashiell Hammett, but I have written about them elsewhere and did not want to repeat myself here. I also thought of later writers in this tradition, such as Nicholas Freeling, whose work I admire, but there is a Post-Modernist quality to Freeling's work, and I wanted someone who clearly belongs to the Modernist tradition. Simenon, it seemed to me, holds a position in Modernist fiction that is similar to that held by Walter Sickert in visual art, as a Neo-Realist working in an era that came to be dominated by other modes of expression. I have chosen to begin with four epigraphs by writers with strong Modernist credentials to indicate that Simenon's work was familiar to his lofty contemporaries and taken seriously by them. The Old Possum, of course, is joking to his Harvard classmates about the important changes in his life (and he is certainly wrong to have shifted from Burgundy to Claret), but even he seems to have taken pleasure in reading Simenon's Maigret novels, which is the main reason I have quoted him here. Ford's comparing of Simenon to Dostoevsky—and not unfavorably—may give us pause, but he is on the mark in noting how the achievements of great writers are assimilated by others who have less exalted ambitions. We should also note that Ford emphasizes the "pity" in Simenon—"pity" being another word for the sentimentality so despised by major Modernists and so prevalent in their best works. And, being Ford, quoting from memory as usual, he slightly misspells both the titles he mentions.

André Gide's praise may seem extravagant, unless we realize that he considers the novel to be a Realistic mode of fiction that Modernism, including his own writing, has surpassed in many respects—a mode capable of flourishing only at the more popular level inhabited by Simenon. But the praise is real enough. New modes of writing do not simply eclipse the old ones, though they may cause a repositioning and revaluing of those older modes. What readers got from Realism and still enjoy they will now find done best at the level of formulaic fiction exemplified by Simenon's novels and stories. Many readers, including Simenon himself, find his best work to lie not in the Maigret novels but in the others, which are less formulaic—or less overtly so. But for my purposes, the more formulaic the better, and besides, I really like the Maigret books myself and am happy to seize this chance to try and show why I have found them so pleasurable. Many of the Simenons in my own library have been literally read to pieces, because they are cheaply printed and bound, and I have read them all at least twice before. On the third reading, they tend to come apart physically, though not aesthetically. But I have also, for this occasion, acquired a number of early Maigrets that I did not have, so that I might discuss how the Maigret formula developed.

Obviously, one cannot attempt to treat seventy-five novels and more than thirty stories in a single chapter. What I do hope to accomplish, however, is to discuss the relationship between formulaic patterns and creativity, looking especially at the early works, in which Simenon is adapting the more general formula of crime fiction to his own purposes. I will also restrict myself chronologically, for the most part, to the first few years of Simenon's work in this genre, which begin, for our purposes, in 1929. We should understand, of course, that this was a writer who produced an average of ten novels a year for a bit more than forty years. He would often crank out a complete work in a week or so of really intense effort, and then rest for a couple of weeks before starting another. We are in the realm of mediocrity here, rather than that of masterpieces. Ernest Hemingway, who wrote thirty or so endings for *A Farewell to Arms,* obviously worked in another mode altogether, which makes his appreciation of Simenon especially relevant for the whole case I have been making about the paradoxy of Modernism. Stuart Gilbert, who first publicized the plan or scaffolding of Joyce's *Ulysses,* translated a number of Simenon's novels into English. T. S. Eliot, Hemingway, Gide, Ford, and Simenon were all working as modern writers at the same time, and we shall understand Modernism and modernity better if we attend to all of them.

As you might expect, there is a vast critical literature on Simenon, which I cannot pretend to have mastered for this occasion. But my purpose is not to contribute to that literature but simply to position Simenon's Maigret fiction in my own argument, demonstrating that formulas and creativity may go together in the creation of durable literary works, and that popular fiction in the modern period reached a range of readers and deserves to be studied as a vital part of the Modernist enterprise. But first, let me be as clear as possible about what I mean by formulaic writing. It would falsify my case if I used the term as a synonym for the constraints that certain experimental writers deliberately set as challenges for themselves, such as Georges Perec in his novel *La Disparition,* a lipogrammatic text, written entirely without using the letter "e" in any word, or Joyce's scaffolding of organs, colors, and so on, used in *Ulysses.* Nor do I wish to use the notion of formula to designate a traditional structure like the sonnet form. What I mean by formula would be more like the use of certain topics and vocabularies *within* the sonnet form, such as the blazon or formulaic description of the beloved's beauties. An extreme use of formulas in modern fiction would be the guides that certain publishers of romances send to prospective writers, telling them exactly what kind of episodes are required, and just how many of them, as well as where they should come in the whole narrative. What I am calling formulaic creativity occurs in that middle ground between large structures established by tradition and the adaptations of structure and texture that a writer uses to make an individual work out of such structures.

Formulas, at this level, belong to genres, and the expression "genre fiction" is often used to disparage various forms of writing that are considered insufficiently creative to be called "literature." Simenon's Maigret novels are written in a subgenre of crime fiction that we now recognize as the "police procedural," which can be distinguished from the "private eye" novel, for example, to which it is clearly related. Simenon, of course, has helped to make the police procedural one of the major genres of formulaic fiction, which, especially in European hands, has produced works of very high quality by such writers as Nicholas Freeling, the Swedish team of Maj Sjowall and Per Wahloo, and their successor Henning Mankell, as well as the American writer of novels set in Italy, Michael Dibden. Both of these modern subgenres (the police procedural and the private eye) emerged from the detective fiction of the nineteenth century and the early twentieth century, against which they were reacting. The private eye subgenre reacted against the aestheticism of its predecessor, giving us gritty detectives walking down mean streets and telling us their own stories, with no Dr. Watson to eulogize them. The police procedural reacted against the elitism of its predecessors, in which the police were usually despised or saved from their ineptitude by brilliant amateurs—or both. But the private eye worked alone, for the most part, without even a Watson for company, whereas the police detective relied on many colleagues for various kinds of support and assistance, and had a whole bureaucratic apparatus to contend with.

The American private eye usually told his own story, as if he were talking to the reader, and his street-smart, wisecracking voice plays a major role in the texture of those novels. The European police officer, however, was normally the object of a narration in the third person. The private eye was, by definition, a maverick, often going where the police would not go and doing what the police would not do. The police officer, on the other hand, was, by definition, a civil servant, what the French call a *fonctionnaire,* constrained in various ways. It is, as they say, no accident that one of these modes is quintessentially American and the other European. But both of them inherited the basic generic structure of the novel of crime and detection, which, as Michel Butor first told us and Tzvetan Todorov reminded us, consists of two different stories—the story of the crime and the story of the detection—superimposed on one another in various ways. This structure, based on a double plot, offers a formula with plenty of room for creative variation.

The basic formula for the double plot begins when the story of the crime is over—with a corpse, for example—and the story of the solution is just beginning. In this way the chronological unfolding of the detection allows the story of the crime to be reconstructed achronologically, with bits and pieces of the criminal narrative turning up in the order of their discovery. This also allows for a separation between the events of that narrative and their significance, which gives the narrative of detection another level of complexity, with a bit of information often being found at one point in that story but not being understood until the process is further along. Just in terms of structure then, without even considering texture, there is room for considerable creativity in these formulaic genres.

Texture in these novels is visible mainly at two levels: the level of characterization, especially the characterization of the detective, and the level of language itself, which plays a role in characterization, to be sure, but a different role in the first-person private-eye novel and the third-person police procedural. As I have already suggested, the voice of the private eye characterizes that figure even as it gives us a picture of the world as perceived by the detective. In the police procedural, however, the world and the characters are presented to us by an invisible narrator, who has much of the authority possessed by the great nineteenth-century omniscient voices of Realistic fiction. These narrators, with their moral authority, were missed by Georg Lukács in the Modernist fiction he deplored—and by many ordinary readers as well. But the grandeur of Balzacian or Tolstoyan omniscience was not really available to Modernist novelists, who turned toward Impressionism for sound epistemological reasons. Writers like Simenon, then, belong with the Neo-Realists in that they adopted a more perspectival Realism, turning back toward Realism with the lessons of Impressionism in mind.

Understanding this process is crucial to understanding Modernism itself. In the narrative voice of a Tolstoyan narrator we find an authority akin to that which enabled Hegel to write his *Philosophy of History*. This is a period voice, shared by Stendhal and Balzac in France, for example, and by Dickens, Thackeray, and George Eliot in England, as well as by Dostoevsky and Tolstoy in Russia—different as each of these individual writers may be from all the others. After Impressionism and Nietzschean perspectivism, such an assumption of narrative authority sounded hollow. As it migrated from authors aspiring to original masterworks to those with the more modest aims of genre fiction, the voice of Realistic narration had to limit its omniscience, generalize less, avoid claiming to be everywhere and to know everything—and this more modest posture suited the forms and aims of genre fiction very well, especially the aims of detective fiction, where the last thing needed is a narrator who knows everything and flaunts this knowledge. No one writing in the modern period understood this better than Georges Simenon, or used the techniques of a shifting but limited omniscience with greater skill, as has been duly noted by such francophone critics as Alain Bertrand (see esp. 30–33). In the developed Maigret novel we are almost always with Maigret, seeing the world through his eyes, but also seeing him from the outside. We sometimes are given information about his feelings, often in the form of external physical signs that can be read by those who know him, including the detectives who work under him, but we never really know the bottom level of his thoughts.

We can best grasp the workings of creativity in the Maigret formula by looking at some specific texts in which both the formula and the creativity are on display, but before that, we should review the unusual circumstances of this character's literary birth. By the late 1920s Simenon had moved from his native Belgium to France, had toured that country as private secretary to a man of wealth and position, and had purchased a boat with which he toured the canals of northern France, Belgium, and the Netherlands. He knew this part of the world thoroughly, and he had mingled with people at all levels of society. He was also writing journalism and popular fiction under several assumed names, including Christian Brulls and Georges Sim. In 1929, at the age of twenty-six, Simenon composed a novel called *Train de nuit* (Night train), which appeared the following year as a work by Christian Brulls. In that novel we have the first appearance on record of a Commissaire Maigret in the work of Simenon. The novel is a story of crime and romance, about a young sailor from Normandy, on leave from a naval vessel in Toulon, who gets innocently involved in a crime on the train taking him to Marseilles from his home in Normandy. Having left his family and his girlfriend back in Yport, he meets a young beauty on the train who lures him into helping her conceal a theft that turns into a murder.

The story is about their flight, their falling in love, and the young sailor's ultimate return to his childhood sweetheart and a reconciliation with his parents, while the dark beauty, after renouncing her claim on the youth she had mesmerized and then protected, is reunited with a father she didn't know she had. The book is a crime novel and a romance, mixing these two genres deftly, and not a police procedural at all, but we can learn a lot from it about Simenon's ability as a writer of fiction and the use he made of it in the later Maigret novels.

Aristotle himself could not ask for more recognitions and reversals than Simenon provides in this short novel, which makes us wait and weep as much as anyone could wish. As a romance, it follows the ancient formula of bringing the hero back to his first love after vicissitudes that include a romance with an older seductress—also used by Fielding in *Tom Jones*, to be sure, as it had been in ancient times by Longus in *Daphnis and Chloe*. And with its renunciation for the sake of love, and its parent/child reunions, it is as sentimental as one could wish. But the crime is brutal and the punishment looks as if it will be severe indeed. If we ask what it is that turns this apparent tale of crime and punishment into a romance, the answer comes in the form of one word: Maigret. And what he does in this preliminary novel holds the key to all of his great success as a character and the success of these novels in general.

Maigret enters the fictional world in the least conspicuous manner possible, as a name in a newspaper report about the crime on the night train. "Tandis que des agents essayaient de s'assurer qu'aucun voyageur du rapide n'avait pu sauter sur la voie à la faveur d'un ralentissement comme il s'en produit à certains endroits, le commissaire Maigret recevait d'abord, vers deux heures de l'après-midi, la visite d'un cafetier des environs de la gare" (72; While some officers tried to make sure that no passenger on the express had been able to jump down on the tracks when the train slowed, as happens at certain spots, Commissaire Maigret was first visited, around two o'clock in the afternoon, by a coffee-seller from the area near the station). A commissaire, in most French police forces, held a position somewhere between lieutenant and captain in American forces—definitely someone who had come through the ranks, rather than a political appointee, as American commissioners sometimes are—but there is no handy equivalent for the translator to use. As a commissaire in Marseilles, Maigret would have been in charge of a district within the city, and supervising the investigations assigned to that district. In Simenon's novel, however, he was something else as well, something essential to the generic structure of this crime/romance novel and to all the later police procedurals involving Maigret. One of the classic expressions of this function appeared in a novel of 1949, called *La Première Enquête de Maigret* (Maigret's first case), which takes us back to 1913, long before Maigret became a commissaire, when he was serving as secretary to the commissaire of a Parisian police station and was allowed to undertake a very unpromising case. In the course of this novel, we are given a fuller exposition of the motivations behind Maigret's career than we would normally receive in a novel about the mature Commissaire Maigret. This is sufficiently crucial for extended quotation here:

> Pour tout dire, le métier qu'il avait toujours eu envie de faire n'existait pas. Tout jeune, dans son village, il avait eu l'impression que des tas de gens n'étaient pas à leur place, prenaient un chemin qui n'était pas le leur, uniquement parce qu'ils ne savaient pas.
>
> Et il imaginait un homme très intelligent, très compréhensif, surtout, à la fois médecin et prêtre, par example, un homme qui comprehendait du premier coup d'oeil le destin d'autri. . . .
>
> On serait venu consulter cet homme-là comme un consulte un docteur. Il aurait été, en quelque sorte, un raccommodeur de destins. Pas seulement parce qu'il était intelligent. Peut-être n'avait-il pas besoin d'être d'une intelligence exceptionnelle? Mais parce qu'il était capable

de vivre la vie de tous les hommes, de se mettre dans la
peau de tous les hommes. (91–92)

To tell the truth, the trade that he had always wanted did
not exist. While still young, in his village, he had had the
impression that a lot of people were not in the right place,
following a path that was not theirs, just because they did
not know.
    And he imagined a man, very intelligent, and, above
all, very understanding, both doctor and priest, for example, a man who comprehended at first glance the destiny of others. . . .
    You would come to consult this man as you would con-
sult a doctor. He would have been, in some way, a mender
of destinies. Not just because he was intelligent—perhaps
he wouldn't even need to be exceptionally intelligent?—
but because he was capable of living the life of every man,
of putting himself in the skin of any man.

    This was a childish dream, to be sure, but it remains the
motivation of the character Maigret wherever he appears, and
this motivation extends to the very formula that governs this
series of novels. Maigret's presence, as it develops from the first
novels in the sequence of seventy-five books, is a guarantee to
the reader that things will end as well as possible for the sympathetic characters, with something close to justice being done—
and often something well beyond what the legal system would
provide if its machinery were allowed to grind away without hu-
mane intervention. This description—an arranger or mender
of destinies—also suits the author, of course. Simenon divided
his novels into "hard or tough" fiction and others that were

softer. The tough novels often end badly, though the author extends his sympathy and understanding to a wide range of characters. The softer novels include the Maigret series, and it is Maigret himself who creates a world around him that is more just—poetically just—than the actual world, which has no Maigret to mend our broken destinies and set us on the right path if we have strayed.

The reader who picks up a Maigret, then, knows that the formula requires Maigret to provide as just an ending to events as may be found, and much of the reader's pleasure comes from the richness and complexity of the obstacles that Maigret must surmount in getting things sorted out properly. And this is where Simenon's creative fecundity comes into play. We shall look at some examples of this later on, but first we should notice how much of the developed character of Maigret was already in Simenon's mind when he first introduced him in *Train de nuit* as a minor figure who appears in only three of twenty chapters. After his mention in the newspaper, we see him first through the eyes of Rita, the young femme fatale who is already familiar with the law in Marseilles: "Celui-là était Maigret, un homme calme, au parler rude, aux manières volontiers brutales" (176; That was Maigret, a calm man, who spoke rudely, with deliberately brutal manners). But we also see him, a bit later, through the eyes of the young man she has led astray, who is recovering from wounds in a hospital: "Il lui avait parlé presque durement, mais d'une façon telle qu'on sentait sous cette dureté une chaude sympathie" (191; He had spoken to him rather harshly, but so that you could sense a warm sympathy under that toughness). And this sympathy emerges even more clearly in his deeds, as he sends the femme fatale back to her father and intercedes to save the young sailor from punishment by the French navy, sending him back too, ultimately, to his childhood sweetheart, his loving mother, and his tough but now sympathetic father. Maigret's role as a mender of destinies was thoroughly in place, then, from the beginning, though his function in the work of Simenon still remained to be settled, and the whole backstory of his life had yet to be created.

Maigret played a similar function in the second novel in which he appeared, *La Jeune Fille aux perles* (The girl with the pearls), also credited to Christian Brulls. This, too, is a romance with criminal aspects, not unlike the popular works of E. Phillips Oppenheim in English. Maigret appears in it as a Parisian commissaire, described this way on his first appearance: "C'était un personnage immense et large, au cou puissant, qui avait dans toute sa personne quelque chose d'à la fois bourru et attendri" (27; He was a tall, broad person, with a powerful neck, whose entire appearance had something in it at once churlish and tender). From the beginning, then, Maigret's character was founded on a paradoxical combination of toughness and tenderness—and that is not the only paradox in his construction. He is both a fonctionnaire and a maverick. He operates within the judicial bureaucracy but he is a loner. He has a brilliant record of solving crimes, but he has no method. As he puts it himself, in *La Jeune Fille aux perles*, when asked what he thinks about the case, "Du calme! Je ne crois rien! Je ne pense rien! Je cherche à savoir, et c'est déjà bien assez" (132; Calm down! I don't believe anything! I don't think anything! I'm trying to know, and that's plenty). Maigret's nonmethod is very much akin to that of the novelist himself. What he is "trying to know" is how the characters involved in a crime live, what motivates them. And this lends interest to his investigations, which are not so much procedural as psychological and sociological. Maigret immerses himself in the milieu of the crimes he investigates, and Simenon's writing makes the most of this immersion by representing the surface of each milieu eloquently and providing nuanced representations of the individuals concerned.

As the character of Maigret began to interest him, Simenon wrote a novel in which he was the central figure and sent it to his publisher. The publisher didn't think it would sell, but agreed, with some reluctance, to promote the book if Simenon would give him four more Maigret novels, so that all five could be publicized together. A few months later he had his five, and Maigret was launched with a big publicity ball in Paris, at which the guests had to be fingerprinted as a kind of initiation into the world of police procedure. The rest, as they say, is history. And Simenon went on to write another seventy Maigret novels and some thirty shorter works involving him, which led to many films, and, ultimately, television shows as well. The tough and tender *raccomodeur de destins* became the most popular detective in the world. In the course of his literary career, he acquired a childhood (son of an estate manager in the provinces), a failed career (forced to leave medical school when his father died), a quick rise in the police (due to a combination of his own unusual abilities and the patronage of a family friend), a happy though childless marriage to the maternal Mme Maigret (to whom he is perfectly faithful), a modest apartment in Paris (on the boulevard Richard Lenoir), a retirement cottage near the river Loire, neighbors and relatives who become involved in crimes, a loyal staff of inspectors and technical experts, and a mixture of competent and interfering superiors.

Simenon varies the locales of the novels, moving Maigret all over France on various pretexts, and into other countries as well, including the United States. But he often returns to Paris, where his repetitive gestures become a repertory of familiar moves in which readers take comfort, as he stirs up the little stove he has kept in his office despite the introduction of central heating, or has sandwiches sent in from the Brasserie Dauphine while interrogating a witness or a suspect, or goes into a sulky phase before reaching the solution to the case under investigation, causing his subordinates to tiptoe around him cautiously. He is, then, in certain respects the kind of flat character described by E. M. Forster long ago, as typical of Dickens and exemplified by Mr. Micawber. But he is also what Forster called a round character, capable of surprising us, and in this, too, he remains consistent from the early works to the last. Which should alert us to the fact that Forster's absolute distinction between flat and round characters is a bit of High Modernist paradoxy itself, a clarification bought at the cost of obscuring the complex middle ground, where many of the most interesting characters in fiction actually live.

At this point I will try to demonstrate more fully the various ways in which formula and creativity interact in these novels, by choosing a single text as an example, though I doubt that I can do justice even to one in the brief compass of this chapter. Rather than pick one arbitrarily, I will use one of the two Maigrets mentioned by Ford Madox Ford in the epigraph to this chapter, *Le Pendu de Saint-Pholien* (The hanged man of Saint-Pholien), which happens to be one of the original five used to launch the literary career of Maigret in 1930. The basic elements of the formula are all present in this work. There is a crime, an investigation, and a solution. But this formula is elaborately distorted, so that none of the formulaic elements works in a predictable manner.

There is a crime near the beginning of the novel, but it is committed by Maigret himself, who steals the suitcase of a sus-

picious man, causing the man to kill himself when he discovers his loss. The investigation that follows this suicide is conducted by a Maigret who is troubled in his conscience for having caused the death himself. His major clue is the contents of
the purloined suitcase—an old suit several sizes too large for
the victim to have worn it. The investigation, which is quite
complex, leads to the discovery of a real crime committed a
decade earlier and concealed by a group of men who were students at that time, flirting with anarchic ideas and living in a
bohemian manner. But the investigation also reveals that, except for the one whose death Maigret caused, who had become
mentally unstable, all those former bohemians had grown up
to lead decent and productive lives. Maigret keeps encounter-
ing their children: a boy of four getting a violin lesson from his
mother in Reims; a daughter, his third child, being born to a
hardworking father in Liège; the forlorn son of the dead man
in Paris. When Maigret has dragged the truth out of this reluctant group of conspirators, reunited in Liège, where the
original murder had been committed, he makes no move to
charge anyone with a crime. Facing the three major figures in
the affair, who don't know what to expect from him, he mutters, under his breath, so that they can't be sure they have heard
him, "Il y a cinq gosses dans l'histoire" (185; There are five kids
in the story)—meaning that these innocents would suffer if
"justice" were to be done. But, of course, justice is being done.
These men, who were on the wrong path, have, for the most
part, found their proper roads. Returning to Paris, having a
drink at the Brasserie Dauphine with Lucas, a brigadier in his
service, he mutters, "Dix affaires comme celle-ci et je donne
ma démission. . . . Parce que ce serait la preuve qu'il y a là haut
un grand bonhomme de Bon Dieu qui se charge de faire la
police . . ." (186–87, ellipses in original; Ten affairs like this one

and I will turn in my resignation. . . . Because that would be proof that there is a great big fellow of a God who has put himself in charge of policing . . .).

It is not altogether clear what Maigret is saying about God, since "faire la police" is left unfinished and can mean doing something *to* the police or simply doing their job *for* them—or both. What is clear is that in this story destinies have been mended without any need for Maigret to interfere with them—and he has the compassion and great good sense to recognize that and accept it. Of course, there is a "grand bonhomme" in the picture—or just out of the picture—and it is Georges Simenon, who has arranged all these destinies, including Maigret's. I have not mentioned all the intricacies of the plot, including the fact that the "hanged man" of the title refers to an image painted over and over again by one of the group, who started as a bohemian artist and has since become a working photo-engraver, with a family, including three children. This image of a man hanging from some point on the old church of Saint-Pholien is in fact a clue, but a clue to the artist's conscience rather than a pointer to an actual hanging. One could go deeper into the clever plotting of the book, but I hope I have shown enough to indicate that the formula of the police procedural has been used creatively here. And we will find a similar level of creativity no matter what aspect of the novel we study—as we will in many of the other Maigret novels.

The handling of point of view, for example, is a deft combination of external and internal perspectives confined to Maigret himself. Sometimes we see him from the outside, even as others see him. Sometimes we merely see through his eyes, as when he looks through a keyhole and sees the man whose valise he stole pull out a gun and shoot himself through the mouth. And sometimes we learn what he is thinking or feeling, as in the moments after that startling death, when we are told, "Il n'était pas loin—il était même bien près de penser—qu'il venait de tuer un homme" (16; He wasn't far—he was even very close to thinking—that he had killed a man). But we never are taken too deeply into his thought processes. We learn, for example, that he is seeking to establish a connection between the dead man and another who has come to look at his body, but that is about as far as we are allowed to penetrate into his thought processes. Even when we see through Maigret's eyes, Simenon reminds us that we are not necessarily getting this information from some omniscient source: "Le commissaire ne fut-il frappé par une ressemblance confuse entre elle et le mort" (40; The commissaire, wasn't he struck by a confused resemblance between her and the dead man). This refers to the wife of the dead man, who is calling on Maigret in his Parisian office. We learn what he thinks he is seeing, but the negative, "wasn't he struck" turns this information into something more like a question. But who is "confused" here? Simenon's narrator merges into and out of Maigret's perspective, bringing us into a sympathetic alignment with him. And then, at other moments, we see him from the outside, as when he leaves the three guilty but not charged men on a street in Liège near the end of the novel: "Et on ne voyait plus que son dos large, son pardessus noir à col de velours qui s'éloignait" (185; And one saw only his broad back, his black overcoat with the velvet collar, which distanced itself). These are signature features of Maigret the "flat" character, metonymic signifiers of the man himself, seen by the French "one" in this case, which manages to give us the perspective of the three guilty parties without explicitly indicating as much.

Simenon's narrator also shares with Maigret a certain ability to generalize about character, to "place" an individual in a rich and nuanced social scheme, as in this example from *Le Pendu:*

> Il appela le garçon, paya. Et, pour tirer son portefeuille de sa poche, il eut un geste que Maigret avait vu souvent aux hommes d'affaires de son espèce qui prennent l'apéritif aux environs de la Bourse, un geste inimitable, une façon de se renverser en arrière en bombant la poitrine, en rentrant le menton, et d'ouvrir avec un néglgence satisfaite cette chose sacrée, cette gaine de cuir matelassée de billets. (30)

> He called the waiter, paid. And, as he drew the wallet from his pocket, he used a gesture that Maigret had often seen in businessmen of his type having an aperitif in the neighborhood of the Stock Exchange, an inimitable gesture, a way of leaning back, inflating the chest, pulling in the chin, and opening with a satisfied negligence that sacred thing, that leather sheath stuffed with banknotes.

Passages like this—and there are many—ensure, as Lionel Trilling said of Scott Fitzgerald, that Simenon would be welcomed to the heaven of novelists by Balzac himself. This is physical description that gives us both an individual and a type, along with an attitude toward the type—but does the attitude belong to Maigret, the narrator, or Simenon? To all of them, no doubt, but the eloquence belongs to Simenon, who followed the Realist masters of France in seeking *le mot juste.*

The character being described, Joseph Van Damme, has found his destined road as an obnoxious materialist, whose oppressive bonhomie grates on Maigret, in whose path the man always seems to turn up. But as the novel continues, we learn that this is not so much a destiny as a role he has learned to play. He is a hollow man, lacking the anchor in marriage and family life that some of his coconspirators have. At one point he actually makes an impulsive attempt to kill Maigret, and the way this plays out casts an interesting light on Simenon's method. Van Damme rents a car and driver in Reims and offers Maigret a ride back to Paris, where he has business. On the way there, while the driver is fixing a flat tire, and the two passengers are looking at the river Marne in flood, Van Damme tries to push Maigret into the river. Maigret recovers, and holds a gun on Van Damme during the rest of the trip. When they reach the office of the police in Paris, Van Damme refuses to pay the driver for the car he hired, saying that this has become Maigret's responsibility. It is a moment that is funny and rings very true, revealing a depth of doggedness behind the hearty surface of the businessman—and Maigret actually prefers this. Little things like this episode are responsible for the durability of these books, for in them flatness and roundness merge into formulaic creativity. And we will find the same thing if we look closely at the descriptions of places and the weather, which are always given careful and deft attention.

As Maigret follows the man whose death he is about to cause at the beginning of the novel, they both wait for a train in the buffet of a provincial railroad station on the Dutch/German border. The local color here, to which Simenon always attends, comes in two national flavors, so that inside the glass counter one sees Dutch chocolate and German cigarettes. And the atmosphere is heavy with the smell of schnapps and gin. The sites and sounds are utterly banal: "C'était familiale, et pourtant il suffisait de quelques détails pour épaissir l'atmosphere d'une touche trouble d'aventure et de mystère" (9; It was familial, but there were enough little things to thicken the atmosphere with a disturbing touch of adventure and mystery).

The "little things" are then mentioned specifically, but the passage functions as an advertisement to the reader of what to expect. Simenon is good at atmosphere, but he will sometimes align it with the events and sometimes against them. There are little mechanical details, to be sure, like the man sitting at the buffet, who is "grand et lourd, large d'épaules. Il portait un épais pardessus noir à col de velours" (10). This tall and heavy, broad-shouldered man, in the thick black overcoat with the velvet collar, is of course Maigret, and these obvious marks will always stay with him throughout the books, though he will take off the overcoat in the warm weather.

My point is that Simenon mixes the flat, the obvious, and the mechanical with elements of fiction that are round, subtle, and creative, so that these books themselves deconstruct the paradoxy of Modernism. They are neither high nor low, but both. Hemingway insisted that he could divide them into good and bad, almost at a glance, and there is something to what he says, but there are good things in all of them, which is why he could read even the bad ones on a rainy day. And the fact that he liked Simenon and Kiki makes me fonder of Hemingway himself, who also wrote good and bad books, though not nearly so many of either as Simenon. I could go on illustrating aspects of this writer's achievement, but his incredible fecundity defeats all attempts to surround him with criticism. Still, he was clearly formulaic, and clearly creative. He reached an audience that ranged up and down and far and wide. And he added one imperishable character to the repertory of human culture, along with many sketches of others that have considerable merit. We students and teachers of Modernism should claim him, study him, teach him. And we should recognize that formulas and creativity do not make some neat binary opposition but are locked in the grip of an inevitable paradoxy.

Part III
Doxies

According to most dictionaries, a "doxy" is a floozy or prostitute, and in this part we shall look at figures who inhabited that part of modern culture or explored its bohemian borders. As we shall see at the end, however, the real doxy of Modernism was the middlebrow audience, along with the artists who wrote for it and the texts that were written for it. Like the paradoxes of Part II, the discussion of doxies in Part III is meant to provide an antidote to the toxic critical discourse of Modernism.

8

Model Artists in Paris: Hastings, Hamnett, and Kiki

*Elle prend ma place devant le chevalet, me demande de ne pas
bouger et tranquillement commence à dessiner mon portrait.
[She took my place in front of the easel, told me not to move,
and tranquilly began to draw my portrait.]*
—Foujita in Kiki's Souvenirs

*We women have to learn to write as we feel. We, of this age, do
not know how! The stupidity of the time has made of us
something between a precieuse and a school-boy. We give way,
break down, undress—and then you see what ruins we be!*
—Beatrice Hastings in The New Age

By "model artists" I mean models, women who posed for painters, but crossed over to the other side of the easel, either as painters or writers, and also painters or writers who moved in the other direction and posed for artists, allowing themselves to become objects for the gaze of others. My examples will be three women who produced some very interesting writing about the world in which Modernism flourished, and especially about the bohemian underside of that world. In the epigraphs for this chapter are hints of different stories, about women who crossed the artist/model line in different directions, with Kiki moving easily from model to artist, and Hastings describing a move in the other direction as a kind of breakdown. Kiki, who literally crossed over to the other side of Foujita's easel, also joined Hemingway on the writer's side of the desk. She was the most famous model of her day as well, familiar to us in many images, whether we always know her name or not. The other two subjects of this chapter also posed, famously, for major artists, though they did not make their living as models, as Kiki did. Nina Hamnett was herself an artist by training and accomplishment, who posed for friends frequently, and Beatrice Hastings was a writer, who posed mainly for Modigliani, when they were living together in Paris in 1914 and 1915. Kiki published her *Souvenirs* in 1929. Nina Hamnett wrote an engaging memoir of her early life, called *Laughing Torso*—the title referring to a sculpted torso of her by Henri Gaudier-Brzeska—published in 1932. And Beatrice Hastings wrote a series of Paris Letters for *The New Age* in 1914 and 1915 which ought to have been collected and published as a book, but never were.

Hastings, who was an important presence on the *New Age* editorial staff before the war, had an unhappy life that ended in suicide, never receiving the recognition as a writer that she sought. Hamnett had considerable success as a writer, with *Laughing Torso* and a sequel, but is still best known as a talented minor painter. She, too, came to a bizarre and possibly suicidal end. Kiki's book is as imperishable as the images of her by Man Ray, Brancusi, and others that appeared in it, though the translation that we have does not do her justice. The hard, rackety life of a model in Montparnasse took its toll on her as well. My main point, however, is that our picture of Modernism is incomplete if it does not include these women and others who do not fit into the High Modernist paradigm. I am thinking of writers like Katherine Mansfield and her cousin Elizabeth von Arnim, the author of *Elizabeth and Her German Garden* and *Enchanted April,* of Stevie Smith, whose poems and *Novel on Yellow Paper* reject high seriousness but have proved very durable, of Gwen Darwin Raverat, whose woodcuts and engravings, as well as her charming memoir, *Period Piece: A Cambridge Childhood,* have worn very well. Of all these, only Mansfield has approached canonization as a Modernist, and the shortness of her life and of her works has too frequently relegated her to minor status.

Elsewhere I have described the achievements of Vera Brittain, Rebecca West, and Anaïs Nin in writing what I call monstrous personal chronicles (*Crafty Reader,* 104–37), but here I am interested in a different phenomenon, the relationship between being a model, an object for the gaze of others, and being an artist or a writer, a speaking subject rather than an object. In the three cases under consideration here, modeling played a very different role. Kiki gloried in it and missed it when it stopped; Nina Hamnett did it casually, moving from one side of the easel to the other and on to the writing desk with effortless nonchalance; but modeling seems to have played a part in the destruction of Beatrice Hastings. What Hastings,

Hamnett, and Kiki have in common is that we have nude images of all of them, made by famous male Modernist artists. How many nude images of male Modernists do we have? Offhand, I can think of Egon Schiele's ruthless self-portraits and not much else. And male nude artists painted by others than themselves? Painted by female artists? I think this would be a very short list. Gaudier's torso of Nina Hamnett says it all. The body has no head but it expresses itself clearly enough to provide a title for Hamnett's first memoir: *Laughing Torso*. Hamnett accepted her status, went on modeling and painting, dancing nude at parties, refusing to be repressed. Kiki, too, was irrepressible, sold out all her works at a show of her art, illustrated her memoir herself, sang in the cabarets, and was, as Hemingway said, a queen in Montparnasse for a time. Hastings had higher aspirations, and tried to write in all the modes available: poems, stories, novels, plays, and journalistic articles, using at least sixteen pseudonyms. But despite her aspirations and her talent, she never succeeded as the others did. She had come to England from South Africa, been briefly married, and taken the name Hastings for reasons never explained. She became an editor and contributor to *The New Age*, a lover, apparently, of A. R. Orage, the editor of the magazine, and a close friend of Katherine Mansfield, who did a lot of writing for *The New Age* in those days. Hastings's name did not appear on her novel of 1911, *The Maid's Comedy*, though she put her name to—and published herself—a *Defence of Madame Blavatsky* before taking her own life in her flat in Sussex. But her most interesting writing, in my opinion, is in the letters she wrote from Paris for *The New Age*, just before the war and during its first year and a half. We can begin there.

Hastings arrived in Paris in May of 1914 and began writing letters about her experiences there for *The New Age* shortly after her arrival, using one of her many pseudonyms: Alice Morning. The tone and quality of her letters can be judged by this excerpt from the first, which she called "Impressions de Paris":

> I fear that I must have been a bore in one of my past lives, I am so often bothered by bores. An awful French one pinched me at dejeuner. . . . "It is not a bad country," the Bore was saying for the tenth time. "These are not bad people altogether, Messieurs les Anglais—but they are detractors of all the earth. Moi, I have made only a little proposition of an excursion to a lady not young, not beautiful, not rich—and there followed a great scandal." "Ah, monsieur," I said, "we run our Empire on just this tongue-waggery. We rule the earth, we govern our masses by permitting them to say what they please. Our nobles are not such fools as to snip off the tongues of the canaille. We oblige ourselves to suffer this that not in the least incommodes us and makes resigned to the others. I, for instance, recently left London a grand example. Last week, I was drunk only three times. On but one occasion did any slight violence occur. A knife and a broken glass found their billets, but, I assure you on my salvation, only skin-deep! Believe me, monsieur, the world made this four times drunk, and the total loss of an ear! I am *not* a violent woman, monsieur! I could not have done it even in my cups! I will never believe that the G.B.S. ear was more than pierced!" I sank into a glowering reverie over my wrongs. At least, I reflected, while he paid his bill— whatever my dear friends in London may be saying about me, they will scarcely beat this—which that bore will publish all over the Mont. (*NA* 15.3:68)

This is typical Hastings, mocking the English, the French, and herself with biting good humor, bending her syntax to parody

her own poor French. And her pseudoviolence, against someone
with George Bernard Shaw's initials, is grounded in a real dis-
like of Shaw and his works, and real feelings of violence, which
she mainly directed against herself. This is lively, accomplished
prose, as good as any journalism being written at that time. I
am sorely tempted to quote from these letters extensively but
will confine myself to a few choice passages. My main point,
however, is that Hastings deserves better than to be a footnote
to Modigliani's self-destructive life, which is all she seems to be
at present. Consider, for example, this report on her first ball:

> It is to-morrow dawn, and I have not been to the Lux-
> embourg, but to an artists' bal. You can't walk home at
> dawn in Paris, even two hundred yards. The streets are all
> being washed. Much laughter, much applause for your
> frock if it is chic, three hundred people inside and outside
> the Rotonde, very much alive! Models arrayed in a flame
> or a half-moon dancing down the boulevarde to the bal,
> and absolutely unmolested, an Indian in full war-paint,
> Spaniards, Chinese, Bacchus, everybody you can think of!
> No old fat men, no painted women; all young, agreeable,
> and spirited. I set out, upon my innocent, prejudiced soul,
> half expecting to have my deposition taken somewhere
> about the small hours! Well, at five o'clock, the leisurely,
> roomy "Pardou's" were as calculable as ever. Those people
> understand amusement. They stood in circles to applaud
> fine dancers; they crowded to the platform, absolutely
> silent, to hear the singers; very few drank very much; and
> they smoked so as not to blind your eyes. They agacéd
> from start to finish, but not to set your teeth on edge—
> nothing maudlin, no sleepy couples; all quick and fire-
> worky, impressionist. (15.4:91)

She gives us "impressions" indeed. What she does not give us is any clear sense of her own life. Hamnett and Kiki, as we shall see, tell us about their backgrounds and their daily lives. Hastings is more reticent. Hamnett has been called a "Queen of Bohemia" and Kiki "as close as people get nowadays to being a Queen," but Hastings never really became a part of the bohemian life around her, let alone a ruler of even a province in Bohemia. Her Paris letters are valuable, I believe, because they add to our view of that world, which was at the center of Modernism, and perhaps especially because they add the perspective of someone who was always an outsider even when she was at or near the center of it. But there is much Hastings might have told us which she never thought of doing. Nina Hamnett, who cannot write nearly as well as Hastings, drops as many famous names as we find in *The Autobiography of Alice B. Toklas* and had the honor of being sued by Aleister Crowley for mentioning him as a practitioner of black magic—which he certainly was. In all her Paris columns, Hastings mentions Modigliani by name only three times. He first appears, however, without being named, in her Impression of June 4, 1914, where Hastings notes that a "fair and pure English bourgeoise came with a bodyguard to see life" in the Rotonde, and "was satisfied when she saw me wake up from a sulk to be very glad with the bad garçon of a sculptor. He has mislaid the last thread of that nutty rig he had recently, and is entirely back in cap, scarf, and corduroy. Rose-Bud was quite shook on the pale and ravishing villain" (15.5:115). Hastings does not quite tell us that "Rose-Bud" was not the only one who found this bad boy of a sculptor "pale and ravishing," but there is no doubt that she herself joined that far from exclusive club. She first mentions him by name a month later, discussing her reaction to some works of the Douanier Rousseau she had seen at an exhibition. She can't understand why people like Walter Sickert and Modigliani praise Rousseau.

O bother Rousseau! But it is difficult to drop him for the moment. What beats me is when, for instance an unsentimental artist like Modigliani says, Oui, tres joli, about him. One of Modigliani's stone heads was on a table below the painting of Picasso, and the contrast between the true thing and the true-to-life thing nearly split me. I would like to buy one of those heads, but I'm sure they cost pounds to make, and the Italian is liable to give you anything you look interested in. No wonder he is the spoiled child of the quarter, enfant sometimes-terrible but always forgiven—half Paris is in morally illegal possession of his designs. "Nothing's lost!" he says, and bang goes another drawing for twopence or nothing, while he dreams off to some cafe to borrow a franc for some more paper! It's all very New Agey, and, like us, he will have, as an art-dealer said to me, "a very good remember." They say here that he will do no more of these questionless, immobile heads, as his designs begin to set the immobile amidst the mobile. He is a very beautiful person to look at, when he is shaven, about twenty-eight, I should think, always either laughing or quarrelling à la Rotonde, which is a furious tongue-duel umpired by a shrug that never forgets the coffee. If he only hadn't said thingamy was tres joli, I would have left off without remarking that he horrifies some English friends of mine whose flat overlooks his studio by tubbing at two hour intervals in the garden, and occasionally lighting all up after midnight apparently as an aid to sculpturing Babel. (15.10:235–36)

Perhaps the most important thing in this early portrait of
Modigliani is the information that his "designs"—that is, his
drawings and paintings—are being noticed to the extent that
people are saying he will abandon sculpture to concentrate on
them. For that, of course, is just what he did, setting, as Hastings observed, "the immobile amidst the mobile." He made the
transition from sculpture to painting as his major medium
during the time when he and Hastings were together, and she
sat for a number of his paintings of that period. It is typical of
her that, because he disagreed with her view of Rousseau, she
gossiped about his taking baths in the garden and shocking her
English friends. She liked to shock people herself, but she remained a bit shocked by the bohemian world of Montparnasse
herself, right to the end.

At this time she made a brief trip back to England, re-
cording Modigliani's woefulness at her departure in her next
Impression de Paris:

Modigliani, by the way, was very much so when I was
coming away. He arrested the taxi as it was crossing the
Boulevard Montparnasse and implored to be allowed to
ride with me—it was so chic, like being his rich uncle
who was dead of the gout! But I didn't know what to do
with him on the station when he fainted loudly against
the grubby side of the carriage and all the English stared
at me. I had to keep calm because, if I get cross, I can't remember my French. I reflected how other people had
played the stick, how I once pretended to be mad when
two females cackled all through a tunnel, how a female
friend and I grimaced everybody out of a carriage which
was wanted all to oneself from Brighton to London, how

I held Valerie's head while she implored me to put her hat
on because these policemen "always connected fair hair
with dissolution," how Shakespeare affronted the passersby
at Stratford, how Krishna astonished the bourgeoisie of
his time by puffing out his cheeks and smacking them
hard—but all this while the English were staring at me
and Modigliani was gasping, "Oh, Madame, don't go!" I
said, "Modigliani, someone says you've been three years
fiddling about with one type of head, and you'll be another three on the new design." He came round. "Cretin!"
he glared at me as though I had said it. "Mais, ma-a-a-is,
ma petite, he is right! I might have grown asparagus in the
time." (15.11:259)

She wants to join the great company of shockers, which includes Shakespeare, Krishna, and Modigliani, and she recounts
a story of herself and a friend assuming that role, but she
brings Modigliani to order by playing the critic. In the process,
she gives us a valuable sketch of him pretending to faint with
sorrow at her departure and then admitting that the critic who
said he worked too slowly was right.

Her last mention of Modigliani is a remark about a
sculptured head by him that she owned:

For example, I possess a stone head by Modigliani which
I would not part with for a hundred pounds even at this
crisis: and I routed out this head from a corner sacred to
the rubbish of centuries, and was called stupid for my
pains in taking it away. Nothing human, save the mean,
is missing from the stone. It has a fearful chip above the
right eye, but it can stand a few chips. I am told that it
was never finished, that it never will be finished, that it

is not worth finishing. There is nothing that matters to finish! The whole head equally smiles in contemplation of knowledge, of madness, of grace and sensibility, of stupidity, of sensuality, of illusions and disillusions—all locked away as matter of perpetual meditation. It is as readable as Ecclesiastes and more consoling, for there is no lugubrious looking back in this effulgent, unforbidding smile of intelligent equilibrium. What avail for the artist to denounce such a work? One replies, that one can live by it as by great literature. I will never part with it unless to a poet; he will find what I find and the unfortunate artist will have no choice as to his immortality. (16.15:401)

She was right about Modigliani's durability, but her own mortality and fragility were too much in evidence. Modigliani made a pencil sketch of her at some point toward the end of their relationship. It is a nude image (Fig. 20), in which she is holding a cloth that does not conceal anything from the viewer. Her eyes are downcast and she looks infinitely sad. We should compare this to Gaudier's sculpted torso of Nina Hamnett (Fig. 21), which is a body without a head, but Hamnett herself saw that torso as expressing itself through laughter. She and Kiki, as we shall see, responded differently to the gazes of artists; both of them liked to be looked at. Hastings did not, and her own bitter introspective gaze gives her writing a depth that should command our attention even now. Modigliani's drawing links Hastings to Hamnett and Kiki, but this torso is not laughing. Kiki laughed a lot, and even made a joking sketch of herself posing (Fig. 22).

Hastings wrote ten Impressions de Paris, all appearing in the Pastiche section of *The New Age*. The last one, all too brief, appeared on July 30, 1914. Here it is, in its entirety:

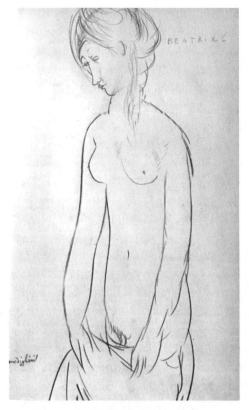

Fig. 20. Amadeo Modigliani, *Beatrice*
(Claude Roy, *Modigliani* [New York: Rizzoli,
1985], 34, Photo Giraudon, Paris)

It is all over. I'm finished. I've been to the Louvre. I only
meant to pretend to go. I never dreamed that the door
would be open. No door has ever before been open when
I have turned up. But it was one of the Days. Farewell,
reader! I bought a guide—within half an hour I had
bought a guide. It cost a franc, or five francs—I don't
know. I can only vow to have been surprised at its cheap-

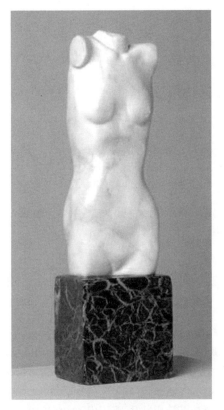

Fig. 21. Henri Gaudier-Brzeska, *Torso*
(©Tate, London 2005)

ness. Heaven help me! For next day I went back. To-day, I
mean. It's no use shuffling matters. I shall go again to-
morrow. But no more impressions. (15.13:307)

It makes a nice swan song, with the Old Masters erasing all the
Impressionists, including the author herself. But history had
other ideas. The day after her last Impression appeared, the
charismatic Socialist leader of France, Jean Jaurés, who had

Fig. 22. Kiki (Alice Prin), *Je Pose* (*Souvenirs*
[Paris: Henri Broca, 1929], opposite 160)

been in Brussels, trying to persuade workers to go on strike, returned to Paris, only to be assassinated by a royalist. Three days
later Germany declared war on France, and two weeks later
Alice Morning's first in a new Impressions of Paris series appeared in *The New Age*, picking up from her previous farewell.
Here is an excerpt that gives us a vivid picture of the city at the
start of the war:

> I begin to fill my diary again. All is war now and art is
> under worse than lock and key. I shall stay if the Prefect
> of Police is persuadable, though there is no more salt to
> be had in my district. I have some sardines, some bad rice,
> and sixteen eggs against the siege. There was an intense
> moment in Paris after Jaurés was slaughtered. The politi-

cians acquired a style in their anxiety. The note issued to
the workmen was a clean document, simple, truthful. We
all wondered what would happen on Saturday when the
gendarmes were about, some carrying revolvers in the
hand. But it was too clear how much the Government re-
sented the assassination at such an hour for the people to
quarrel about it. Out in the streets last night I heard cries
against La Caillaux, but nothing about Jaurés. The gendarmes, so far, have nothing to do here but arrest any
drunken canaille, and laugh and applaud the processions
manifesting in favour of the war. They broke up the anti-
war meeting with no trouble, simply running the men off
the spot, beating a few. You wouldn't wonder if you could
see the frenzied faces laughing for war. The men are
bright as birds, though most of the women are crying.
I thought all the Germans were gone, but I saw two
within a few streets of each other being battered for saying Vive Allemagne! Courageous, too courageous! "It is
not the moment for that!" as a gendarme remarked to
me. (15.15:350)

"La Caillaux" is the wife of the government official Joseph
Caillaux, who shot and killed the editor of *Le Figaro* for publishing letters between her and her husband, written a dozen
years earlier, while she was still married to another man. She
was tried and acquitted, with the verdict being handed down
on July 28. But Hastings is not interested in her. The "frenzied
faces laughing for war" and "the men . . . bright as birds,
though most of the women are crying"—these "impressions"
tell us all we need to know about how it felt to be in Paris at the
start of this terrible conflict. And all we need to know about
the quality of Hastings as a writer and an observer.

She remained at her post, occasionally offering insights like this one: "The bombs fell again yesterday, wounding a man, a woman, and a little child of seven years. There is something sneakish in this form of warfare, but then a good deal of sneakery seems to distinguish modern warfare. The ideal seems to be to strike your enemy from a safe hole!" (15.25:599). How right she was! And the little details didn't escape her, either: "I have seen English and American women frantically trying to seem Parisian on the boulevards (it is easy enough in London or New York) and being out-Parisianed by any little work-girl with the local figure skin and eyes" (16.26:693). As the year 1915 went on, and the war with it, Hastings gradually retreated from impressions of the life around her. She took refuge in literary criticism, writing about French authors that the English might not know, and becoming a much less interesting writer in the process. Her personal life, too, was disintegrating, though we know very little about the details of this. A poignant comment from an Impression of October 1915 is painfully revealing: "We women have to learn to write as we feel. We, of this age, do not know how! The stupidity of the time has made of us something between a precieuse and a school-boy. We give way, break down, undress—and then you see what ruins we be!" (17.24:568). She is certainly talking about herself, here, and she is ruthless—as ruthless as Egon Schiele, Vanessa Bell, or Gwen Raverat in a visual self-portrait. She has given way, broken down, undressed, for Modigliani and Raymond Radiguet, among others, and been revealed—to herself at least—as something between a precieuse and a school-boy, to her infinite regret. Then, in late November 1915, she returned to observation of Paris, but this time, what she reported was an allegory for her own situation. Here is her final Impression of Paris, in its entirety:

A furious cow got loose, yesterday morning, at a quarter past ten from a herd which was being led, by Mr. Adolphe Moiron, from the station of Vaugirard towards the slaughter-house of this quarter, and she ran at a mad pace along the avenues of Chatillon and the Maine.

In front of number ten of the first-mentioned road, she flung herself against a vehicle belonging to Mr. Goudert, potato merchant of Malakoff, wounding the horse on the shoulder. Then the enraged animal made a hole with her horn in the left leg of a horse harnessed to a spring-van belonging to Mr. Godefroy, carrier, of Montrouge. Continuing her course, she charged, with head down, trams and passers-by who tried to bar her route.

A wagoner, Mr. Georges Girod, 25, Rue Croulebarbe, was struck in the chest. The policeman, Mathurin Cohallan, parried with the aid of his bicycle an attempted charge at his head and received no more than a slight wound in his left hand.

Finally, at about number ninety-five of the Avenue du Maine, the sergeant Bourgoin succeeded, not without trouble, in mastering the frantic cow by seizing her horns. He conducted her back to the herd. (18.4:84)

This reads like an item from a newspaper, just translated by the weary foreign correspondent. But clearly, it is she who is the frantic cow, now being conducted back to the herd, leaving some wounded in her train, to be sure, though no one more deeply damaged than herself. The last words on this shall be hers: "We give way, break down, undress—and then you see what ruins we be!" Hastings continued to write articles for the journal for a while, though she never resumed her personal relationship with the editor, A. R. Orage, breaking with him and

with the magazine before his departure in 1922. She returned
to France for a few more sporadic notes, the last of them appearing in 1920. In it we find the following terrifying confes-
sion, uttered casually, almost comically: "I can't help coming in
with the reflection that I have never succeeded in being a well-
informed person. Life, the great affair, is very difficult to get
any information about" (26.19:302). Hastings's death in 1943
was apparently a suicide: the last, large, self-destructive act of
a life made up of small ones. She lives for us in her writings and
in the images of her recorded by Modigliani. The names she
wrote under include the following: Alice Morning, A.M.A.,
E.H., B.L.H., Beatrice Tina, Cynicus, Robert a Field, T.K.L., D.
Triformis, Edward Stafford, S. Robert West, V.M., G. Whiz, J.
Wilson, and T.W. There may be others. In a poem she called
herself a "Lost Bacchante," which seems fair enough. In the
gas-filled apartment in which her body lay, the remains of her
pet mouse were found along with her own.

Nina Hamnett undressed all over the place, but she never
broke down until the end of her life. Her phenomenal irre-
pressibility is the most important feature of her memoir, and
it compensates for considerable slackness—in the writing as
well as in the life. *Laughing Torso: Reminiscences of Nina Hamnett* is still very much alive, and it needs to be read alongside
the work of the other two writers I am discussing here because
all three of them offer us glimpses of the bohemian core of
Modernism, and, in particular, perspectives on the roles open
to women in that dark center of Modernist art. Hamnett begins with herself in another dark center, the womb, with her
mother being frightened by a man with "dark, hypnotic eyes"
who stared at her from a distance—offering this as a possible
explanation for her own rackety, bohemian life. She kept a
diary most of her life and based her reminiscences on that,

though, presumably, she had not yet begun it when the dark stranger entered her life. About her actual birth, she says, "Everybody was furious, especially my Father, who still is. As soon as I became conscious of anything I was furious too, at having been born a girl: I have since discovered that it has certain advantages" (1). She never elaborates on the advantages, but the implication is that having a female body could be useful, if you were the one who used it. She and Kiki both flaunted their bodies while never allowing themselves to be reduced to them. Beatrice Hastings, as we have seen, just could not manage that particular trick. She was a woman who hated suffragists and wanted to be respected and protected. There was a strong Victorian streak in her makeup, and, though she is said to have put notches on her bedpost for the men who shared that bed, she never really adapted to the bohemian life as the other two women we are considering actually did.

Nina Hamnett discovered her own body when she was sixteen—and she liked what she saw: "I drew from the nude at the Art School, but I had never dared to look at myself in the mirror, for my Grandmother had always insisted that one dressed and undressed under one's nightdress using it as a kind of tent. One day, feeling very bold, I took off all my clothes and gazed in the looking-glass. I was delighted. I was much superior to anything I had seen in the life class and I got a book and began to draw" (19). Hamnett loved the human body. She once borrowed some bones from an anatomy student, keeping the chain of vertebrae on a string hung over the end of her bed and putting the skull on her night table. She soon left the Royal Academy Schools and moved to the less stodgy London School of Art. At about this time she discovered Arthur Ransome's book *Bohemia in London,* and, like Alice going through the looking-glass, she entered the world of that book: "I walked into a friend's room and a man in knickerbockers, with a very large moustache, was there. He produced a flute from his pocket and I danced. We were later introduced. This was Ransome. I went to his flat one day; as he opened the door there was an awful smell of shag and beer" (23). On the other side of that door, in addition to shag and beer, lay the whole world of artistic bohemia in London and Paris, which Hamnett documented better than anyone, with the possible exception of Kiki.

In 1911 Hamnett reached the ripe age of twenty-one. At that point, as she says, "I now began to feel that having finished with Art Schools I must leave the student stage and become an artist. This I realized was a difficult thing to do as many students at the Art School—and they were of all ages—seemed to have remained students all their lives" (35). A shrewd observation, which applies to many other fields as well. As we have seen, Beatrice Hastings felt that she and other women were caught in that net, positioned as "something between a precieuse and a school-boy." But Hamnett did indeed leave school, and, in the next two years in London, she met Carrington, Mark Gertler, Walter Sickert, Lucien Pissaro, Wyndham Lewis, T. E. Hulme, Jacob Epstein, and Henri Gaudier-Brzeska, who

> one day came to my room and said, "I am very poor and I want to do a torso, will you sit for me?" I said, "I don't know, perhaps I look awful with nothing on," and he said, "Don't worry." I went one day to his studio in the Fulham Road and took off all my clothes. I turned round slowly and he did drawings of me. When he had finished he said, "Now it is your turn to work." He took off all his clothes and made me draw and I had to. I did three drawings and he said, "Now we will have some tea." From the drawings he did two torsos. (39)

At that time Gaudier told Hamnett that the "elderly woman" living with him was his sister. Later he admitted that she was not his sister but his mistress, and Hamnett "choked down some sobs." She reports that Ezra Pound bought a block of marble and told Gaudier to sculpt him, and to "make me look like a sexual organ." Gaudier "chipped and chipped and it was magnificent and it has been offered to and refused by many museums" (41). The sculptor and Hamnett went to weekly meetings of an anarchist group. "I did not know much about anarchy," she wrote, "but I thought that any kind of revolt against anything was good" (42). Her perspective on her life is naive and ruthless at the same time, which is what makes these pages live, despite their consisting of nothing but anecdotes. And the attitude she describes in her youthful self is still alive and well, recurring every decade or so.

Needing money, Hamnett sought work at Roger Fry's Omega Workshops. Fry hired her and she started learning "how to do Batiks" (42). Then she got Gaudier some work there as well. It seems surprising to us, perhaps, in this work of casual sexuality, but, when she turned twenty-two, Hamnett "was almost completely ignorant" about sex: "I went to an elderly woman in Chelsea and asked her what happened. She gave me such a terrifying description that when the moment arrived for the presentation of my virginity I required more courage than a soldier has when 'Going over the top'" (44). But she met a "beautiful creature" and selected him for the task. "I did not think much of it," she says, "but the next morning I had a sense of personal freedom and that something important had been accomplished" (44).

It turned out that the rooms in which she went over the top had been occupied by Verlaine and Rimbaud on their visit to London. "One day I said to Walter Sickert, 'Do you think that they will put up a blue plaque on the house for me or will they put up one for Verlaine and Rimbaud?' and Walter said, 'My dear, they will put up one on the front for you and one on the back for them'" (44–45). Witty fellow, Sickert, and it's hard to think of Jack the Ripper making a joke like that. At about that time, Hamnett made her first visit to Paris. Through Epstein and his wife she met Brancusi. Epstein's monument to Oscar Wilde had just been put up in the Père Lachaise cemetery. The French found it indecent and covered it with a tarpaulin, "so every afternoon Epstein, his wife, Brancusi, a Spanish painter, his wife and I, would go off to Père Lachaise and snatch the tarpaulin off" (45). The police put an end to this little stunt, but it is typical of Hamnett to have been there, revolting.

Back in London, Hamnett decided that she wanted more of Paris and was delighted to accept money from a friend to return there. Eating dinner alone in a little restaurant recommended by Epstein, run by a woman who had been a great beauty and a model for Whistler, she had the following encounter:

Suddenly the door opened and in came a man with a roll of newspaper under his arm. He wore a black hat and a corduroy suit. He had curly black hair and brown eyes and was very good looking. He came straight up to me and said, pointing to his chest, "*Je suis Modigliani, Juif, Jew,*" unrolled his newspaper, and produced some drawings. He said, "*Cinq Francs.*" They were very curious and interesting, long heads with pupil-less eyes. I thought them very beautiful. Some were in red and blue chalk. I gave him five francs and chose one of a head in pencil. He sat down and we tried to understand each other and I said that I knew Epstein and we got on very well, although I could not understand much of what he said.

He used to drink a great deal of wine, and absinthe when he could afford it. Picasso and the really good artists thought him very talented and bought his works, but the majority of people in the Quarter thought of him only as a perfect nuisance and told me that I was wasting my money. (48–49)

Hamnett met everybody. She had an introduction to Marie Wassilieff, who ran an academy where Fernand Léger taught. She danced nude in Van Dongen's studio, where Arthur Craven used to spar in a boxing ring in one corner, and she met Zadkine there. When Wyndham Lewis came to Paris he walked down the Boulevard Montparnasse with her, speaking French and tutoyer-ing her, which posed a problem for her shaky grammar, since she had not used the intimate form before. "I did not paint Cubist pictures," she wrote, "though Léger had given me two lessons" (60). She remained a Neo-Realist to the end, but that did not prevent her from admiring the work of the Geometrists—nor did it prevent them from praising her work. That arch-Neo-Realist, Augustus John, had bought two of Modigliani's sculptures and had them in his Chelsea house—bought them before Hamnett had known either one of them.

It was Hamnett who introduced Beatrice Hastings to Modigliani: "One day Beatrice Hastings came to Paris. She had been a great friend of Katherine Mansfield's and was a very talented writer. She edited *The New Age* with Orage. It was about the most interesting and well-written paper in London before the War. She had an introduction to me. She was very amusing. I introduced her to Modigliani and we all spent the evening together at the Rotonde. They drank absinthe, as Beatrice had some money" (69). Hamnett kept on drifting, even after the war started, spending time in both London and Paris, meeting new people in London, like Augustus John, Richard Aldington, the Stracheys, the Sitwells, Aldous Huxley, and Roy Campbell, spending time with Walter Sickert and teaching at his art school. She also met Diaghilev, Massine, and Lydia Lopokova of the Russian Ballet. But she longed to get back to Paris, even after Modigliani died in 1920.

Returning there she called on Wassilieff, who asked how her figure looked, so she took off her clothes. Wassilieff said, "*Oui, la même chose*" (121), and Hamnett got dressed again, noting that the artist was satisfied "that I had not dropped to pieces." My point is simply that she was at home in Bohemia in ways that Hastings never could be, for whom the act of getting undressed amounted to breaking down, revealing oneself as ruined. This is very much the same world, being seen by two women who knew each other and lived in the same orbit, but it does not look the same. Among other things, Hastings held on to a Modernist reverence for art itself, as we can see in her thoughts about the stone head she got from Modigliani: "What avail for the artist to denounce such a work? One replies, that one can live by it as by great literature. I will never part with it unless to a poet; he will find what I find and the unfortunate artist will have no choice as to his immortality." Hamnett liked to paint and draw and she enjoyed the work of her fellow artists—but she doesn't go into raptures about it. To her it is as natural as breathing—or taking off your clothes when someone asks how you are looking. We need both of these perspectives in order to understand this world, and we need to know how permeable were all the divisions that critics and the makers of manifestos sought to impose on that world. Hastings and Hamnett can help us learn that important lesson. Hamnett, like many other artists, enjoyed the work of the

Douanier Rousseau, though, as we have seen, Hastings hated it. But Hamnett also went to Brancusi's studio after the war and saw there "a bronze bird that was very beautiful. It was highly polished and shone in the corner of the studio" (123). No raptures, just an act of attention. That bird gets its raptures now in the Museum of Modern Art in New York.

Hamnett fell in love with a young Polish artist in Paris and gave him her money, which he used it to run off with a friend of hers. Her reaction? "One has to pay for all one's stupidities, and they are very expensive, so perhaps one day I will learn some sense" (127–28). And we want to say, with St. Augustine, "but not yet, please!" Her stupidities are too interesting. When the Pole returned and was waiting for Hamnett's friend to come back and marry him, he offered to live with her platonically for three months until her friend arrived to claim him. She took him to lunch, and "I told him in French what I thought of him. I had a fine vocabulary, which I had learnt from Modigliani, and I should think that if anyone who had not been such a complete monster had been spoken to in the way that I did to him, I should have been strangled. After lunch I paid the bill and gave him ten francs" (129). So Modigliani lived on in her vocabulary—a different kind of immortality from that envisioned by Hastings. This chronicle continues for another decade, extending to the south of France, where she spent some time with Darius Milhaud and Rudolph Valentino, among others, but I will not follow Nina Hamnett through the rest of her adventures, which end with her wondering what the future had in store for her—which was, of course, more of the same.

The cast changes, but the experiences are similar, and she never learns too much sense. Her sequel, *Is She a Lady?* (1955), continues in the same vein, but her end, in 1956, was as bizarre as that of Hastings. Like Virginia Woolf's Septimus Smith, Hamnett fell from a window of her flat in Paddington and was impaled on the railing below. She died a few days later in the hospital. Tougher than Hastings, in the end she too succumbed to the bohemian lifestyle of Modernism. She lived it, she reported on it for the rest of us, but she paid a price for those adventures. Reviewing *Laughing Torso* when it first came out, Rebecca West compared Hamnett to Agatha Runcible in Evelyn Waugh's *Vile Bodies*, but the person she really needs to be compared with is Alice Prin, a young lady from Burgundy, who took Paris by storm during this same period.

Alice Prin was born in Burgundy in 1901, came to Paris to live with her mother when she was twelve, and at the age of fifteen started posing for artists to make a little money. In a few years she had met and posed for many of the best painters and sculptors working in Paris. But she was not a passive model. This is the way the artist Leonard Tsuguharu Foujita described her first posing session with him:

Quand elle a quitté son manteau, elle était absolument nue. . . . Elle prend ma place devant le chevalet, me demande de ne pas bouger et tranquillement commence à dessiner mon portrait. . . . Elle m'a demandé l'argent de sa pose et triomphalement est partie, son croquis sous le bras. Trois minutes après, au café du Dôme, un riche collectionneur américain lui avait acheté un prix fou ce croquis. (*Souvenirs*, 10)

When she took off her coat, she was absolutely naked. . . . She took my place in front of the easel, told me not to move, and calmly began to draw my portrait. . . . She asked me for money for posing and left triumphantly,

carrying her sketch with her. Three minutes later at
the Café du Dôme a rich American collector bought this
drawing for a crazy price.

Kiki was not the first model who was also a painter, but her
way of displacing the artist from his own easel puts her in a
very special class, and the drawing of Foujita by her in the *Souvenirs* is excellent. Kiki drew and painted a lot, and when she
had a show, her work sold in a way to make the "real" artists
envious. She was untrained, of course, and remained a "primitive" in all her work, but she was a primitive at a time when the
Douanier Rousseau was admired by many artists, and painters
like Matisse were exploring techniques derived from African
and Oceanic art. Kiki's visual art can sometimes remind the
viewer of Matisse's, but she is naturally primitive rather than
self-consciously so.

But Kiki not only drew and painted. She also wrote. In
1929, after much persuasion, she produced a series of short autobiographical sketches that traced her life from its Burgun-
dian beginnings to its Montparnassian present. Published as
Souvenirs (a word best translated, perhaps, as "recollections")
and including a preface by Foujita as well as pictures of her and
by her, the book caused a small sensation. The following year
an English translation—with some additions by Kiki and, in
place of Foujita's original statement, new introductory material by Ernest Hemingway, Samuel Putnam (the translator),
and Edward Titus (the publisher)—was published in Paris,
causing yet another stir, though censorship problems prevented an American edition. The result, in English, is a short,
jolly book, in which we hear a voice that is usually silenced—
and therein lies much of this text's importance for those interested in modern culture. Can the sexual subaltern speak? Kiki's

Souvenirs may be as close as we will ever come to hearing this voice as it existed in the twenties. And from it we may learn many things, including the startling fact that, after a few conventional pages on her first twelve years, she speaks of the past in the present tense. Chapter 2, for instance (each chapter is a few tiny pages long), begins with the following paragraph: "J'ai douze ans" (81; I am twelve).

When this particular sexual subaltern writes, she writes as if she were speaking. Her style is both lively and laconic. She uses the present tense not because she lacks grammar—she is perfectly capable of the past when she needs it, as in the following passage from chapter 3: "My mother had noticed that I had a big mark the color of eggplant on my neck. I spit on my handkerchief, but it wouldn't go away. I was wondering what it could be, when I got such a box on the ear that it knocked me silly. . . . I hadn't thought that kisses left marks, too; I'll know better after this" (*Memoirs*, 56; this passage is not in the French original). Between the past and future tenses in this passage is the one in which Kiki lives and writes. She is rethinking her life in the historical present tense, used by Virgil and others for rhetorical effect. For Kiki it is just her way of telling stories. She is comfortable in the present. It is tempting to suggest that her way of living in the present was part of the effect she had on those around her, which was extraordinary. But let us return to the question of her writing.

Most Americans read Kiki in translation, which poses certain problems—and not just for us. Ernest Hemingway, in his introduction, indicated that he had not seen the translation but was convinced that it would be a failure. His final paragraph summed up a number of things:

> This is the only book I have ever written an introduction for and, God help me, the only one I ever will. It is a crime

to translate it. If it shouldn't be any good in English, and reading it just now again and seeing how it goes, I know it is going to be a bad job for whoever translates it, please read it in the original. It is written by a woman who, so far as I know, never had a Room of Her Own, but I think part of it will remind you, and some of it will bear comparison with, another book with a woman's name written by Daniel Defoe. If you ever tire of books written by present day lady writers of all sexes, you have a book here written by a woman who was never a lady at any time. For about ten years she was about as close as people get nowadays to being a Queen but that, of course, is very different from being a lady. (*Memoirs*, 14)

In addition to the difficulties involved in translating Kiki, Hemingway drew our attention to her status. She was definitely not a "lady" and she never had a "Room of Her Own." The allusion to Virginia Woolf's discussion (1929) of what a woman needs to write was quite deliberate on Hemingway's part. He meant to remind us that we are not hearing the voice of a cultivated bourgeoise, here, but that of a woman who knows and says things that her privileged counterpart could neither know nor say.

There are also things that Kiki does not say. Her reticences are as much a part of her cultural construction as her utterances. In chapter 12, one of those Hemingway recommended particularly, she recounts bits of her grandmother's life, including an adventure with an American soldier. Here it is in Putnam's translation:

One day, when she had been a long way from home and was coming back, she caught sight of a woman who was running away for dear life, and behind a tree, she saw a

young American soldier making a bed of leaves on the
ground. She came up close to find out what he was up to,
when the American came over to her with some money in
his hand. He finally made her understand that, in spite of
her age, he'd like . . . My grandmother understood at last,
and had such a scare that she forgot all about her cartload
of wood and began running as hard as she could tear
across a field of beets, which is not exactly an easy thing
to do.

> "That young brat," she would say, "wanted to rape me
> right there in the woods." (*Memoirs*, 109–10)

The ellipsis in the passage is Kiki's. She doesn't need to tell us
what the soldier would like, and she has a certain delicacy that
goes with her frankness. The last sentence, however, betrays
the translator's inability to solve his problems. It was not
"rape" that was in question, but a commercial transaction. In
the French text Kiki writes, "'Ce sagouin-là,' disait-elle, 'il
voulait me souiller dans les bois'" (*Souvenirs*, 121). Which
translates literally as "'That prick,' said she, 'he wanted to dirty
me in the woods.'" *Sagouin* is a word that means pig, slob, bas-
tard, and prick, with connotations of both dirtiness and sex—
connotations that are reinforced by *souiller*, which means to
dirty, soil, or sully. In the most recent edition of Kiki's text
there are notes, some of which correct Putnam's translation,
but not in this case. Putnam's has become the English version
of record, but there is a case for a completely new translation
that might come closer to giving us Kiki's own voice in English.

The case I am making at the moment, however, is for
Kiki's *Souvenirs* as an important text for the study of modern
culture, and, in particular, the artistic life as enacted in Montparnasse in the twenties. The chapter titles alone tell part of

the story. There are individual chapters called "Epoque Sou-
tine," "Mon entrée dans les milieux artistiques," "En plain
Montparnasse," "1918," "Kisling," "1922 Foujita," "Man Ray,"
and "Le Jockey," as well as many others that recount aspects of
Montparnasse life during its high period. There is also a fascinating episode in the south of France. Chapter 24 begins, "Je
suis arrivée à Villefranche" (150; I have come to Villefranche).
She writes about the women from Marseilles and Nice—and
once again she is betrayed by her translator. Among the women
who follow the sailors in this part of the world are some prostitutes: "Ce sont des putains très gentilles, qui ont de bonnes
manières, de l'élegance et qui sont fort sentimentales" (153;
There are some very nice whores, who have good manners, el-
egance, and are very sentimental). Putnam translates this sentence as follows: "There are some nice whores among them,
with good manners, even elegant, you might say, but a bit
sloppy" (152). Kiki thinks the hookers are nice, elegant, and
fond of their sailors. Putnam knows that whores can't really be
elegant, and he substitutes "sloppy," with its connotations of
dirt, for "sentimental," which is purely emotional. And he in-
troduces his own expression "you might say" and the telling
conjunction "but" to distort Kiki's perspective and bring it
closer to his own. All the women, including the whores, line
the wharf when their sailor lovers leave on their ship. Kiki
finds that sweet. Then, her friend Treize arrives with the artist
Per Krogh:

> Treize and Per Krogh have just arrived. They are crazy
> about the good-looking sailors. We've adopted five or six
> of 'em, and we're together all the time.
>   Per Krogh never gets tired of sketching sailors. For
> recreation, he gives me a few pinches in the rump. That

tickles Treize, but it leaves me cold. I've got a behind that's
proof against anything. (*Memoirs*, 152)

Once again, we must stop and look at the French text, the last
sentences of which read: "[Per Krogh], pour se délasser, me
donne des fessées aidé de Treize. Ça me laisse froid: j'ai un der-
rière à toute épreuve" (153). In this version Krogh gives Kiki
some *fessées* (spanks), helped by Treize, who is not a spectator
but a participant. There is a casual bisexuality here that is part
of the general ambiance, though Kiki is not moved.

What does indeed move her, but in a different way, is
being called a whore herself. When the manager of an English
bar tells her "No whores allowed here!" ("Pas de putain ici!"
154), she does not hesitate: "I make one leap for him and shove
a pile of saucers in his face" (*Memoirs*, 153). The line between
prostitution and the level of sexual activity just above it is crucial for women in Kiki's world. It is a line that appears, with all
its threatening aspects, in much of the writing of Jean Rhys, for
instance, and in stories such as Katherine Mansfield's "Je ne
parle pas français." It is a line, once crossed, that is difficult to
recross in the other direction. Jean Rhys, like many of her characters, sometimes lived very close to the line, which embodies
all the sexism and exploitation of women that are near the center of Modernist art and life. Part of Kiki's importance, and the
importance of her book, may be found in the way she lived as
close to that line as possible without ever being pushed over it.
Her response, it should be noted, is not to weep or complain
but to fight. Yet no one would accuse her of a lack of feminin-
ity. Fighting is not a gendered response here, but a response of
class, in that she comes from a class in which women were not
considered fragile. Because she is threatened in her respect-

ability as a working girl—but not *that* kind of working girl—
she goes on the attack.

These are the sorts of issues that come up when one reads
Kiki along with the texts of women brought up more gently,
like Rhys and Mansfield, and even Nina Hamnett, and this is
why she must be read alongside them. Her fight leads to the arrival of the police, and a brief imprisonment, followed by a
trial. There is a moment while she is in jail that is revealing
about her feelings and about Putnam's translation of them:

> They take me down into a dark cellar, where there is
> nothing but a board, what's left of a bicycle, and a lot of
> other old junk . . .
>
> I've been there long enough to think things over
> plenty, when the door opens and one of my girl-friends
> comes in sobbing, with a basket on her arm, followed by
> a big copper.
>
> When I looked at that copper's neck, my fingers
> twitched, I can tell you! (156)

From the English text we expect the "copper" to be called
something equivalently colloquial (like "flic") in the French
text, but this is far from the case. He is merely a "gros gendarme"—a big policeman, about whom she says, "J'ai regardé
le cou du gendarme, et mes doigts se serraient machinale-
ment" (156)—literally, "I looked at the neck of the policeman
and my fingers squeezed mechanically." Putnam hides the big
word, *mechanically,* and throws in the colloquial "I can tell
you." Hemingway was right to worry about the translation.
The temptation to make Kiki into what she should have been,
to hide the mixture of discourses that in effect constitute her

being, must have been sometimes too great for the translator
to deal with. He wanted a lively gamine. We want something
else, a textual Kiki as close to reality as we can get it—if only
to her textual reality. What comes across in both the original
and the translation, of course, is that Kiki reacts to the police
not in flight mode but in fight mode. Her friend is crying, but
Kiki's body wants to choke the guy.

The translation both censors Kiki and colloquializes her
clean French prose. When she is moved to a prison cell, she
notes that her "pot de chambre en fonte, qui n'est jamais net-
toyé, parfume la cellule" (159). Putnam's Kiki says "my thun-
der-mug, which is never cleaned, stinks up the whole cell"
(160). In the French text, the chamber pot is "en fonte" which
means something like congealing. The word is used in smelt-
ing and casting metals, and, by painters, for mixing colors.
Here it gets lost in translation, as does "parfume" which is col-
loquialized to "stinks." It might have been better to translate
the piece from scratch, or, as Hemingway suggested, to read it
in French. On the other hand, this is the English version that
was read by all those who were not comfortable with the
French. It is a text of record and has a certain status. But the
persistent dumbing down of Kiki's text is annoying, as in her
final chapter, *Montparnasse aujourd'hui*, in which she describes this quarter as a land of liberty, where "Les gens ont les
idées large et ce qui, aillers, serait un crime, ici, c'est simplement une peccadille" (168). Which Putnam turns into "Folks
here are broad-minded, and what would be a crime anywhere
is simply a little false pass" (174). "Broad-minded" is fine for
idées large, but to translate *peccadille* as "false pass" is really a
crime, since it suggests that Kiki had written *faux pas,* instead
of the more elegant and precise word she used, for which we
have an exact equivalent in English: peccadillo.

This is like touching up one of the photos of her to give her a little more pubic hair. (She always complained about being deficient in that department.) The girl from Burgundy's working class entered the bohemia of Montparnasse from the bottom, as Hastings and Hamnett had entered it from the top—or perhaps the side—but she learned the language and customs of the place and spoke like a native, which is why it is wrong to deny her expressions like *en fonte* for her congealing chamber pot. It hides from us a woman who never wanted to hide. To really recover Kiki, of course, we need to see her own artworks, in color, if possible. When she had her show of drawings and paintings at the Galerie du Printemps in 1927, the *Paris Times* wrote: "Ceux qui ignoraient que Kiki possédât un réal talent de peintre étaient surpris de manière plaisante" (*Souvenirs,* 22; Those who didn't know that Kiki possessed a real talent as a painter were in for a pleasant surprise).

Kiki had the shortest life of these three model artists, dying in 1953, and wrote the shortest work about her experiences in Montparnasse, but she made the most powerful and enduring impact on Modernism of the three. She had the fewest advantages of the three women, and depended most on her body as well. Lou Mollgaard, who has given us the best biography of Kiki, described her last phase, in these words: "Mais pour Kiki, l'art a moins été un combat et un métier qu'un miroir dans lequel elle ne peut plus se voir. Et elle n'a rien trouvé de bon pour remplacer le regard des artistes" (298; But for Kiki art was not a struggle or a trade, but a mirror in which she could no longer see herself. And she found nothing that could replace the gaze of artists). A new edition of the Putnam translation of *Souvenirs* was brought out a few years ago, edited by Billy Kluver and Julie Martin. The edition has some shortcomings, in addition to the translation itself, which were discussed by Mark Gaipa and myself in the *Hemingway Review*, but it is good to have the book available for English readers in any form.

Hastings came from South Africa, Hamnett from Wales, and Kiki from Burgundy. All three were outsiders in Montparnasse, but together they have given us a lively and memorable portrait of that vanished bohemian country, where real art flourished, in spite of everything, but where the model could never quite make it to the other side of the easel and stay there. The world of Modernism seemed open to the talents and the genders, but it was far less open for women than it seemed. Very few succeeded, and those who did all paid a heavy price for success. Of the three whose writing we have looked at in this chapter, Hastings was the one who realized this most acutely and expressed it most clearly, Hamnett the one who left us the fullest record of her work as an artist, and Kiki the one who almost turned posing itself into a work of art. The least we can do, it seems to me, is to give the work they actually did our serious attention, for they all produced texts that are still very much alive and speak to us about Modernism in a different voice from the those we usually hear.

9
The Aesthete in the Brothel: Proust and Others

—Votre théâtre . . . , commença-t-il d'une voix flûtée.
Bordenave l'interrompit tranquillement, d'un mot cru,
en homme qui aime les situations franches.
—Dites mon bordel.

"*Your theater . . . ,*" *he began in a fluty voice.*
Bordenave calmly interrupted him with a raw word,
a man who liked clear situations.
"*Call it my brothel.*"
—Emile Zola, Nana

I t is time to return, now, to the theme of High and Low, with which we began this series of probes into the paradoxy of Modernism—but High and Low in a different sense. Modernism was the era in which a particular combination of High and Low reached its apogee in the Never Land called Bohemia, given textual form by Henri Murger's *Scènes de la vie de Bohème* in 1846 and a permanent place in modern culture by Puccini's operatic version in 1895. In Bohemia the High and the Low rubbed elbows and other body parts, sang and danced together, and the artists made textual objects of those around them. We explored that world through the texts of women embedded in it in Chapter 8, but now it is time to look at the ways in which some major literary Modernists chose to enter and represent a central feature of the Lower urban world: the modern brothel.

Some years ago, in an essay called "In the Brothel of Modernism," I investigated the significance of prostitution in the work of certain modern artists and writers, concentrating on Picasso's *Demoiselles d'Avignon* and Joyce's "Circe" chapter in *Ulysses,* while glancing at some other uses of the brothel in the visual and verbal texts of Modernism (see *In Search of James Joyce*). There were some criticisms of my original essay, largely on the grounds of its alleged political incorrectness. I believed then, and still believe, that the political incorrectness was real enough, but that it was a feature of Modernism itself, not something I imported into the topic. I return to the topic now, however, neither to praise my original essay nor to bury it but rather to see what the brothel has to tell us about the paradoxy of Modernism, by looking at the strange spectacle of the most antiseptic of Modernists, Marcel Proust, in those haunts of grubby naturalism. The brothel, in fact, is a space that links the Naturalists to the Modernists, extending, in visual art, from

Toulouse-Lautrec and Degas to Picasso and Kirchner, and, in literature, from Zola and the Goncourts through Wedekind, Isherwood, Miller, and Genêt. But the Naturalists and the Modernists do things differently there, and this difference interests me. So let us follow Proust out of his cork-lined room and into this very different fictional space.

Before turning to Proust, however, I want to draw attention to an important precursor text, from which I have drawn this chapter's epigraph: Emile Zola's *Nana*. The brief exchange I quoted above appears two more times in the first chapter of Zola's novel, with the impresario Bordenave insisting each time that what he is running is not a theater but a brothel, though it is in fact a theater called the Parisian Variety, based on an actual place that Zola knew very well. As we shall see, Bordenave's equation runs in both directions—the theater may indeed be a kind of brothel, as he insists, but the brothel is just as certainly a theatrical space, a place of enactment, performance, artifice—a point not lost on Zola's Modernist successors, from Joyce to Genêt. "Circe," for example, is by far the most theatrical section of *Ulysses*. In *Nana*, however, the theater is also a place dominated by fleshly appetites, a place of flirtation and assignation, in which lust triumphs over art at every turn, and especially in the turn of Nana herself, who, in the role of Venus in a comic opera, sings and dances badly but dominates the audience by the sheer power of her sexual allure, so that "all Paris" feels obliged to come and gaze at her, and all the "gentlemen" of Paris feel obliged to seek her sexual favors.

What happens to Nana, it is worth noting, is just the opposite of what happened in one of the first brothel episodes in English literature, presented in book 8 of Gower's *Confessio Amantis* (c. 1390), which Shakespeare and his collaborators followed in *Pericles*. In that play (c. 1607), the virgin Marina argues that she can make more money for the bawd who owns her by using her art than by using her body. As the poet Gower, now Shakespeare's on-stage narrator, puts it:

> *She sings like one immortal, and she dances*
> *As goddess-like to her admired lays;*
> *Deep clerks she dumbs; and with her needle composes*
> *Nature's own shape, of bud, bird, branch, or berry,*
> *That even her art sisters the natural roses;*
> *Her inkle, silk, twin with the rubied cherry:*
> *That pupils lacks she none of noble race,*
> *Who pour their bounty on her; and her gain*
> *She gives the cursed bawd. (act 5, Prologue)*

The captive Marina, offered as a virgin prostitute to the bawd's public, escapes this fate by singing and dancing like a goddess, while poor Nana debases her role as a goddess to the level of prostitution. Marina earns her keep, but the person Gower called the "bordeller" keeps what she earns. This story has its roots in Greek romances and traveled through Latin and Old English versions before reaching the Middle English of Gower. We are indeed dealing here with one of the oldest professions. I mention all this by way of prelude, before turning to the use made of brothels in Modernist texts, to indicate that I am not claiming that the Modernists were the first to take up the brothel as a scene of art but am rather attending to the special inflection they have given to the brothel in their texts. As we shall see, the common thread from early to late uses of the brothel in literature is the parallel between the fleshly arts of the brothel and the representational arts of the stage. Zola's theater manager indicates that the theater is in fact a brothel.

The Modernist writers, on the other hand, are more interested in the brothel as theater.

Perhaps the most glaring omission in my earlier discussion of the literary brothels of Modernism was that of Proust, which occurs at roughly the same point in the *Recherche* that "Circe" does in *Ulysses*—near, but not at, the end of the book, about a third of the way through the final volume of the six or more (depending on the edition) volumes that make up Proust's text (starting on p. 173 of vol. 6 in the Modern Library translation). As you will remember, time moves quite rapidly in this final volume. The narrator (whom I call "Marcel," following tradition) informs us in the beginning that he has spent "long years" receiving treatment in a sanatorium, from which he returned to Paris in 1916, right in the middle of the Great War. And by the end of this volume we are in the postwar world, where Marcel is seeing people he has not seen for years—and finding them altered in ways that astonish him, transformed by Time, who is the great Circe of this novel. The war years, and the war experience, then, are mainly presented by Proust in the section of the book that is dominated by Marcel's visit to Jupien's brothel. And that is one of the points I wish to make about the function of the brothel in literary Modernism. There is often a military connection, a connection with war or revolution, though I must leave the nature of that connection open on this occasion.

Proust's brothel sequence itself is preceded by a conversation between Marcel and the Baron de Charlus, who waxes rhapsodic about the beauty of soldiers, seeing the English as "Greek athletes . . . the young men of Plato, or rather . . . Spartans" (170), and then admires a passing young Parisian "with his knowing expression, his alert and humorous face" (171), going on to praise even "that splendid and sturdy fellow the Boche soldier" (171). In the course of the conversation the narrator's imagination turns Orientalist: "It was a transparent and breathless night; I imagined that the Seine, flowing between the twin semicircles of the span and the reflection of its bridges, must look like the Bosporus. And—a symbol perhaps of the invasion foretold by the defeatism of M. de Charlus, or else of the cooperation of our Muslim brothers with the armies of France—the moon, narrow and curved like a sequin, seemed to have placed the sky of Paris beneath the oriental sign of the crescent" (172). As a prelude to the brothel episode, this invocation of the Orient is entirely appropriate, since in French visual art throughout the nineteenth century the Oriental harem and odalisque constituted a displaced representation of the European brothel and prostitute, in which the sordid could be represented as exotic. The Naturalists, led by Zola, pushed the exotic back in the direction of the sordid. The Modernists did something else. One of the things they did was revealed in Picasso's *Demoiselles d'Avignon,* in which he made the sordid savage and primitive. Proust and Joyce did other things, which need more careful investigation.

In the scene from the *Recherche* that we are considering, the thoughts of both Marcel and his interlocutor, M. de Charlus, are in fact thoroughly Orientalized. The Baron continues his rhapsody on male beauty while holding and squeezing Marcel's hand:

Perhaps he thought that he was merely shaking my hand, as no doubt he thought that he was merely seeing a Senegalese soldier who passed in the darkness without deigning to notice that he was being admired. But in each case the Baron was mistaken, the intensity of contact and of gaze was greater than propriety permitted. "Don't you see all the Orient of Decamps and Fromentin and Ingres and Delacroix in this scene?" he asked me, still immobilized by the passage of the Senegalese. "As you know, I for my part am interested in things and in people only as a painter, a philosopher. Besides I am too old. But how unfortunate that to complete the picture one of us two is not an odalisque!"(173)

Marcel is making fun of the baron here, to be sure, but his own Orientalism had depicted this scene as Turkish before the baron invoked the painters of Oriental canvases, and this orientation remains operative as the brothel episode begins, after a break in the text. The narrator continues, "It was not the Orient of Decamps or even of Delacroix that began to haunt my imagination when the Baron had left me, but the old Orient of those *Arabian Nights* which I had been so fond of; losing myself gradually in the network of those dark streets, I thought of the Caliph Harun al-Rashid going in search of adventures in the hidden quarters of Baghdad" (173). Thus Marcel enters an Orientalist Nighttown in the midst of Paris: "One felt that poverty, dereliction, fear inhabited the whole quarter" (174). This is the kind of anarchy that Matthew Arnold believed to be the alternative to culture, the abyss which culture should help us to avoid. But culture seems to like the abyss. Joyce and Proust were drawn there, and sent their main characters there, but as observers like Harun al-Rashid rather than as participants.

Marcel, in particular, is so keen an observer as to approach the status of voyeur. Wandering like the Caliph of Baghdad, he notices amid the derelict houses one that seems full of activity and life. Soldiers are going in and out, including an officer he almost recognizes whose rapid departure "had almost the air of a sortie from a besieged town" (175). This person is in fact Saint-Loup, Marcel's aristocratic friend, who has lost his *croix de guerre* in leaving and will soon die in the war. Wondering whether this curious hotel may be a "meeting place of spies," Marcel is led by a combination of curiosity and thirst to approach the open door and lurk unobserved, listening to sailors and soldiers discussing the war with other men "of the working classes." Then "patriotic" discussion takes a turn that shocks Marcel, as the men discuss the work they are actually doing in this place, which is tying up someone in chains and "beating the stuffing out of him." Thinking that "an appalling crime was about to be committed," but also observing that "the whole scene . . . was like a dream or a fairy-tale," he enters the open door "with the pride of an emissary of justice and the rapture of a poet" (177).

What he discovers, of course, is that he has entered a rather specialized brothel, in which men of the working classes cater to the erotic fantasies of their social superiors, especially those who require that they be chained and beaten to experience bliss. Ordering a drink and wandering in the corridors of the "hotel," Marcel finds a peephole and gazes into a room in which he has heard a man abasing himself and begging for mercy: "And there in the room, chained to a bed like Prometheus to his rock, receiving the blows that Maurice rained upon him with a whip which was in fact studded with nails, I saw, with blood already flowing from him and covered with bruises which proved that the chastisement was not taking place for the first time—I saw before me M. de Charlus" (181–82). Unobserved at his voyeuristic perch, Marcel then overhears a conversation between the baron and his factotum, Jupien, through whom he actually owns and runs this brothel. In the course of this conversation, Charlus complains that the young man assigned to him is not "sufficiently brutal. He has a charming face, but when he calls me a filthy brute he might be just repeating a lesson" (184). Jupien assures the baron that this is not the case and goes on to claim that the young man was involved in the murder of a concierge in La Villette, which makes the baron smile approvingly, after which Jupien says he will get the baron someone even better, a man who kills oxen in the slaughterhouses. Both of these young men, it turns out, are perfectly respectable in actuality, and both share a resemblance to the love of the baron's life, Morel, which leads Marcel to remark that the baron is faithful to a particular type.

As Marcel observes and learns, he reflects on the parallels between love and war, in which victories seldom lead to peace on the terms desired by the victor. Leaving his vantage point, he makes his way downstairs, where everyone is talking about a medal, a *croix de guerre*, which has been dropped just outside the door of the hotel. This leads to more patriotic discussion, revealing further just how simple and decent the young men are who are called upon to play the roles of thugs and murderers in this theater of a brothel. Meanwhile, new customers keep coming in, men of the upper classes who will be served by men of the working classes, and these customers bring with them exotic tastes: "Clients could be heard inquiring of the *patron* whether he could introduce them to a footman, a choir-boy, a negro chauffeur. Every profession interested these old lunatics, every branch of the armed forces, every one of the allied nations. Some asked particularly for Canadians. . . . Scots too. And . . . an old man in whom curiosity of every kind had no doubt been satisfied was asking insistently to be introduced to a disabled soldier" (193). The young men who are asked to meet these demands for wickedness are often ludicrous failures in the roles assigned them, as in this instance:

Occasionally Jupien warned the young men that they ought to be more perverse. Then one of them as if he were confessing something diabolical, would hazard, "I say, Baron, you won't believe me, but when I was a kid I used to watch my parents making love through the key-hole. Pretty vicious, wasn't it? You look as if you think that's a cock and bull story, but I swear it's the truth." And M. de Charlus was driven at once to despair and exasperation by this factitious attempt at perversity, the result of which was only to reveal such depths both of stupidity and of innocence. (198)

The baron leaves, finally, through a secret door, still complaining to Jupien about "the young man's virtuousness," which leads Marcel to reflect that the baron could not complain too much, because "if he wanted others to prepare his pleasures for him, he wanted to give himself the illusion that they were unprepared" (200). Excessive complaint would put him in the position of directing a play that he hoped to appear in as a character convinced of the reality of the whole scene.

There is much more to this scene, which is one of a number of comic tours de force in Proust's great novel, but we must leave it now in order to pause and reflect on what we have seen before moving to Joyce and "Circe." First, this is an unusual brothel scene, because there is not a single woman in it. The crucial difference here is not that between sexes or genders, but that between classes. Second, the lower figures in this socioeconomic situation are not being paid to suffer but to inflict suffering on those who pay them. And they are not very good at this, because they are, in general, too nice, too honest, and too unimaginative. But it is imagination that the customers are demanding. The body alone will not suffice. The mind must play a major role in this kind of satisfaction. That is, perhaps, one reason why the major action in these representations of the brothel seems to take place not in the bed rooms but in the rooms where people sit and talk. But let us look at Joyce's "Circe" through the peephole provided by Proust.

We enter Nighttown, with its "flimsy houses and gaping doors," on p. 429 of the Vintage *Ulysses*. Stephen, expounding to Lynch on the virtues of gesture as a universal language, proposes to demonstrate in gesture "the loaf and jug of bread and wine in Omar" (433), introducing an Oriental motif by way of the *Rubaiyat* of Omar Khayyam. This motif will be continued just a bit later on by the appearance before Bloom of a fantastic Molly "in Turkish costume" with a camel beside her (439). In fact, there is a constant flow of Oriental motifs and references throughout the chapter, ranging from J. J. O'Molloy's claim that Bloom's "native place" is "the land of the Pharaoh" (463) to the transformation of the whore Zoe into an odalisque and Nighttown itself into an Oriental "womancity, nude, white, still, cool, in luxury" (477). Even the famous Caliph Haroun Al Raschid makes two appearances in this scene. He appears first as a bidder for the prostituted Bloom, who is ordered by Bello to "Pander to their Gomorrhan vices," causing him to simper and say, "O, I know what you're hinting at now" (540); and then Bloom himself assumes the caliph's role as he flees from the brothel: "Bloom . . . draws his caliph's hood and poncho and hurries down the steps with sideways face. Incog Haroun al Raschid, he flits behind the silent lechers" (586).

The brothel episodes of both Proust and Joyce, then, carry similar signs of Orientalism, which both transform their sordid surroundings and bring their sordid qualities into high relief. In the *Recherche*, Marcel goes upstairs and peers through a peephole at the degradation of Charlus. In "Circe," Bloom himself is degraded in a similar manner. He is thoroughly feminized, declared by Dr Mulligan to be *virgo intacta* and by Dr Dixon to be "a finished example of the new womanly man" (493). This fantasmagoric Bloom resembles Proust's baron in many ways. Approached by Bella Cohen and her domineering fan, Bloom has this to say: "Exuberant female. Enormously I desiderate your domination. I am exhausted, abandoned, no more young. I stand, so to speak, with an unposted letter bearing the extra regulation fee before the too late box of the general post-office of human life" (528). And Bella, metamorphosing into Bello, proceeds to gratify Bloom's extremest wishes for domination and degradation: "*(With bobbed hair, purple gills, fat moustache rings round his shaven mouth, in mountaineer's puttees, green silverbuttoned coat, sport skirt and alpine hat with moorcock's feather, his hands stuck deep in his breeches pockets, places his heel on her neck and grinds it in.)* Feel my entire weight. Bow, bondslave, before the throne of your despot's glorious heels, so glistening in their proud erectness" (531). How the poor Baron de Charlus would have loved this one can only think, but no one in that dismal, imagination-starved brothel of his could provide it for him. And Proust himself was not about to lift a hand or pen to assist him. Proust's brothel is all about the failure of the imagination, and Joyce's is all about its triumphs. No wonder that, when these two met, as legend has it, they had nothing to say to one another. And yet, as these two episodes demonstrate so powerfully, they are in agreement about one thing, and that is the importance of the imagination and the abject failure of naturalistic attempts to capture reality "directly."

We are in a position, now, I think, to consider more carefully the function of the brothel episodes in Proust and Joyce, and, therefore, in Modernism itself. Proust uses this episode to prepare us for his fullest discussion of the functions of art and literature in human life, which comes when Marcel is waiting in the Guermantes library for a musical performance to end so that he can enter the drawing room and join the party without disturbing anyone. We have traveled only a few pages, but years have passed for Marcel, in a new sanatorium which "was no more successful in curing me than the first one" (238). He has been reflecting on "the vanity, the falsehood of literature" (238) and his own lack of talent for it, but as he waits in the library he formulates a better concept of literature that suits his own sense of a literary vocation. This is developed in a long passage of literary theory, in the course of which Proust observes that "a work in which there are theories is like an object which still has its price-tag on it" (278)—but goes right on theorizing nonetheless. And the theory that he develops reads like a Modernist manifesto. In it he attacks "the falseness of so-called realist art" (277) which deals with "superficial appearances" and lacks the strength and quality of language to force an impression "through all the successive states that will culminate in its fixation, the expression of its reality" (279, translation modified).

It seems to me that these words of Proust's describe to a remarkable degree the process at work in Joyce's "Circe" episode, in which impressions are forced to pass through successive states of transformation until a reality is revealed that goes beyond anything the eye can see. Which reminds me of that day long ago when William Faulkner came to my seminar on *Absalom, Absalom!* When I had a chance to add a question of my own to those being posed eagerly by my students, I told Faulkner that it seemed to me that as the book went along, and we got farther and farther from the eyewitness narrators, we got closer and closer to the truth. And he confirmed that he saw it that way, too. It was not the case that the Modernists rejected the notion of truth. But they did indeed reject the notion that it could be read on the surface of events. Thus, as in Virginia Woolf's quarrel with Arnold Bennett and the Edwardians, Proust is quarreling here with Zola, the Goncourts, and all the Naturalists. He has already given us in this volume a long parody of a Goncourt journal, which captures all the surface objects of a milieu but never gets near its reality. And he has taken us to a brothel, which is the ur-site of Naturalism, the lowest of the low, where humans are most like animals, or ought to be—and he has shown us just how unreal this social space actually is. And in Nighttown Joyce has done something very similar in spirit though different in method. So that if we can't see the similarity between these two brothels, we are guilty of a failure of imagination ourselves.

The brothels of Joyce, Proust, and Picasso need to be seen against two backgrounds—the Orientalist images of Romantic art and the Naturalistic representations of Degas, Toulouse-Lautrec, Zola, and the Goncourts. Modernism will use both of these traditions, but in its own way. What has not changed, what has never changed, is the artist's pursuit of that elusive quarry—reality itself. Stephen Dedalus emerges from the brothel, let us not forget, a drunker but a wiser man, tapping his brow and saying, "But in here it is I must kill the priest and the king" (589), which, along with other things, leads Private Carr to knock him unconscious, and Bloom to bring him back to consciousness by calling him by his first name—a fatherly act for which he is rewarded with a vision of Rudy, his own dead son, "dressed in an Eton suit with glass shoes and a little bronze helmet, holding a book in his hand" (609). In *Ulysses*, too, war enters by way of the brothel, in this case the recent Boer War, as Private Compton urges his fellow soldier, "Do

him one in the eye. He's a proboer," and the coming Irish re-
bellion, signified by the Citizen's encouraging shout of "Erin
go bragh!" (596).

It is worth noting that Joyce and Proust were working on
their brothel episodes at virtually the same time in the same
city—1920–21 in Paris. We should note as well that they both
had strong roots in the aesthetic movement of the late nineteenth century, as did Virginia Woolf. Joyce's debts to Pater are
obvious in his early prose, and Proust translated Ruskin. Each
wanted to capture the reality of his own time, but both believed that this reality lay beneath the naturalistic surface of
things—as did Woolf, who could not follow them into the
brothel. Erich Auerbach, you will remember, grouped Proust
and Woolf together, and he found them both hostile to reality,
which was by no means the case. What they were hostile to was
Realism, especially in its Naturalistic manifestation, but their
hostility was on the grounds of the failure of Realism to reach
the Real. Joyce and Proust, sharing this hostility, chose to take
the struggle to that quintessentially Naturalist place, the brothel,
and to show there what imagination could accomplish. In the
case of Proust this demonstration was so powerful that it led
his translator to make him say something he did not say at all.
Let us pause for a moment and look at the passage in question:

Gradually, thanks to its preservation by our memory, the
chain of all those inaccurate expressions in which there
survives nothing of what we have really experienced comes
to constitute for us our thought, our life, our "reality," and
this lie is all that can be reproduced by the art that styles
itself "true to life," an art that is as simple as life, without
beauty, a mere vain tedious duplication of what our eyes
see and our intellect records, so vain and so tedious that

one wonders where the writer who devotes himself to it can have found the joyous and impulsive spark that was capable of setting him in motion and making him advance in his task. The greatness, on the other hand, of true art, of the art which M. de Norpois would have called a dilettante's pastime, lay, I had come to see, elsewhere: we have to rediscover, to reapprehend, to make ourselves fully aware of that reality, remote from our daily preoccupations, from which we separate ourselves by an even greater gulf as the conventional knowledge which we substitute for it grows thicker and more impermeable, that reality which it is very easy for us to die without having ever known and which is, quite simply, our life. *Real life, life at last laid bare and illuminated—the only life in consequence which can be said to be really lived—is literature, and life thus defined is in a sense all the time immanent in ordinary men no less than in the artist.* (297–98, emphasis added)

It's very eloquent, but it's not what Proust wrote. The last sentence quoted here makes a statement that sounds more like Whistler or Oscar Wilde than Proust—"Real life . . . is literature." In the French text, there is no separate last sentence and no such statement. The previous sentence just continues. I give the end of it here, with a literal translation:

cette réalité que nous risquerions fort de mourir sans l'avoir connue, et qui est tout simplement notre vie, *la vraie vie, la vie enfin découverte et éclaircie, la seule vie par conséquent réellement vécue, cette vie qui en un sens, habite à chaque instant chez tous les hommes aussi bien que chez l'artiste.*

> this reality that we strongly risk dying without having known, and which is simply our life, *the true life, the life finally discovered and made clear, the only life consequently really lived, this life that in a sense, lives at every instant in all men as well as in the artist.*

This mistranslation is preserved, I should note, in the latest translation of Proust, which is prevented by copyright laws from being sold in the United States. We seem to want that perverse statement—that life is literature—badly enough to refuse to part with it no matter how many opportunities arise for its correction. But Proust is not saying that life is literature. He is saying that only literature can give us access to real life, and that it does so by getting beneath the surface of conventional representation. This is a theory of defamiliarization, which is in fact familiar to us as part of an aesthetic that extends from the British Romantics to the Russian Formalists and reaches its apogee in literary and artistic Modernism. But this same license to turn away from surfaces extends from the High Modernists to the writers of durable fluff and iridescent mediocrity as well, who are partners in the endless search for the true, the good, and, of course, the beautiful.

The aesthete in the brothel is perhaps the most concrete and powerful representation of the paradox of Modernism that we can find. The Modernist writers and artists keep returning to this scene because it is the place where the flesh and the spirit are brought into the closest proximity, where the question of what is Real is posed most powerfully. And here we must return to that other tormented scene, the essay "Middlebrow," in which Virginia Woolf defined the highbrow as all mind and the lowbrow as all body (152–54). She then positioned the middlebrow as a person who tried to mediate between these two extremes, having neither a proper mind nor a proper body of his (or her?) own. Woolf's refusal to allow the middlebrow a genuine position in this system is a quintessentially Modernist move, carried, in this case, to a point where its absurdity is quite plainly visible:

> But what, you may ask, is a middlebrow? And that, to tell the truth, is no easy question to answer. They are neither one thing nor the other. They are not highbrows, whose brows are high; nor lowbrows, whose brows are low. Their brows are betwixt and between. They do not live in Bloomsbury which is on high ground; nor in Chelsea which is on low ground. Since they must live somewhere presumably, they live perhaps in South Kensington, which is betwixt and between. The middlebrow is the man, or woman, of middle-bred intelligence who ambles and saunters now on this side of the hedge, now on that, in pursuit of no single object, neither art itself nor life itself, but both mixed indistinguishably, and rather nastily, with money, fame, power, or prestige. (135)

One may wonder just what a "middle-bred intelligence" may be. Are we really talking about intelligence, here, or breeding? But the last words of this quotation offer us a different picture. These rascally middle-bred creatures are interested in money, fame, power, and prestige, whereas the pure highbrows and lowbrows want none of those nasty things. Oh, really? That's not what we learn from reading your diaries, Mrs. Woolf. Of course, reading another person's diaries is just what one would expect of a nasty middlebrow to begin with. So I must plead guilty to mediocrity—again.

This entire book has been, among other things, an attempt to find a place for the excluded middle in Modernist studies, by exploring some of the complexities underlying the powerful binaries of Modernist critical dogma. To that end I have examined the major binaries themselves, explored some of the paradoxes that undo them, and finally returned to the ultimate binary of High and Low. A "doxy," as I indicated at the beginning of this section, is a floozy or prostitute, which makes this the proper chapter for a discussion of that element of my title. Many Modernists, it is clear, have welcomed such creatures into their pages or onto their canvasses. And I think of Kiki's elegant whores, with their good manners and sentimental feelings about sailors, in addition to the other examples discussed in this chapter. But the real doxy of Modernism, as Woolf's "Middlebrow" makes so eloquently clear, is not the prostitute, male or female, but the writer and artist who insists on trying to please a broad audience. "Para-" means against, so that paradoxy can mean against doxa (or dogma) or against doxies. Personally, I am against the Modernist orthodoxy that makes a doxy out of any artist who does not aspire to the production of masterpieces.

Modernism, after all, has been the very heaven of manifestos, including Woolf's own "Mr. Bennett and Mrs. Brown," produced in pursuit of fame, prestige, and even money. And the general tendency of those manifestos—and of the critical interpretations that came in their wake—was to define Modernism as High, Experimental, and Hard, while positioning texts aimed directly at readers as Low, Conventional, and Soft—entirely unworthy of attention. This positioning of Modernism itself generated those middlebrows, the critics and teachers, who defined their role as explaining the great texts of Modernism. The exclusion of the true Middle generated this false Middle, which complacent critics have inhabited for a century or so. It is time for them—or rather for us, since I have languished in that comfortable space in my day—to get up and get out.

As we have seen, writers as different as Beerbohm and Woolf argued for a direct connection between the producers of art and its consumers. And we have seen this kind of connection in the fiction of Simenon and Dornford Yates, in the personal writings of Hastings, Hamnett, and Kiki, and in the durable fluff of Oscar Wilde. When we looked for it, we have even found it in the fiction of Joyce and Proust, and in the poetry of Eliot and Pound. It is also there in the art of Walter Sickert and even, when they are at their best, in the more geometrical Epstein, Nevinson, and Gaudier. The Modernists were grappling with the same modernity which we inhabit, though ours is a more extreme case of it, to be sure. But what we can learn from them, what we must learn from them, is the folly of trying to exclude the middle by positioning it as low—and despising both equally. Perhaps Dr. Johnson went too far, in insisting that "mediocrity is best," but it is good, it is necessary, and it is folly to exclude it.

I began this effort by borrowing from L. P. Hartley the notion that the past is a foreign country, where "they do things differently." But it is also our own country, which means that the very causes for this foreignness are waiting there for us to find and understand them. In this book I have tried to act as a guide to that country, carrying the red umbrella of paradoxy so that I might be followed through High, Low, and Middle. I have tried to make this tour different from the others, however, resisting the temptation to make the guide book itself the focus of attention. I have tried instead to say, "Look up, see what is really there, listen to what they are really saying"—whether this meant recovering the lost texts of Beatrice Hastings, the academically ignored fiction of Dornford Yates, or the

mistranslated phrases of Kiki and Proust. When we manage
this kind of attention, what we learn is that they are not so different from us after all. The process that sorts out the works
that continue to survive does not function according to manifestos and modes. It functions according to the persistent concerns for human values that shine through the gloss of High
Modernist technique and the more modest language of comic
romance and bohemian memoir.

As I was finishing this book I happened to be given a copy
of a novel I had read before and remembered with pleasure,
the tenth work in Anthony Powell's post-Proustian sequence
The Music of Time. This volume is mainly about the publishing world, and is called *Books Do Furnish a Room.* Near the end
of the novel, I came across a passage I had forgotten, in which
the Naturalistic novelist, X. Trapnel, is holding forth in a pub
on the subject of fiction and the Real. I should note in passing
that the title of the novel refers to the nickname of a character,
usually shortened to "Books" in conversation, so that Trapnel,
who seems in this exhortation to be addressing the volumes
themselves, is actually talking to a character known as Books:

> But, Books, you said Tolstoy wrote "like" life, because he
> was naturalistic. I contend that his characters aren't any
> more "like"—in fact aren't as "like"—as, say Dostoevsky's
> at their craziest. Of course Tolstoy's inordinately brilliant.
> In spite of all the sentimentality and moralizing, he's never
> boring—at least never in one sense. The material's incon-
> ceivably well arranged as a rule, the dialogue's never less
> than convincing. The fact remains, *Anna Karenin's* a glori-
> fied magazine story, a magazine story of the highest genius,
> but still a magazine story in that it tells the reader what he
> wants to hear, never what he doesn't want to hear. (216)

Well, yes. That is, from a certain perspective, it is possible to call Tolstoy kitsch. And Vladimir Nabokov would say even worse things about Dostoevsky—did say them. I heard him when I sat in on some of his lectures when I was a graduate student at Cornell in the fifties. But my point is that the character Trapnel—who may or may not have his author's support in this—is right about Tolstoy. Right about the brilliance, right about the sentimentality and moralizing, and right that *Anna Karenina* is glorified magazine fiction of the highest genius. And my main point, which is the point of this whole book, is that Trapnel is uttering not paradoxes but home truths that seem paradoxical only because we, his audience, are so steeped in the paradoxy of Modernism ourselves. Under the instruction of the Modernist critics and writers of manifestos, we have been led to believe that works of art and literature must be either High or Low, Old or New, Hard or Soft, serious or trivial, popular or elite, creative or formulaic. But when we unravel the paradoxy of Modernism, we find that this is not the way things actually are. The interesting and durable works of the period we call modern are mixtures of these qualities, and they resist insertion into that ultimate binary opposition: Good or Bad.

As I listen to all those voices from the past that we have been considering, I find myself asking why they are so interesting to me, why I care about their problems, and why I want others to attend to them. The answers to these simple questions are far from simple themselves. But they have to do with learning and with pleasure. The Modernist critics and writers of manifestos insisted on difference, on the newness of the New, the highness of the High, but they could not sustain those distinctions, and their failure is instructive. In the long run, the continuities count for more. And that most modest attribute, affording pleasure to viewers and readers, turns out to be crucial for the survival of works of art in all the modes and media. From the tea table of Cecily Cardew to the brothels of Circe and Charlus, we can learn similar lessons about human desires and the role played by imagination in those desires. The scene of Nina Hamnett with Constantin Brancusi and other friends pulling the cover off Jacob Epstein's monument to Oscar Wilde in the Père Lachaise cemetery in Paris tells us something about the importance of Wilde to the young Modernists, and about the importance of a book like itself. (A friend reports, by the way, that Epstein's monument to Wilde is now covered with the lipstick marks of kisses.) I care about these people and their works because they cared themselves, and recorded their care for us in words, pictures, and even stone. It is a rich world, vividly realized in all the various modes we have considered. In that world, even the critics were interesting. And that may be the ultimate paradoxy of Modernism.

Works Cited

Adorno, Theodor, and Max Horkheimer. "The Culture Industry: Enlightenment as Mass Deception." In *Dialectic of Enlightenment,* trans. John
Cumming, 120–67. New York: Continuum, 1982.

Aristotle. *The Rhetoric of Aristotle,* trans. Lane Cooper. New York: Appleton-
Century, 1960.

Beckett, Samuel, et al. *Our Exagmination Round His Factification for Incam-
ination of Work in Progress.* New York: New Directions, 1939.

Beerbohm, Max. *Letters of Max Beerbohm, 1892–1956,* ed. Rupert Hart Davis.
New York: Norton, 1989.

———. *Zuleika Dobson.* London: Penguin, 1988.

Bertrand, Alain. *Georges Simenon.* Lyon: La Manufacture, 1988.

Breton, André. *Manifestes du surréalisme.* Paris: Gallimard, n.d.

———. *Manifestoes of Surrealism,* trans. Richard Seaver and Helen R. Lane.
(This text includes *Soluble Fish.*) Ann Arbor: University of Michigan
Press, 1972.

———. *Poisson soluble.* Paris: Gallimard, 1996.

Calinescu, Matei. *Five Faces of Modernity: Modernism, Avant-garde, Decadence, Kitsch, Postmodernism.* Durham: Duke University Press, 1987

Christian Remembrancer, The. London: Printed for F. C. and J. Rivington,
1819–68.

Connolly, Cyril. *The Condemned Playground.* London: Routledge, 1946.

———. *The Unquiet Grave.* New York: Harper and Brothers, 1945.

Danson, Lawrence. *Max Beerbohm and the Act of Writing.* New York: Oxford
University Press, 1989.

Eisenstein, Sergei. *The Film Sense,* trans. and ed. Jay Leyda. New York: Harcourt Brace Jovanovich, 1975.

Eliot, T. S. *The Complete Poems and Plays.* New York: Harcourt, 1952.

———. *On Poetry and Poets.* London: Faber, 1984.

———. *The Sacred Wood.* London: Methuen, 1960.

Forster, E. M. *Aspects of the Novel.* New York: Harcourt, n.d.

Greenberg, Clement. "Avant-Garde and Kitsch." In *Art and Culture: Critical Essays,* 3–21. Boston: Beacon, 1965.

Hamnett, Nina. *Laughing Torso.* London: Virago, 1984.

Hart, Clive. "James Joyce's Sentimentality." *Philological Quarterly* 46, no. 4 (October 1967): 516–26.

Hartley, L. P. *The Go-Between.* London: Penguin, 1981.

Hueffer, Ford Madox. "The Saddest Story," in *Blast 1.* Santa Barbara: Black Sparrow, 1981.

Hulme, T. E. *Speculations: Essays on Humanism and the Philosophy of Art.* London: Routledge and Kegan Paul, 1987.

Hume, David. *Of the Standard of Taste and Other Essays.* Indianapolis: Bobbs-Merrill, 1975.

Huyssen, Andreas. "High/Low in an Expanded Field." *MODERNISM/modernity* 9 (2002): 363–74.

Johnson, Samuel. *The Rambler.* London: J. M. Dent, 1953.

Joyce, James. *Ulysses.* New York: Vintage, 1990.

Kames, Henry Home, Lord. *Elements of Criticism.* London: Johnson Reprint, 1970.

Kiki (Alice Prin). *Kiki's Memoirs,* trans. Samuel Putnam. Paris: Black Manikin, 1930.

———. *Souvenirs.* Paris: Henri Broca, 1929.

Kipling, Rudyard. "The Three Decker." <http://www.everypoet.com/archive/poetry/Rudyard_Kipling/kipling_the_three_decker.htm>.

Levenson, Michael. *A Genealogy of Modernism.* New York: Cambridge University Press, 1984.

Longenbach, James. "Randall Jarrell's Legacy." *Literary Imagination* 5, no. 2 (Spring 2003): 358–68.

Lukács, Georg. "Narrate or Describe." In *Writer and Critic,* 110–48. New York: Grosset and Dunlap, 1971.

———. *The Theory of the Novel,* trans. Anna Bostock. Cambridge: MIT Press, 1971.

Macdonald, Ross. *Find a Victim.* New York: Bantam, 1979.

Marivaux, Pierre Carlet de Chamblain de. *Le Prince travesti, L'ile des esclaves, Le Triomphe de l'amour.* Paris: Flammarion, 1989.

Mollgaard, Lou. *Kiki, Reine de Montparnasse.* Paris: Robert Laffont, 1988.

Nelson, Cary. *Repression and Recovery: Modern American Poetry and the Politics of Cultural Memory, 1910–1945.* Madison: University of Wisconsin Press, 1989.

New Age, The. Ed. A. R. Orage. London, 1907–22 <www.modjourn.brown.edu>. Citations of *The New Age* are all given in the format Volume.Issue: Page(s), thus: 11.8:191.

Perkins, David. *Is Literary History Possible?* Baltimore: Johns Hopkins University Press, 1993.

Pound, Ezra. *Literary Essays of Ezra Pound.* New York: New Directions, 1968.

———. *A Memoir of Gaudier-Brzeska.* New York: New Directions, 1978.

———. *Personae: Collected Shorter Poems.* New York: New Directions, 1950.

Powell, Anthony. *Books Do Furnish a Room.* Boston: Little, Brown, 1971.

Proust, Marcel. *Finding Time Again.* London: Penguin, 2002.

———. *Ouvres romanesque complètes.* Paris: Champion Électronique, 1998.

———. *Time Regained.* New York: Modern Library, 1993.

Ress, Laura Jane. *Tender Consciousness: Sentimental Sensibility in the Emerging Artist—Sterne, Yeats, Joyce, and Proust.* New York: Peter Lang, 2002.

Scholes, Robert. *The Crafty Reader.* New Haven: Yale University Press, 2001.

———. *In Search of James Joyce.* Urbana: University of Illinois Press, 1992.

Shakespeare, William. *The Complete Works.* New York: Walter Black, 1937.

Simenon, Georges. *La Jeune Fille aux perles.* Paris: Julliard, 1991.

———. *Le Pendu de Saint-Pholien.* Paris: Presses de la Cité, n.d.

———. *La Première Enquête de Maigret.* Paris: Presses de la Cité, n.d.

———. *Train de nuit.* Paris: Julliard, 1991.

Stein, Gertrude. *Tender Buttons.* Los Angeles: Sun and Moon, 1991.

Stone, Dan. *Breeding Superman: Nietzsche, Race, and Eugenics in Edwardian and Interwar Britain.* Liverpool: Liverpool University Press, 2002.

Tate, Allen. "Tension in Poetry." In *Critiques and Essays in Criticism,* ed. R. W. Stallman, 55–65. New York: Romald, 1949.

Usborne, Richard. *Clubland Heroes.* London: Barrie and Jenkins, 1974.

Wilde, Oscar. *The Writings of Oscar Wilde,* vol. 3. London: A. R. Keller, 1907.

Wimsatt, W. K. "The Affective Fallacy." In *The Verbal Icon,* 20–39. Lexington: University of Kentucky Press, 1954.

———. "The Concrete Universal." In *The Verbal Icon,* 68–83.

Windsor Magazine, The. London: Ward, Lock, 1895–1939.

Wollen, Peter. *Signs and Meaning in Cinema.* Bloomington: Indiana University Press, 1972.

Woolf, Virginia. "How It Strikes a Contemporary." In *The Common Reader,* 236–46. New York: Harcourt, 1964.

———. "Middlebrow." In *The Death of the Moth and Other Essays,* ed. Leonard Woolf, 152–60. London: Penguin, n.d.

———. "Mr. Bennett and Mrs. Brown." In *The Captain's Death Bed and Other Essays,* ed. Leonard Woolf, 94–119. New York: Harcourt, 1950.

———. "Walter Sickert." In *The Captain's Death Bed and Other Essays,* 187–202.

Wordsworth, William. *The Poetical Works of Wordsworth.* New York: Oxford University Press, 1933.

Worringer, Wilhelm. *Abstraction and Empathy.* Cleveland: World, 1967.

Yates, Dornford. *Berry and Co.* 1920; London: Ward, Locke, 1921.

———. *The Berry Scene.* 1947; London: House of Stratus, 2001.

———. *Blind Corner.* 1927; New York: Harper and Row, 1985.

———. *The Brother of Daphne.* 1914; electronic version published by <amazon.com>.

———. *The Courts of Idleness.* 1920; London: Ward, Lock, 1929.

———. *Maiden Stakes.* 1927; London: Ward, Lock, 1931.

———. *Perishable Goods.* 1928; London: J. M. Dent, 1984.

Yeats, William Butler. *Yeats's Poetry, Drama, and Prose,* ed. James Pethica. New York: Norton, 2000.

Zola, Emile. *Nana.* London: Penguin, 1972. The French text may be found at <http://www.gutenberg.org/etext/5250>.

Index

Abstract Expressionism, 75, 85, 178
abstract forms, and Modernism,
    51, 75, 80–81, 84–87, 90, 93
Adorno, Theodor: and High/Low
    Modernism, 4, 5, 9, 23, 28, 29;
    with Max Horkheimer, "The
    Culture Industry: Enlightenment
    as Mass Deception," 14–16, 18
aesthetic movement, 271
Aldington, Richard, 103, 244
Anarchism, and Surrealism, 116
anarchy, as alternative to culture, 263
Aristotle, 26–27, 98–99, 150, 151
Arnim, Elizabeth von, 193, 223
Arnold, Matthew, 17, 144, 151, 263
art, and culture industry, 14–16, 18,
    26–28
Auerbach, Erich, 6, 271
Austen, Jane: artistic formulas of,
    10, 196–97; *Mansfield Park*, 155,
    194; *Pride and Prejudice*, 144, 194
avant-garde art, and cultural di-
    vide, 7–9

Babbitt, Irving, 20, 23
Bacon, Francis, 93, 94

Bakst, Léon, 39
Balzac, Honoré de, 6, 202, 203, 215
Barr, Alfred, and Museum of Mod-
    ern Art, 92
Baudelaire, Charles-Pierre, 20
Beerbohm, Max, 154–55, 193, 276;
    Auleika Dobson, 191–92; and
    Virginia Woolf, 23–25
Beethoven, Ludwig van, *Fidelio,* 161
Bell, Clive, *Art,* 68–69, 80
Bell, Vanessa, 38, 59, 80, 93, 236
Benjamin, Walter, 9, 44
Bennett, Arnold, 169, 270
Bertrand, Alain, 203
Beyle, Marie-Henri (Stendhal), 203
Blake, William, 49, 85
Blast, 77, 88, 137, 138, 139
bohemia, and Modernism, 73, 222,
    238–39, 240, 246, 258
Bomberg, David, 76, 87–88; *Chin-
    nereth,* 88, 89
Boughton, G. H., 167
Brancusi, Constantin, 223, 242,
    245, 279
Braque, Georges, 8, 87
Breton, André, 112–13, 114, 115–16

Brittain, Vera, 223
brothels, and Modernism, 139,
    258–73
Brown, Ford Madox, 167
Butor, Michel, 201

"La" Caillaux, 235
Caillaux, Joseph, 235
Calinescu, Matei, *Five Faces of
    Modernity*, 11–12, 18, 189–90
Camden Town Group, 73
Campbell, Roy, 244
Cantor, Paul, 26
capitalism: and avant-garde art, 9;
    and Modernity, 34–35, 41–42
Carrington, Dora, 240
Carroll, Lewis, 100
Carter, Huntly, art and drama
    critic, *The New Age*, 36, 38–39,
    58, 66, 68
cartoons, and Modernism, 90
categorical terms, and description, 17
Cézanne, Paul, 52, 67, 68–69, 83,
    85, 89–90, 164
Chandler, Raymond, 111, 197
Chaplin, Charles Spenser, *Modern
    Times*, 17
characterization: in detective fic-
    tion, 202; and novels of Georges
    Simenon, 210–11, 214–15
Chesterton, G. K., 197
Clark, Suzanne, *Sentimental Mod-
    ernism*, 125
class, and gender, in Berry books
    of Dornford Yates, 174–83
Classicism, 20, 57–58
Cleobulus the Lindian, 194
Coleridge, Samuel Taylor, 31, 100
comedy: and "durable fluff," 153;

and High/Low distinction, 17;
    and iridescent mediocrity, 193
communications, and Modernity, 35
Communists, 116
Concrete forms, of representation,
    and Modern art, 84–85
Connolly, Cyril, 127; *The Con-
    demned Playground*, 163, on
    Dornford Yates, 163–67, 174, 177,
    184; *The Unquiet Grave*, 163
Conrad, Joseph, 81
Coomaraswamy, Ananda, 80
Craven, Arthur, 243
creativity, formulaic, 200, 217
crime genre novels, formulaic cre-
    ativity in, 200–203
Crowley, Aleister, 227
Cubism, 67, 73–75, 80, 84, 87, 89

defamiliarization, as aesthetic the-
    ory, 273
Degas, Edgar, 91, 259, 270
Derrida, Jacques, 146
detective fiction, 201
Dias, B. H. *See* Pound, Ezra
Dibden, Michael, 201
Dickens, Charles, 149, 203, 211
Doolittle, Hilda (H.D.), 103, 107
Doré Gallery, 42, 83, 86
Dostoevsky, Fyodor Mikhailovich,
    203, 278
"doxy," and middlebrow audience,
    219, 275
"durable fluff," as paradox of Mod-
    ernism, 143–61, 273
Dyson, Will, 94; *Progress*, 60, 62,
    86, 90

The Egoist magazine, 106, 110

Eisenstein, Sergei, 97–106; *The Film Sense,* 100–105
Eliot, George (Mary Ann Evans), 203
Eliot, T. S., 8, 20, 87, 276; as High Modernist, 163–64, 168; "Love Song of J. Alfred Prufrock," 110, 134–35; as Neo-Realist, 88; and objective correlative, 103–5, 107; and Royalism, 40, 43; and Virginia Woolf, 24–25
Ellmann, Richard, 121
entertainment novel, 5–6, 13–14
Epstein, Jacob: discussion of, in *The New Age* magazine, 46–50, 54–55, 57, 76, 86–87; monument to Oscar Wilde, 242, 279; and Nina Hamnett, 240, 242–43; *The Rock Drill,* 50, 51, 93
Etchells, Frederick, 76, 84
Expressionism (Vorticism), 84, 87

Fascism, and Modernism, 44–45, 91, 115–16
Faulkner, William, 269–70
Fauves, 89
Fawlty Towers, 17
Fergusson, John Duncan, 39
fiction: and entertainment, 5–6, 13–14; and "iridescent mediocrity," 191, 192; and literary formulas, 196–97, 198, 200–202, 204–17
Fielding, Henry, 154–55
figuration, and Modernism, 92–93
film, and montage, 96–103
Fitzgerald, F. Scott, 215
Flanner, Janet (Genêt), 259
Flaubert, Gustave, 5; *Madame Bovary,* 13

Flint, F. S., 103
Ford, Ford Madox (Ford Hermann Hueffer), 81, 163; and the *English Review,* 169; on Georges Simenon's characters, 196, 198, 211; *The Good Soldier,* 137–38; *Parade's End,* 170
formulaic patterns: and art, 9–10; in crime and police procedural novels, 200–202; of fiction, 196–97; and Georges Simenon, 198, 204–17
Forster, E. M., 191, 211
Foujita, Leonard Tsuguharu, 246–47
Freeling, Nicholas, 197, 201
French, Cecil, 36
Freud, Lucien, 93, 94
Fry, Roger, 38, 58, 59, 93; and Omega Workshops, 241; as organizer of "Manet and the Post-Impressionists," 35–38
Futurism: and Modernism, 83–86; and Primitive Art, 83–84
"Futurist Manifesto" (Marinetti), 82
Futurists, exchange of views on, in *The New Age,* 41, 42, 54–55, 56, 63, 83–84, 86

Gass, William, 117
Gaudier-Brzeska, Henri, 39, 76; *A Dancer,* 72–74, 76, 87, 93, 94; and Nina Hamnett, 240–41; *Torso,* 224, 231, 233
Gauguin, Paul, 37, 39, 52, 85, 90
gender, and class, in Berry books of Dornford Yates, 174–83
Genêt (Janet Flanner), 259
genre fiction, of crime, 200–202

geometrical art, and Modernism, 64–66, 72, 77, 80–81, 164

Geometrists, 62, 67, 87–88, 94, 167

Georgian culture: and Dornford Yates, 169–70; and Virginia Woolf, 187

Gertler, Mark, 240

Gide, André, on Georges Simenon, 195, 198

Gilbert, John, 167

Gilbert, Stuart, 199

Ginner, Charles: *Leicester Square*, 58, 59, 93; on Neo-Realism, 52–53, 58, 67, 81

Godwin, Mary, *Ethel*, 77, 78

Gombrich, E. H., *Art and Illusion*, 10

Goncourt, Edmond de, 188, 259, 270

Goncourt, Jules de, 188, 259, 270

Gore, Spencer, 77

Gorman, Herman, 123

Gosse, Sylvia, *The Doctor*, 81, 82

Gower, John, *Confessio Amantis*, 259, 260

Grant, Duncan, 38, 93, 164

graphic arts and posters, 42–44

Great Divide, and Modernist critical theory, 20–26

Greenberg, Clement: "Avant-Garde and Kitsch," 7–9, 10, 11, 18, 23, 166; and High Modernism, 5, 7, 28, 29, 30, 66, 179

Greene, Graham, 186

Guest, Edgar, 8, 20–21

Haggard, H. Rider, 168

Hamilton, C. F., 76

Hammett, Dashiell, 111, 197

Hamnett, Nina, 73, 227, 253, 276, 279; *Is She a Lady?* 245; *Laughing Torso*, 222, 223, 224, 238, 246; as model artist, 222, 223–24, 238–46; and Modigliani, 242–43, 245

Hardy, Thomas, 138

Hart, Clive, "James Joyce's Sentimentality," 122–23, 125–26, 134

Harte, Bret, 137

Hartley, L. P., 276

Hastings, Beatrice, 222, 223–24, 276; *Defence of Madame Blavatsky*, 224; as editor and contributor, *The New Age*, 224–38, 243; "Impressions de Paris," 225–37; *The Maid's Comedy*, 224; and Modigliani, 222, 227–31, 238, 243, 244; and Nina Hamnett, 243

H.D. (Hilda Doolittle), 103, 107

Hegel, Georg Wilhelm Friedrich, *Philosophy of History*, 203

Hemingway, Ernest: *A Farewell to Arms*, 199; on Georges Simenon, 195–96, 199, 217; and Kiki, as model artist, 217, 222, 224; on Kiki's *Souvenirs*, 247, 248–49, 253

High/Low distinction, and Modernism, 103, 278; and Bohemia, 258–77; and formulaic writing, 195–217; history of, 26–32; and mediocrity, 162–94

Hockney, David, 94

Home, Henry (Lord Kames), *Elements of Criticism*, 27–28

Hopper, Edward, 91

Horizon magazine, 164

Horkheimer, Max, and Theodor Adorno, "The Culture Industry: Enlightenment as Mass Deception," 9, 14–16, 18, 23, 28

Hughes, Herbert, 120, 121

Hulme, T. E., 23, 40, 165, 240; as art critic, *The New Age* magazine, 46–51, 55, 56–58; "Contemporary Drawings" series, 72–79, 82, 88, 93–94; on David Bomberg and abstraction, 86–88; on divisions of modern art, 63–68, 70; as Imagist poet, 103, 107; "Mr. Epstein and the Critics," 47–50

Hume, David, "On the Standard of Taste," 27

Huxley, Aldous, 244

Huyssen, Andreas: *After the Great Divide*, 4–5; and "suggestive intertextuality," 171

Imagism, and poetry, 76, 87, 100, 103–9

The Importance of Being Earnest (Wilde), 17, 144–51, 155–61, 167

Impressionism: and entertainment, 13; and literary narrative, 81–82, 202–3; and visual arts, 35–36, 53

industrialization, and Modernity, 35

"iridescent mediocrity," 163, 188–94, 273

irony, and sentiment, 138, 159

Isherwood, Christopher, 259

James, Henry, 5

James Joyce Quarterly, 122, 126

Jarrell, Randall, and sentiment, 124–25, 134

John, Augustus, 45, 49, 243, 244

John, Gwen, 92

Johnson, Samuel, on mediocrity, 193–94, 276

Joyce, James: "Circe" chapter, *Ulysses*, 129, 139, 259, 261, 267–68, 270–71; "The Dead," 126, 137; *Dubliners*, 80, 123, 137; *Finnegan's Wake*, 126, 136–37; and Modernism, 14, 80, 81, 100, 103, 276; and Orientalism, 267–68, 270; *A Portrait of the Artist as a Young Man*, 123, 126, 131–32, 137, 139; and sentimentality, 121–26, 136, 139; *Ulysses*, 90, 126–34, 137, 139, 163–64, 199, 200

Kain, Richard M., and Robert Scholes, *The Workshop of Daedalus*, 121–22

Kames, Lord (Henry Home), *Elements of Criticism*, 27–28

Kandinsky, Wassily, 39, 75–76, 84, 85, 87, 88

Kenner, Hugh, 25

Kiki (Alice Prin): and Ernest Hemingway, 217, 222, 224, 247, 248–49, 253; *Je Pose*, 234; as model artist, 222, 224, 227, 231, 246–56; *Souvenirs*, 222, 223, 247–56, 276

Kinross, Albert, 168

Kipling, Rudyard, 168, 172–73

Kirchner, Ernst Ludwig, 259

Kitsch, and High/Low cultural divide, 7–12, 179, 188–90

Krogh, Per, 251–52

Kuleshov, Lev, 98

La Thangue, H. H., 83

Léger, Fernand, 84, 243

Leverson, Ada, 193

Lewis, Wyndham, 55, 76, 165, 240, 243; as artist, 84, 93; and *Blast*, 77, 139; *The Enemy of the Stars*, 138–39; and sentiment, 124, 132, 138–39; *Tarr*, 132 "light art," and culture industry, 14–16

literary montage, as rhetorical device, 106–15

literary narrative, and Modernism, 80–81

literary terminology, origins of, 26–27

"literature of description," and reality, 186–87

Ludovici, Anthony: admiration of Nietzsche, 39, 40, 48, 67, 68; as art critic, *The New Age*, 38–50, 52, 66–67, 73; on Jacob Epstein, 46–50, 54–55, 57; *The Jews, and the Jews in England*, 45; and Old/New Modernism, 39–45, 178; political views of, 40, 44, 45

London Group, 73, 76, 86

Longenbach, James, "Randall Jarrell's Legacy," 124–25, 134–35

Lowell, Amy, 103

Lukács, Georg, 5, 18, 23, 25, 202; "Narrate or Describe," 12–14; *Theory of the Novel*, 5–7

Macdonald, Ross, *Find a Victim*, 111

Maillol, Aristide, 37–38

Mankell, Henning, 201

Mann, Thomas, 21

Mansfield, Katherine, 193, 223, 224, 243, 253; "Je ne parle pas français," 252

Marinetti, Emilio, 42, 55, 82, 84

Marivaux, Pierre de, *Le Triomphe de l'amour*, 153–54, 159

Matisse, Henri, 37, 52, 58, 67–70, 247

mechanical reproduction, and Modernism, 9

mediocrity, iridescent, 162–94; and

Dornford Yates, 165–71, 173–86, 193; and *kitsch*, 189–90; and Marcel Proust, 186–89

Merritt, Anna Lea, 167

metaphor, and montage, 97

Michelangelo, 8, 49

middlebrow culture: and mediocrity, 190–91; Virginia Woolf's view of, 26, 167–68, 173, 273–75

Millais, John Everett, 167

Milton, John, 100, 101–2, 104, 105, 170–71

Modernism: bohemian core of, 73, 222, 238–39, 240, 246, 258; and the brothel, 139, 258–73; "durable fluff" paradoxy, 143–61, 273; and formulaic fiction, 9–10, 196–97, 217; High/Low dialogue, 90, 258, 278; High/Low distinction, 26–32, 103, 151, 165, 167–68, 197, 275; and "iridescent mediocrity," 163, 189–94, 273; Old/New polarity in, 22–23, 34–35, 63–67, 88–94, 278; and Orientalism, 262–63, 267, 270; and reality, 186–87, 270, 273; and sentiment, 121–26, 134–39, 198; and women as writers and artists, 222, 223, 252–53, 256

Modernist critical theory: division between the Old and the New, 63–66, 72–73; and the Great Divide, 20–26; and Museum of Modern Art (MoMA), 91–94

Modernity: conditions of, 34–35; and cultural break, 91, 178; and middlebrows, 167–68; and nostalgia, 176–77, 179–80; shadings and variations of, 90–91

Modigliani, Amadeo: *Beatrice,* 231, 232; and Beatrice Hastings, 222, 226, 227–31, 238, 244; and Nina Hamnett, 242–43, 245

montage: and film, 96–99; as modernistic technique, 171–73; as rhetorical device, and poetry, 100–110, 112–14

Morning, Alice. *See* Hastings, Beatrice

Mozart, Wolfgang Amadeus, 16

Murger, Henri, *Scènes de la vie de Bohème,* 258

Murry, John Middleton, as editor of *Rhythm,* 39

The Museum of Modern Art (MoMA), 85, 91–93, 245

Nabokov, Vladimir, 278

narrative authority: in novels of Georges Simenon, 214–15; and Realism, 202–3

Naturalism: and the brothel, 258–59, 270; and Émile Zola, 6, 262, 270; within Modernist context, 90; and Realism, 52–53, 271

nature: and the artistic imagination, 67–68; and Realism, 52

Nazism, and political New Order, 91

Nelson, Cary, 128

Neo-Realism: defense of, by Charles Ginner, 52–53, 58, 67, 81; T. E. Hulme's opinion of, 67–68; and *Ulysses,* 90; and Walter Sickert, 52, 61–63, 67, 81–82

Neo-Realists, 61–63, 73–74, 94, 169, 203, 243

Nevinson, C. R. W., 90, 276; *The Chauffeur,* 76, 82, 83, 93; "Vital English Art," 83–86

The New Age magazine, 34–94; "Contemporary Drawings" series, 72–79, 82, 88, 93–94; "Impressions de Paris," 225–37; "Modern Drawings" series, 53, 68; Old and New Modernism in, 34–35, 38–40, 120–21, 167. *See also* Ginner, Charles; Hulme, T. E.; Ludovici, Anthony; Nevinson, C. R. W.; Orage, A. R.; Sickert, Walter

New Criticism, and Allen Tate, 19–22

New Critics, 5, 20, 21–22, 31, 123

New Geometricism, 77, 87, 94

New Humanists, 20–22

Nietzsche, Friedrich Wilhelm, 39, 40, 41, 48, 137

Nietzschean perspectivism, 203

Nin, Anaïs, 223

Noon, William, 121

nostalgia, and Modernity, 176–77, 180–82

novel, as literary art, 5–7. *See also* fiction

objective correlative, and literary montage, 103–8, 115, 116

Omega Workshops, 241

omniscience, and Realistic fiction, 202–3

opera buffa, 16

opera seria, 16

Orage, A. R.: and Beatrice Hastings, 224, 237–38, 243; as editor of *The New Age,* 34, 55; on poetry of Ezra Pound, 108–10, 114

Orientalism, and Modernism, 262–63, 267, 270

Ortega y Gasset, José, 20

Pater, Walter, 271

Pavlov, Ivan, 98, 103

Perec, Georges, *La Disparition,* 200

phaulos, 26, 153, 158

Picasso, Pablo, 39, 58, 69–70, 85, 103; and the brothel, 259, 270; and Cubism, 74–75, 84, 87, 89; defense of, by Victor Reynolds, 36–37; *Demoiselles d'Avignon,* 139, 258, 262; sentimentalism of, 139

poetry: and film montage, 96, 99–105; and the Great Divide, 19–26; and rhetoric, 96, 105–6, 109–10, 114, 118–19; and *Windsor Magazine,* 168

police procedural novels, 200–202, 206, 211–17

politics: and Anarchism, 116; and art criticism, 18–23; and Fascism, 44–45, 91, 115; and the New Order, 91

Post-Impressionism, 13, 52–53, 59, 80, 93, 164

Pound, Ezra, 34, 88, 165, 168, 276; and Fascism, 44, 91, 115; and Henri Gaudier-Brzeska, 241; *Hugh Selwyn Mauberley,* 114–15; and Imagism, 87, 103, 104, 105, 106–7; "In a Station of the Metro," 107–8, 114–15, 118–19, 135; "Pisan Cantos," 135; "The River Merchant's Wife: a Letter," 135; and sentimentality, 135

Powell, Anthony, *Books Do Furnish a Room,* 277

Pre-Raphaelite Brotherhood, 167

Primitive art, and Modernism, 83–84

Prin, Alice. *See* Kiki (Alice Prin)

private eye novel, as genre fiction, 200–202

prostitution, 252, 258. *See also* brothels, and Modernism

Proust, Marcel, 276; *À la Recherche de temps perdu,* 188–89, 261–73; brothel episode in *Recherche,* 261–73; narrative theory of, 186–89; and Orientalism, 262, 267–68

Putnam, Samuel, 247

Radiguet, Raymond, 236

Ransom, John Crowe, 124

Ransome, Arthur, *Bohemia in London,* 239–40

Raverat, Gwen, 236; *Period Piece: A Cambridge Childhood,* 223

Ray, Man, 223

Reade, Charles, 124

Realism: and the Maigret novels of Georges Simenon, 198, 203, 215–17; and Naturalism, 52–53, 268, 271

À la Recherche du temps perdu (Proust), 188–89, 261–73

Ress, Laura Jane, *Tender Consciousness: Sentimental Sensibility in the Emerging Artist—Sterne, Yeats, Joyce, and Proust,* 125

Reverdy, Pierre, 112–13

Reynolds, Victor, 36–38, 68

rhetoric, and poetry, 96, 105–6, 109–10, 114, 118–19

Rhys, Jean, 252, 253

Rhythm, 39

Rhythmistes, 39, 41

Richards, Fred, *Temple of the Sibyl,* 68, 69, 93

Richards, I. A., 123
Richardson, Dorothy, 124
Roberts, Charles G. D., 168
Roberts, William, 76, 87, 88;
    A Study, 78–79, 88
Rockwell, Norman, 8, 176
Rodin, Auguste, 38, 39
Romanticism, 20, 71, 76; High/Low
    divide, 28–29; Orientalist im-
    ages of, 270; and subjectivity, 87
Rossetti, Dante Gabriel, 167
Rousseau, Henri (Le Douanier),
    227–29, 245, 247
Rousseau, Jean-Jacques, 20
Royalism, 40, 43
Ruskin, John, 271

Sassoon, Siegfried, 169–170
Schaffer, Talia, *The Forgotten
    Female Aesthetes,* 125
Schiele, Egon, 224, 236
sentiment: and "durable fluff,"
    149–50; and irony, 138, 159; and
    Modernism, 121–26, 134–39,
    198; and novels of Georges
    Simenon, 205
Shackleton, William, 36
Shakespeare, William: allusions to,
    181–82, 183; *As You Like It,* 150,
    154; comedies of, 150–53, 159;
    Henry V, 181–82; *Pericles,*
    259–60; *Twelfth Night,* 150,
    151–53, 158, 161; works of, and
    High/Low Divide, 30, 151
Shaw, George Bernard, 226; *Arms
    and the Man,* 165
Sickert, Walter, 93, 276; *Londra
    Benedetta,* 59, 61; and medioc-
    rity, 191; *The Music Lesson,*

61–62, 63; as Neo-Realist, 52–53,
    67, 169, 197; and *The New Age,*
    36, 52–54, 58, 68–71, 77, 80–86
    passim; and Nina Hamnett, 240,
    241–42, 244; *Portrait of Miss
    Enid Bagnold,* 53, 54; *Reconcilia-
    tion,* 68, 70
Simenon, Georges (Christian
    Brulls; Georges Sim), 276; fic-
    tional formulas of, 204–17; *La
    Jeune Fille aux perles,* 209; Mai-
    gret novels, 195–217; *Le Pendu de
    Saint-Pholien,* 211; and physical
    description, 217; *La Première
    Enquête de Maigret,* 206–8;
    Train de Nuit, 204, 208; use of
    sentiment by, 205
Sjowall, Maj, 201
Smith, Stevie, *Novel on Yellow
    Paper,* 223
Souvenirs (Kiki), 222, 223, 247–56, 276
spoudaios, 26, 153, 157, 158
Stalinism, 91
Stein, Gertrude, 81; and Surreal-
    ism, 116–19; *Tender Buttons,*
    116–17
Stendhal (Beyle, Marie-Henri), 203
Stephen, Leslie, 24
Sterne, Lawrence, 125
Strauss, Richard, *Elektra,* 120–21
Stravinsky, Igor, *The Rite of
    Spring,* 73
suggestive intertextuality, as Mod-
    ernist device, 171, 173
Surrealism, 90, 178, 179; and
    Gertrude Stein, 116–19; and
    montage, 106, 112–13; and Pierre
    Reverdy, 112–13
Swift, Graham, *Last Orders,* 127

Taste, as critical term, 27–28
Tate, Allen: as New Critic, 21, 22, 23, 31; "Tension in Poetry," 19, 20
Thackeray, William Makepeace, 203
theater: and the brothel, 259–61, 265; and "durable fluff," 17, 153–61
Three Stooges, *Pop Goes the Easel,* 17
Titt, Tom (Jan Junosza de Rosciszewski), 55, 94; *Anthony Ludovici,* 63, 65; *Charing Cross Road: 11 P.M.,* 55, 56, 90; *New Oxford Street and Holborn,* 58, 60; *St. Paul's Churchyard,* 62–63, 64, 90
Titus, Edward, 247
Todorov, Tzvetan, 201
Tolstoy, Lev, 100, 277–78; *Anna Karenina,* 277, 278; and omniscient narrators, 202–3
Tompkins, Jane, *Sensational Designs,* 125
totalitarianism, and New Order, 91
Toulouse-Lautrec, Henri de, 259, 270
translation problems: in *À la Recherche du temps perdu,* 271–73, 276–77; in *Souvenirs,* 248–50, 276–77
Trilling, Lionel, 215
Le Triomphe de l'amour (Marivaux), 153–54

Ulysses (Joyce), 163–64, 199, 200; brothel episode in, 267–68, 270–71; and sentiment, 126–34
urbanization, and Modernity, 35

Van Gogh, Vincent, 52, 85
verbal art, and Modernism, 81, 82
Vertov, Dziga, 98
visual art, and Modernism, 34–36, 64–65, 73, 77, 81–94, 258–59

von Schwind, Moritz, *Morgenstunde,* 71, 72, 73, 87, 93–94
Vorticism, 76, 77, 84, 88, 91
Vorticists, 39, 84
Vuillard, Édouard, 91

Wadsworth, Edward, 76, 84
Wahloo, Per, 201
Wallace, Edgar, 168
Wassilieff, Marie, 243, 244
Wedekind, Frank, 259
Wells, H. G., *Tono-Bungay,* 169
Wells, Muriel, 42
West, Rebecca, 223, 246; "Indissoluble Matrimony," 138
Wilde, Oscar, 193, 276, 279; "The Ballad of Reading Gaol," 149; "De Profundis," 149; *The Importance of Being Earnest,* 17, 144–151, 155–161, 167; *The Soul of Man Under Socialism,* 156
Wimsatt, W. K., 20–21, 22, 23
Windsor Magazine, 164, 167, 168–69, 183
Winfrey, Oprah, 142–43, 150–51
Wodehouse, P. G., 167, 168, 174, 183, 189, 193
Wollen, Peter, *Signs and Meaning in Cinema,* 98
women, impact of, and Modernism, 35, 222, 223, 252–53, 256
Woolf, Leonard, 168
Woolf, Virginia, 169, 270, 271; *The Common Reader,* 25; "Middlebrow" (essay), 26, 167–68, 173, 273–75; and Modernism, 23–26, 34, 80–81; "Mr. Bennett and Mrs. Brown," 23–24, 89, 187, 275; "Mrs. Dalloway in Bond Street," 59; "A Room of Her Own," 249

Wordsworth, William, *Lyrical Ballads,* 20, 28–31, 183
Worringer, Wilhelm, *Abstraktion
und Einfühlung,* 51
Wyeth, Andrew, 91

Yates, Dornford (C. W. Mercer),
86, 163–67, 169–86, 189, 193, 276;
Berry and Co., 170–71, 174–75;
Berry Scene, 176–79; *Blind Corner,* 184, 186; *The Brother of*

Daphne, 164, 169; "Clothes and
the Man," 164–65; *The Courts of
Idleness,* 169; "Letters Patent,"
184–85, 189; *Maiden Stakes,*
185–86; *Perishable Goods,* 184, 185
Yeats, William Butler, 73, 105, 168

Zadkine, Ossip, 243
Zimansky, Curt, 122
Zola, Émile: *Nana,* 259, 260; as
Naturalist, 6, 258–59, 262, 270

DATE DUE